T0319777

Competition Policy and Global Competitiveness
in Major Asian Economies

To Souraya, Danielle, Cybele, Samira and Matthew

Other books published by Tran Van Hoa

Causes and Impact of the Asian Financial Crisis (editor with C. Harvie)

China's Trade and Investment After the Asia Crisis (editor)

Contributions to Consumer Demand and Econometrics
(editor with R. Bewley)

Economic Crisis Management (editor)

Economic Development and Prospects in the ASEAN (editor)

National Income and Economic Progress
(editor with D.S. Ironmonger and J.O.N. Perkins)

Prospects in Trade, Investment and Business in Vietnam and East Asia
(editor)

Sectoral Analysis of Trade, Investment and Business in Vietnam (editor)

The Asia Crisis: The Cures, their Effectiveness, and the Prospects After
(editor)

The Asia Recovery (editor)

The Macroeconomic Mix in the Industrialised World
(co-author with J.O.N. Perkins)

The Social Impact of the Asia Crisis (editor)

Vietnam: Market Intelligence and Business Analysis
(author – in preparation)

Vietnam's Reforms and Economic Growth (co-author with C. Harvie)

Competition Policy and Global Competitiveness in Major Asian Economies

Edited by

Tran Van Hoa
University of Wollongong, Australia

Edward Elgar
Cheltenham, UK • Northampton, MA, USA

Published by
Edward Elgar Publishing Limited
Glensanda House
Montpellier Parade
Cheltenham
Glos GL50 1UA
UK

Edward Elgar Publishing, Inc.
136 West Street
Suite 202
Northampton
Massachusetts 01060
USA

A catalogue record for this book
is available from the British Library

Library of Congress Cataloguing-in-Publication Data

Competition policy and global competitiveness in major Asian economies /
    edited by Tran Van Hoa.
        p. cm.
    Includes index.
        1. East Asia–Commercial policy–Case studies. 2. Australia–Commercial
    policy. 3. East Asia–Foreign economic relations—Case studies. 4. Australia–
    Foreign economic relations. 5. Competition–Government Policy–East Asia–
    Case studies. 6. Competition–Government policy–Australia. 7.
    Globalization–Economic aspects–East Asia–Case studies. 8. Globalization
    –Economic aspects–Australia. 9. Competition, International. I. Tran, Van Hoa.

HF1600.5.C65 2003
337.5–dc21

                                                                            2003049264

ISBN 1 84376 081 9

Printed and bound in Great Britain by MPG Books Ltd, Bodmin, Cornwall

Contents

Figures

Tables

Acknowledgements

The book is the result of our research and training work during 2001 on competition policy and law and international competitiveness in major countries in Asia. The work was partly funded by the Australian Agency for International Development (AusAID) and with the collaboration from economic experts from the University of Wollongong, the University of Melbourne, Kangwon National University (Korea), the Australian Competition and Consumer Commission, National Advanced Training Institute, Vietnam Ministry of Trade, and the Central Institute for Economic Management, Ministry of Planning and Investment.

Competition policy and competitiveness are crucial tools for modern economic, financial and trade management and governance at both the national and international levels. They are also consistent with the principle of free markets in contemporary international trade, development and growth in developed and developing economies alike worldwide. In the context of globalisation and within the framework of the World Trade Organisation, the existence of a competition policy in its implicit or explicit form is often regarded as a requisite for bilateral or multilateral trade agreements among nations and promotion of their mutual commercial and well-being benefits.

In major Asian economies, competition policy is only in its developmental infancy. The book therefore is an important new study surveying first the fundamentals of competition policy and secondly investigating how, in practice, it has been developed in major economies in the Asian region. It also contains previous lessons and experiences in the formulation and implementation of competition policy and the pitfalls that may be avoided in similar future developments. The book is timely and important for current regional and international interest in globalisation, competitiveness, trade liberalisation, economic development and growth, and would be a must-have college and university text and reference in this emerging and important area.

The editor wishes to thank Edward Elgar for his support for the book concept. Discussions with colleagues and government officials in Australia and major Asian countries on the significance, interest and important aspects of competition policy and its development in particular and competitiveness in general had been most useful. The editor also wishes to thank AusAID for its funding and his contributing authors for their great efforts in research and reportage. Thanks

xi

also to Robert Hood for his hard work and dedication on proof-reading the book's manuscript and on professionally preparing all required camera-ready form layout. Again, I am deeply indebted to all members of my family for their support and sacrifice during the preparation of this book.

Tran Van Hoa
University of Wollongong
August 2002

Notes on the Contributors

Charles Harvie, Associate Professor, Department of Economics, and Director, Centre for SME Research and Development, University of Wollongong.

Tran Van Hoa, Associate Professor of Economics, and Director, ASEAN+3 Research Program, Faculty of Commerce, University of Wollongong.

Vu Xuan Nguyet Hong, Deputy Director, Department of Macroeconomic Policy, Central Institute for Economic Management, Vietnam Ministry of Planning and Investment.

Hyun-Hoon Lee, Professor and Chair, Division of Economics and International Trade, Kangwon National University, Korea, and Managing Director of the *Journal of the Korean Economy.*

P.J. Lloyd, Ritchie Research Professor of Economics, Department of Economics, University of Melbourne.

Chaiyuth Punyasavatsut, Associate Professor, Faculty of Economics, Thammasat University (Thailand).

Hank Spier, Director Spier Consulting and Former Deputy Chair, The Australian Competition and Consumer Commission.

Le Viet Thai, Economic Expert, Department of Macroeconomic Policy, Central Institute for Economic Management, Vietnam Ministry of Planning and Investment.

Editor's Biographical Notes

Professor Tran Van Hoa, a graduate from the University of Western Australia, holds higher degrees from Monash University, Victoria, Australia. He has taught widely at universities in Australia, Asia and the USA, and visited major international research institutes and universities (for example, Cambridge University (UK), the London School of Economics (UK), CORE at the Universite Catholique de Louvain (Belgium), Stanford University (USA), the University of Southern California (USA), the University of California in San Diego (USA), the University of Florida (USA), INSEE (France), CEPII (Prime Minister's Office, France), Chulalongkorn and Thammasat Universities (Thailand), the People's University of China (Beijing) and the National Economics University (Vietnam). Dr Tran Van Hoa has published 20 books and over 115 refereed articles in the major applied and theoretical areas of economics, business, finance, energy and econometrics in Australian and international professional journals, and numerous commissioned reports. He is listed in *Who's Who in the World, Who's Who in Asia and the Pacific Nations, Who's Who in Science and Engineering, 2000 Outstanding People of the 20th Century, 1000 Great Intellectuals of the 21st Century, Who's Who in America, Australian Who's Who* and in *Dictionary of International Biography*. He also is a Director of T&M Enterprises P/L (Australia), which provides education and consulting services, and in the past few years, he has been a consultant to a number of organisations and authorities in Australia and China and various ministries in Thailand and Vietnam.

1. Competition Policy and Global Competitiveness in Major Asian Economies: An Overview

Tran Van Hoa

1.1 COMPETITION POLICY, GLOBAL COMPETITIVENESS AND GLOBALISATION

The increasing globalisation of trade, financial transactions and business has highlighted the importance of competition issues on an international scale. Global competitiveness is a crucial ingredient in the support, or even guarantee, of a smooth operation of globalisation. While the determination to pursue globalisation, sometimes claimed by its detractors as a result of the active and effective lobbying by big corporations, has been a public prominent policy of the US and often reiterated by its presidents, the European Union (EU) has not been less active in promoting competition policy and law, and with it, the deregulation of the markets. The Asia–Pacific Economic Cooperation (APEC) forum has not missed out on the growing trend in this area and has set up, in recent years, a number of committees, fora and collective action plans to develop and promote competition policy and law to enhance competitiveness in the Asian region.

Competition policy and law and deregulation are related, directly or indirectly, to the three fundamental principles of the multilateral trading system that underlie the working of the World Trade Organisation (WTO). These principles are: non-discrimination, predictability, stability and transparency. They are supportive of development and essential to serve the interest of all trading partners and members. The new WTO round in Doha in 2001, dubbed the 'development round', is also aimed at benefiting the poor and focusing on issues of direct interest to developing economies.

1.2   OBJECTIVES

The present book contains scholarly studies with a focus on the general theory of competition and competitiveness and their adoption by multilateral and international organisations to improve global business and trade in goods and services. It also contains in-depth analyses on the development and implementation of competition policy and law in a number of major APEC economies in the Asian region in the face of increasing globalisation and the widely recognised need for promoting international competitiveness.

The book thus is a timely and important contribution to this contemporary and high-priority area of intense international study and debates on competition policy and global competitiveness. Its other objective is to report on how all this economic policy interest and development and their implementation experience in developed and developing economies in the past decades has assisted or can assist governments and corporations alike in improving trade and business and economic integration as well as the welfare not only in the context of a global market but also and especially with a focus on major developing economies in the Asian region.

1.3   SCOPE OF STUDY

In Chapter 2, Tran Van Hoa gives, first, a concise description of the theoretical microfoundation underlying the concepts and issues of competition policy and law and, second, how these concepts and issues are related to the companion idea and aspects of global competitiveness. He then goes on to point out that, while competition and competitiveness have principally been the preoccupation and interest of the US and the EU respectively, the development and implementation agenda of these concepts and ideas have become increasingly important in a number of major countries in the Asian region, developed and developing alike. The chapter finally deals with recent activities in these Asian economies, often supported and funded by the APEC organisation and committees, on substantive issues in adopting and adapting competition policy and law and competitiveness to enhance their international trade and economic integration and to improve the welfare of their populations.

Chapter 3, written by Peter Lloyd, a consummate proponent of free trade and globalisation and an adviser to numerous government-appointed committees on trade in Australia, is essentially a review of the general development of competition policy and laws by a number of international organisations and in a number of regions in recent years. These organisations include, in descending order of scope, the WTO, the APEC forum and the Association of the South East Asian Nations (ASEAN). The regions covered are thus, in ascending geographical order, South East Asia, all countries surrounding the Pacific and, finally, the global economy. The chapter also describes in detail the difference in the scope and rules on the cross-border flows of goods and services, domestic and regional trade of the WTO, APEC and ASEAN respectively, and how these areas overlap in a global sense.

In Chapter 4, also written by Peter Lloyd, special focus is on the profound change in competition that has taken place over a decade or so around the world and how this was being reflected in the work of the multilateral organisations such as the Organisation for Economic Cooperation and Development (OECD), the WTO and the World Bank. This work not only deals with competition policies in their member countries but also in the countries that have not had them. The chapter finally discusses the development, promotion and implementation of competition policy and law in a number of major APEC countries including Vietnam in recent years.

In Chapter 5, written by Charles Harvie, special attention is focused on the small- and medium-sized enterprises (SMEs) sector in major transition economies in Asia and how the sector has to adapt to deal with the introduction of competition policy and law. The chapter then goes on to discuss specific aspects and issues of competition policy and laws in the most populous transition and developing economy in the world, namely China, and how they have affected the development and operation of the country's SMEs. The chapter emphasises that the experience from this area of study is of profound importance and can be used to assist other transition APEC economies in Asia in developing and implementing their own competition policy and law in order to raise their living standard and to enhance their international trade relations.

Aspects and issues of competition policy and law in the second OECD country in Asia, namely Korea (the other is Japan), are dealt with in Chapter 6. Written by Hyun-Hoon Lee, the chapter discusses first the objectives and developmental stages of Korea's Monopoly Regulation and Fair Trade Act since its enactment in 1980, and how the content of this Act has been pivotal to the country's economic reform and the benchmark for use in the assessment of its economic efficiency over the past two decades. Aspects of enforcement of the Act and the actions taken by its implementing agency, the Korea Fair Trade Commission, to handle the impact of the Asia economic and financial crisis of 1997 are also discussed. The chapter finally suggests a number of lessons from Korea's 22-year experience in competition policy and law that would be useful to other Asian economies in their process of drafting their own policy and law in this area.

Another country-specific study not on competition policy but on its related field, competitiveness, is given in Chapter 7. Written by Chaiyuth Punyasavatsut, the chapter posits first that the overemphasis of research on the financial sector in Thailand before and after the Asia crisis of 1997 has almost completely neglected the country's important sector, the real or manufacturing sector. It is this sector and its local and international competitiveness characteristics that have played an important role in the face of economic crises, increasing globalisation and growing international competitiveness. The chapter calculates and reports a number of competitiveness indicators for Thailand's manufacturing industry for both the pre- and post-crisis periods and discusses how these indicators can be of interest to economic as well as competition policy and also to informed debates on their related issues.

Chapter 8, written jointly by Le Viet Thai, Vu Xuan Nguyet Hong and Tran Van Hoa, provides a detailed study from a macroeconomic perspective on anti-trust law and competition policy and their recent development in a major transition and APEC economy in Asia, Vietnam. Various aspects and issues are covered and critically analysed. These include the country's traditional perception by the public and officials alike on competition and its recent change after the introduction of the Doi Moi policy in 1987, recent legislations to liberalises local and international trade and business, achievements in economic development and competitive market orientation policy and obstacles and challenges of increasing globalisation and growing international competitiveness influence. The chapter gives numerous examples to substantiate its discussions, and provides practical and concrete policy recommendations to improve the country's competitive business and trade environment, standard of living and international economic integration.

In Chapter 9, Charles Harvie presents a country-specific analysis of the need to have competition policy and law in Vietnam to nurture its continuing growth and development. The analysis specifically focuses on and discusses the possible impact of this competition policy and law on the operation of the private sector, namely the non-state SMEs, in the country. The idea is simply that private entrepreneurship and enterprise reform can play a crucial role in the restructuring of the economy for the benefits of non-farm employment and income enhancement. This reform is one of the objectives implied in the various sections of the competition policy and anti-trust law that were being drafted for Vietnam.

Finally, in Chapter 10, Hank Spier gives a good summary on the history, development and implementation of competition policy and law as stipulated in the Australian Trade practices Act. He also proposes that the vast experience in a number of countries (for example, Australia) that have successfully developed and implemented competition policy and law can be used as a valuable input and contribution to the development in this area in other countries, developed and developing alike. He specifically uses his long-standing experience and observations at the Australian Competition and Consumer Commission (ACCC) to look at many aspects and issues of regulations and their enforcement in Australia over the past 20 years or so, and suggests how these can be integrated as inputs in the work of, for example, Vietnam's Competition Law Drafting Committee to produce a practical, feasible and effective legislation and enforcement regime to assist the country to improve its competitive business environment and to enhance its international economic relations and integration.

2. Competition Policy and Global Competitiveness: Theory and Practice

Tran Van Hoa

2.1 INTRODUCTION

Competition policy and competitiveness are crucial requirements in modern economic, financial and trade management and governance at both the national and international levels. They are also consistent with the principles underlying a free market or a laissez-faire economy in contemporary international trade, development and growth in developed and developing economies alike worldwide.

With increasing globalisation and the prevailing influence of the World Trade Organisation (WTO) and the implementation requirement of its rules on its member and potential member states in recent years, the economies of the world have increasingly had to adopt, in compliance, many aspects of international competition policy and law standards. The expected outcomes of this adoption are to improve their global competitiveness and, subsequently, the economic welfare of their populations, either absolutely in the case of many developed countries or relatively in the case of many developing countries.

In the case of major developed and developing economies in the Asian region, competition policy and global competitiveness are, for the reasons mentioned above, now fast becoming national priority areas of study, development and promotion. These efforts are often assisted by the international organisations or institutions as well as academics and practicing competition experts.

This chapter summarises the fundamentals underlying the concepts of competition policy and law and global competitiveness and briefly describes their development and implementation agenda in a number of major countries in the Asian region. The objective is to provide a balanced view of the theory and practice in this important and growing area of research, discussion and knowledge dissemination. Substantive issues on different views on adopting or not competition policy in a number of countries in Asia are also briefly discussed.

2.2 COMPETITION POLICY AND GLOBAL COMPETITIVENESS

From a theoretical perspective, competition policy is based on the simple idea that a perfectly competitive economic model for a market or economy is best. It is best for a number of reasons: optimal use and allocation of physical and human resources, optimal pricing policies of products and factors of production and optimal distribution of income among its economic agents. Competition law is designed to assist in the achievement, maintenance or operation of a perfectly competitive market or economy in the face of market failures. Market failures occur when the necessary and sufficient conditionality of a perfectly competitive market or economy is violated. Global competitiveness is present when all economies of the world accept and adopt this perfectly competitive economic model and, as a result, also allow for perfect mobility of factors of production and trade.

The resulting outcomes, achieved naturally or through the implementation of competition policy and law are: optimal allocation of physical and human resources, optimal pricing policies, optimal income distribution and optimal welfare for all peoples in all economies in the world. The real obstacles to this economically ideal model are the presence of monopolistic, oligopolistic or duopolistic power in a market or economy or in a global sense involving international trade and business among nations that can seriously hamper the working of a laissez-faire principle or even an invisible hand in the sense of Adam Smith.

An official statement on the need to have a comprehensive competition policy in corporate and government governance of an economy, developed and developing and its effective practical implementation can be, very recently, found in the work of the United Nations Conference on Trade and Development (UNCTAD). The UNCTAD series on issues in competition law and policy has the title of the law 'Anti-monopoly Law' and 'Competition Act' in the elimination or control of restrictive business practices. The series contain draft commentaries to possible elements for articles of a model law or law in 2000 (UNCTAD 2000). This document has possible elements in 12 articles covering diverse subjects such as: the objectives or purpose of the law; definition and scope of application; acts or behaviours constituting an abuse of a dominant position of market power; notification, investigation and prohibition of mergers affecting concentrated markets; and aspects of consumer protection, administering authority, sanctions and relief, appeals and action for damages.

Further reviews of the various articles of the model law or law dealing with more specific issues were published by the UNCTAD in 2002 (see UNCTAD 2002a). To carry out the necessary work, the UNCTAD has established the Commission on Investment, Technology and Related Financial Issues and its agency, the Intergovernmental Group of Experts on Competition Law and Policy. This Group, at its third session on 2–4 July 2001, reviewed proposals for a new article, together with commentaries and suggested how to promote competition in the public utilities and infrastructure industries. It also suggested how to promote efficiencies through the development of appropriate competition law and institutions, how to protect general interest within industries opened to competition and how to organise the relationship between competition agencies and regulatory agencies (see UNCTAD 2001). The rest of this section attempts to summarise the main elements and issues of this work on Articles 5 and 6 by UNCTAD.

More specifically, the Group, at its fourth session in Geneva on 3–5 July 2002, attempted to revise the 2–4 July 2001 document above and discussed a model law on competition and reviewed all aspects of the set of multilaterally agreed principles and rules for the control of restrictive business practices. Of particular focus are strengthening the protection of general interest within industries opened to competition and organising the relationships between competition agencies and regulatory agencies more specifically with respect to local or regional governments. The proposals from this session were presented as Article 5 of the Model Law and commentaries. Article 5 takes into account a number of peculiarities of less mature market structures and focuses mainly on how to increase the efficiencies of regulated industries of developing countries and countries in transition. Possible elements of Article 5 and its commentaries on notification, investigation and prohibition of mergers affecting concentrated markets will become possible elements for Article 6 and its commentaries taking into account recent developments in the field.

This revised model covers possible elements and commentaries on (a) the relationship between competition policy and regulation and (b) aspects of notification, investigation and prohibition of mergers affecting concentrated markets. The final model is expected to be available during 2003.

It has been admitted by experts in their commentaries that followed the review of Article 5 that the purpose of Article 5 is to minimise the economic inefficiencies created in markets by anti-competitive behaviours. Competition policy is seen as consisting of not only competition law enforcement, but also, as we have discussed earlier, of trade liberalisation and deregulation in the interest of consumers' welfare. Competition law and policy are designed to regulate non-competitive behaviours by firms, whereas deregulation is aimed at minimising market-distorting government intervention. The proposal for Article 5 sets out four elements of definitions: the advocacy role of competition agencies, the definitions of regulation, and regulatory barriers to competition and the protection of general interest (UNCTAD 2002a, p. 5).

Other important aspects in the implementation of Article 5 are contained in Article 6. These aspects are concerned with the administration of competition law and policy and involve essentially the notification, investigation and prohibition of mergers affecting concentrated or monopolistic, oligopolistic and duopolistic markets.

Notable in Article 6 is the consideration for notification of mergers, takeovers, joint ventures or other acquisitions of control of business, including interlocking directorships, whether of a horizontal, vertical or conglomerate nature. Especially when at least one of the enterprises is established within the country of its operation and the resulting market share in the country, or any substantial part of it relating to any product or services, will result in a dominant firm or in a significant reduction of competition in a market dominated by very few firms (UNCTAD 2002a, p. 18).

The more practical role of competition in world trade of developing countries has also been recently highlighted by UNCTAD. Here the organisation cautions governments and corporations alike that more export growth and foreign direct investment as a result of more competition and enhanced trade liberalisation may not automatically generate commensurate income or welfare gains. It thinks that these countries are competing among themselves to export similar labour-intensive manufacturing products to the same markets and suggests, as a remedy, that these countries should move into higher-value exports by upgrading technology and improving productivity (see UNCTAD 2002b).

The argument against this assessment is that some technologically advanced countries, such as Japan, may be reluctant, to protect its competitive edge, to transfer its more recent hi-tech innovations to these developing countries (for example, Thailand) to protect its competitive edge. This a another aspect of study in competition policy and law and trade and investment liberalisation at the international level.

2.3   ISSUES IN COMPETITION POLICY

The theory, development, implementation and challenges of competition policy and law are of immense importance to corporate and government governance. They are not only important to business executives appointed by share-holders but also to regulating authorities appointed by the government. They have also been incorporated in the curricula of the specialist courses in many academic institutions around the world.

The aim of these courses is to equip students and participants alike with the economic tools needed for a critical appraisal of the welfare effects of competition, competition legislation and alternative competition policy decisions. Other objectives include intellectual support for academics and independent competition analysts in their work to deliver the economic expertise necessary for the growing political debates, legal disputes and administrative decision-making processes concerning market power and anti-trust, mergers and acquisitions, state subsidisation and so on.

These courses have several topics of focus. First and prominently is the oligopoly theory of Cournot, Bertrand, Stackelberg and Nash and its relevance to competition and efficiency from a Western experience. Emerging public policy issues in this case include an effective regulatory regime for maintaining a healthy level of product market competition and the link between procompetitive firm restructuring and a rise in productivity and profitability and their effects on social welfare. Second, the other topics introduced in the courses deal usually with market power, profit maximisation, the case of effective competition, collusive behaviour, demand elasticities, incentives to innovate and the tension between market power and economies of scale. Emerging policy issues from this second group of focus are the sustainable levels of market power from a social welfare perspective and consumers' benefits when public monopolies are sold to strategic private and foreign investors. Third, the courses also consider the changing market structures, barriers to entry and exit, the interaction of infrastructure regulation, competition and trade policies and the aspects of the European competition policy and the challenges of enlargement (see, for example, the Central European University website 2002).

The general concepts and issues of competition policy and law as described above have been assumed to be applied equally to both developed and developing economies and globally.

2.4   COMPETITION POLICY AND LAW IN MAJOR ASIAN ECONOMIES

Competition policy and law has been particularly of interest to the Western economies especially the European Union and its companion concept to promote international trade and competitiveness, namely globalisation, has mainly been of primary concern for the US. In spite of this policy emphasis of the world's two major trading blocs, most developed and developing economies in the Asian region and perhaps Africa are only in the development and discussion stages of competition policy and law.

In the Asian region, we note an important fact that not all major economies have adopted competition policy and law. The country of interest in this case is Singapore, a newly developed or industrialised economy. Singapore believes that a law on competition is not necessary for it as its policy of openness of the country to international competitiveness is the most effective way to have competition. Korea, an Asian member of the Organisation for Economic Cooperation and Development (OECD), is only fast building its capacity in competition policy and regulatory reform to control basically its top 30 chaebols that practically have run the economy. China, a new member of the WTO, has not got to the stage of development in these areas and Vietnam is also at its very early stage of development and discussion.

To assist the development of competition policy and law, the regional organisations such as the Asia–Pacific Economic Cooperation (APEC) forum have been active in providing funds and experts' meetings for capacity building in this area for major Asian economies. For example, its Committee on Trade and Investment (CTI) has devoted a forum on competition policy as one of its major collective actions plans. This forum is interested in laws and policy that affect the flows of trade and investment in the APEC region. The CTI has also had two fora on deregulation and trade facilitation and a working group on trade promotion. In fact, its Osaka Action Agenda (OAA) combines both competition and deregulation as a focus of study and its priority includes business and academic inputs through the Pacific Economic Cooperation Council (PECC) to enhance technology transfer in this respect. In addition, the CTI, through its fora and collective action plans (CAPs), actively promotes the APEC principles of competition and regulatory reform and seeks cooperative initiatives with the OECD and specifically the European Union on its experience on regulatory reform.

More specifically, as early as November 1994, APEC Ministers had agreed that one of its committees, the CTI, would develop a study to understand better competition issues, in particular competition laws and policies of economies in Asia and how they affect flows of trade and investment in the APEC region. This study would also identify potential areas of technical cooperation among APEC member economies. In 1996, the OAA work programmes for competition policy and deregulation were combined.

In addition, as a result of the damages and contagion of the Asian economic and financial crisis of the late 1990s, APEC Ministers had endorsed, in 1999, the APEC Principles to Enhance Competition and Regulatory Reform and approved a 'road map' which established the basis for subsequent work on strengthening the markets in the region.

In 2001, with more globalisation, a slow economic recovery in Asia and the still volatile situation of the world's financial markets, APEC Leaders agreed that the OAA should be broadened to 'reflect fundamental changes in the global economy' since Osaka, including 'Strengthening the Functioning of Markets'. The implementation of competition policy and deregulation area provides markets with a framework that encourages market discipline, eliminates distortions and promotes economic efficiency. Therefore, competition policy and deregulation area is one of the key elements contributing to both the 'road map' and the broadening of the OAA (see APEC 2002).

The focus of the APEC–CTI work on competition policy and law in major APEC countries in Asia is therefore not an ad hoc or short-term policy project or plan. In fact, in the next two years, the APEC–CTI work involves a number of important activities and programmes. These include: implementation of the APEC principles above, development of APEC competition law for developing economies, building domestic capacity for high-quality regulatory regimes, building and transferring technical skills and knowledge on competition policy and regulatory reform and finally, sharing, exchanging and discussing developments and challenges in competition policy and regulatory reform. For 2002 for example, two workshops were planned. The first one was held in Merida, Mexico in April. The second will be held in Korea in September. The programme Implementation of the Training Program to promote Economic competition in APEC Economies aims at promoting the implementation of the APEC Principles through the organisation of seminars focusing on regulation in the energy, telecommunications, transportation and finance sectors

On other practical capacity-building sides of work on competition and regulatory reform in major Asian economies in the APEC and related to the APEC programmes above, we can mention that, during 2001, a number of training programmes were conducted by international academic institutions to assist major countries in Asia to develop and promote their competition policy and law. One such program was, for example, run by the Vietnam Focus Research Program, the University of Wollongong and led by Prof Tran Van Hoa. This programme, which focused on the APEC principles of competition and regulatory reform and commentaries on drafts or implementation of competition law, was funded by the Australian Department of Foreign Affairs and Trade aid agency, AusAID and also had the collaboration of other national and international institutions and corporations in East and South East Asia, Oceania and North America. These institutions and corporations include the University of Melbourne, the Australian Competition and Consumer Commission (ACCC), Kangwon National University in Korea, the Central Institute for Economic Management, Vietnam Ministry of Planning and Investment and the Drafting Committee of Competition Law of Vietnam Ministry of Trade and Siemens International.

About at the same time, the UNCTAD also ran a series of workshops in Vietnam to help specifically the country to understand better the issues and aspects of this policy and law as well as to provide expert commentaries on Vietnam drafts of its competition policy and law. These workshops' agenda and commentaries complemented the institutional and academic work mentioned above.

2.5   CONCLUSIONS

In the preceding sections, we have briefly discussed the growing trend in the world to embrace increasing globalisation and, with it, the necessity to have international competitiveness. To support globalisation and to promote international competitiveness, the development and implementation of competition policy and law is a pre-requisite for all trading countries. Since the ultimate purposes of globalisation and global competitiveness are to liberalise trade and investment around the world to enhance the welfare of its populations, an effective and well-managed competition policy and law can substantially contribute to achieving these objectives.

We have also discussed the economic foundation of the crucial concepts of globalisation, international competitiveness, competition policy and law. We have, in addition, described their pertinent and essential aspects to assist the development and implementation of competitiveness and regulatory reform in both developed and developing economies. In our view, the idea that singularly motivates these concepts is simply the principle of a laissez-faire state or a perfectly competitive market or a group of markets that carry out trade and business among themselves. Since a laissez-faire state may not be present due to market failures, competition policy and law are an absolute requirement for optimal corporate and government governance, nationally and globally, to achieve economic efficiencies as well as welfare improvement.

In the preceding sections, we have also noted the interest of the US in pursuing globalisation and that of the European Union to promote competition policy and law. We have provided reasons on how this preoccupation of the world's two major economic and trading blocs will make it necessary for developed and especially developing countries alike in the Asian region to embrace these concepts and develop their own competition policy and law to be part of the growing trend and also to gain benefits from a liberalisation of trade and investment.

The following chapters in the present book will provide further detail on the various aspects and issues raised in this chapter and on how the efforts by a number of major countries in Asia have been carried out to deal, at the practical level, with these aspects and issues. The chapters also record the experiences of countries that have had a long history of developing and administering competition policy and law and how these experiences can be effectively used by experts and implementing agencies to assist economies in the Asian region to develop their own appropriate policy and law in this area.

REFERENCES

Asia–Pacific Economic Cooperation (APEC) forum (2002), 'Competition Policy',

Central European University (2002), 'Competition Policy in the Transition: Theory, Implementation and Challenges', <www.ceu.hu/sun/SUN%202001/ Descriptions/competition_policy.htm>

Pacific Economic Cooperation Council (PECC) (2002), 'Trade Forum',

United Nations Conference on Trade and Development (UNCTAD) (2000), 'Model Law on Competition', Geneva, TD/RBP/CONF.5/7.

United Nations Conference on Trade and Development (UNCTAD) (2001), 'Intergovernmental Group of Experts on Competition Law and Policy', Geneva, TD/B/COM.2/CPL/23,

United Nations Conference on Trade and Development (UNCTAD) (2002a), 'Work on the Model Law on Competition', Geneva, TD/B/COM.2/CPL/31,

United Nations Conference on Trade and Development (UNCTAD) (2002b), 'Trade and Development Report 2002: Developing Countries in World Trade', Geneva,

3 Competition Policy in APEC, ASEAN and the WTO

P.J. Lloyd

This chapter reviews the development of competition policy and laws in the WTO (World Trade Organisation), APEC (Asia–Pacific Economic Cooperation forum) and ASEAN (Association of the South East Asian Nations). The rules of the WTO concern cross-border flows of goods and services whereas those of APEC are chiefly concerned with domestic competition trade and those of ASEAN with regional trade but there is considerable and increasing overlap between these flows.

3.1 RULES RELATING TO COMPETITION POLICY AND THE CURRENT DEBATE IN THE WTO

3.1.1 Present Competition Rules and Agreements in the WTO

The WTO is a multilateral organisation which lays down the rules of the world trading system, that is, the system which regulates world trade in goods and services (but not, with some minor exceptions, international trade in capital or labour). Its objective, as set out in the Preamble to the Agreement that established it, is a reduction in barriers to international trade in goods and services and the elimination of discrimination in international trade. As its rules are binding on all member countries, it provides a system of international trade law. This law is enforceable through its Dispute Settlement Provisions. These rules relate to government measures that restrict trade. Thus, it is an organisation which regulates the behaviour of national governments relating to international trade in goods and services.

The WTO does not address 'competition policy' as such. It has no explicit objective relating to the promotion of competition. It does not regulate the competition laws of its members and it imposes no obligation on members to have national competition laws. It does, however, have a number of provisions relating to areas of international competition among private producers who trade goods and services and rules relating to nullification and impairment of negotiated concessions that might in some circumstances be used to enforce national competition laws.

In relation to business conduct, the most important of the specific provisions in the body of law inherited from the GATT (General Agreement on Tariffs and Trade), which is known as GATT 1994, are those dealing with enterprises owned by states or enterprises with import monopolies or exclusive or special trading privileges; and with anti-dumping and subsidised trade. (These are described in WTO 1996, Chapter 4.) The provisions under Article XVII relating to state trading are concerned with enforcing non-discrimination among foreign suppliers and national treatment. Anti-dumping action under international trade law is not normally regarded as a part of competition law but there is concern that it may sometimes have anti-competitive effects. Export subsidies are prohibited except for primary products under Article XVI. The provisions under Article VI relating to subsidised import trade do not prohibit or regulate subsidy levels. They merely permit member countries to take action against subsidised imports for those categories of subsidies that are actionable by means of imposing countervailing duties up to the limit of the rate of subsidy.

The WTO does not prohibit or otherwise regulate any forms of anti-competitive business conduct as such. There are no provisions in the GATT 1994 that put obligations on member countries to take action against horizontal or vertical restraints. There are no provisions concerning mergers. GATT 1994 does not prohibit export or import cartels, which are the most blatant form of anti-competitive conduct based on international trade flows. In the case of import cartels, all it does, under the article dealing with state monopolies, is to require that state monopolies must not operate so as to afford protection in excess of the scheduled tariff rate. It prohibits quantitative restrictions on exports with some exceptions but this prohibition does not apply to cartel activities that raise prices. This lack of action against trade cartels is a clear demonstration that the international trade law of the GATT was not concerned with competition issues. Rather it has been concerned with the trade effects of businesses that dump or trade in subsidised goods or are state traders. To adapt the terminology of the WTO itself, one could say that the GATT 1994 (and the GATS (General Agreement on Trade in Services) and TRIMS (Trade-Related Investment Measures Agreement)) are concerned only with *trade-related* competition problems.

The GATS Agreement of the Uruguay Round introduced new areas of competition-related law into the WTO. The GATS has provisions that apply to enterprises rather than to government measures. In this respect, it departs from GATT 1994 whose only enterprise-specific provisions relate to state trading and these are limited to non-discrimination, as noted. Article VIII of GATS contains a general requirement that, where there is a monopoly supplier, that member shall ensure that the supplier does not abuse its monopoly position to act in a manner which is inconsistent with the national treatment obligations and specific commitments made by the member in respect of the service. Article IX recognises that certain business practices of service suppliers may restrain competition and thereby restrict trade in services.

One specific area of competition in services is subject to further rules in an Annex to GATS. This is the area of interconnection to telecommunications facilities. An important consideration in the Uruguay Round negotiations on services was the recognition that an offer to provide market access in a specific service area (for example, financial services) could be nullified by the failure of a member country to offer to provide for access to a public telecommunications network that is necessary to sell the service. To be offered market access in financial services but denied access to leased lines or facilities may totally undermine the value of the offer. A Telecommunications Annex to the GATS was added to ensure that 'any other Member is accorded access to and the use of public telecommunications transport networks and services on reasonable and non-discriminatory terms and conditions, for the supply of the service'. Similar provisions apply to access to private networks and services. These Annex provisions apply only to those services which member countries have inscribed on their schedules.

These competition-related provisions of GATS came about because market access in the GATS has a much broader definition than in the GATT 1994 which deals only with trade in goods. Trade in services is defined to include supply by the modes of 'commercial presence' and by 'the movement of natural persons' as well as the cross-border supply of services. Consequently, market access can be impeded by restrictions on entry for foreign investors or denial of national treatment to foreign investors who supply services. Article XVI ('Market Access') expressly prohibits limits on the number of service suppliers. This would guarantee the right of establishment to foreign service providers but it only applies to those services listed on the Members' Schedules. (GATT 1996a, Chapter 4.V outlines the investment-related provisions of the GATS.) The fundamental importance of the GATS is that, in the area of services, the WTO has already integrated some instruments of international trade, foreign investment and competition policies.

The enforcement of these competition-related provisions of GATS is based on positive comity and provides for consultation among members and enforcement by means of national laws and regulations. Each member will, at the request of another member, enter into consultations with a view to the government concerned eliminating the restrictive practices within its territory. When a member is approached to enter into consultations, it is necessary to accord full and sympathetic consideration to such a request. The member is to cooperate through the supply of publicly available non-confidential information of relevance to the matter in question. The member is also to provide other information, subject to its domestic law and to the conclusion of a satisfactory agreement concerning safeguarding of its confidentiality by the requesting party.

Other provisions of the GATS address competition concerns. These provisions include transparency, government procurement, the distribution and marketing of services and subsidies. These are important because services are essential inputs into many production activities.

Since the Uruguay Round, the Agreement on Basic Telecommunications was concluded in 1997. This Agreement only applies to those countries that have signed it; to date some 69 countries have opted to do so. The Reference Paper of the Agreement on Basic Telecommunications, which some of the signatory governments have adhered to, contains provisions relating to competition. It states that any new supplier may interconnect with the existing network of a major supplier on non-discriminatory and reasonable terms. The Reference Paper also specifically refers to the prevention of anti-competitive practices in telecommunications. This goes further than the access provisions of the Annex to the GATS. It states that: 'Appropriate measures shall be maintained for the purpose of preventing suppliers who, alone or together, are a major supplier from engaging in or continuing anti-competitive practices' (WTO Negotiating Group on Basic Telecommunications 1996). It lists three practices in particular: 'anti-competitive cross-subsidisation', 'using information obtained from competitors with anti-competitive results' and 'not making available to other service suppliers on a timely basis technical information about essential facilities and commercially relevant information which are necessary for them to provide services'.

The Trade-Related Aspects of Intellectual Property Rights (TRIPS) Agreement has as its objective the protection of intellectual property rights. It contains two articles which relate to aspects of competition: these concern 'effective protection against certain competition' (Article 39) and control of 'anti-competitive practices' (Article 40). Much of it concerns issues of pricing for the use of intellectual property, which is a classic competition issue. As with the GATS, it incorporates positive comity. Enforcement of these provisions is by means of civil and administrative procedures and remedies under national laws. Intellectual property transactions too are an increasingly important part of the international trade in technologies and goods.

The Trade-Related Investment Measures (TRIMS) Agreement is intended to discipline trade-related investment measures that had hitherto escaped any international regulation. In particular, it prohibits TRIMS that are inconsistent with the WTO Articles relating to National Treatment or the General Elimination of Quantitative Restrictions.

One further aspect of the rules of the WTO is relevant to cross-border competition. This is the Dispute Settlement Procedures (DSP) of the WTO. As the WTO (1997, p. 79) observes: 'There has been considerable discussion as to whether the failure of a member to enforce its competition laws to prevent enterprise practices that are impeding market access to trading partners could be successfully challenged under this provision'. The provision cited is the 'non-violation' clause of the DSP that applies to cases where it is alleged that benefits accruing to a member are being nullified or impaired or the attainment of an objective of the Agreement is being impeded by a government measure even if it does not conflict with the provisions of the WTO Agreement. The use of this provision can only occur when private conduct can be attributed to a government measure and proof of nullification or impairment is shown. In fact, only one case concerning the role of government laws and regulations relating to anti-competitive conduct has been brought to the WTO. This was the Kodak/Fuji case brought by the US. In this case the WTO Panel found that nullification or impairment were not proven. (See Lloyd and Vautier 1999, Chapter 11, for a discussion of this case.)

These competition-related rules of the WTO can be compared with the principles-based approach recommended in Section 1. The international trade law of the WTO does not have a set of principles that apply consistently to all of the rules but some principles are applied selectively. The principle of *non-discrimination* is enshrined in Article I of GATT 1994, the body of trade law inherited from the GATT at the time of the creation of the WTO in 1996. But the scope of non-discrimination in this article is restricted to non-discrimination among foreign nations, which is called Most Favoured Nation (MFN) treatment. Furthermore, there are exceptions to MFN treatment, most importantly the provisions in Article XXIV and the Enabling Clause that permit the existence of discriminatory regional trading arrangements. National Treatment on a 'no less favourable' basis is required under Article III and under GATS though in the latter case it applies only to those sectors inscribed in a Member's GATS Schedule. Non-discrimination in the sense of the removal of all border barriers that discriminate against foreign suppliers of goods and services would require free trade.

The principle of *transparency* is recognised in several of the Uruguay Round Agreements including GATS Article III ('Transparency') and TRIMS Article 6 ('Transparency'). The WTO is striving to be a more transparent organisation and encourages transparency in the international trade laws of its members through the Trade Policy Review Mechanism.

The principle of *comprehensiveness* is clearly breached in regard to those provisions of the WTO that affect competition in international markets. The GATS and later agreements on trade in services are the major occurrences in the WTO of the new dimensions of policy at the interface of international trade and competition policy. There are no competition provisions in the WTO applying to goods trade. Within the GATS, there is differential treatment of service sectors. We have noted the special provisions in the Annex to GATS and in the Basic Telecommunications Agreement that apply to the telecommunications sector. Similar problems of interconnection arise in other service industries but these are not addressed in GATS.

With respect to the list of business conduct that is covered, the WTO still addresses only a small fraction of the conduct and competition problems that might be addressed by multilateral competition law. There are no provisions at all in the WTO that relate to horizontal restraints involving collusion (such as price-fixing or bid-rigging), abuse of dominance, vertical restraints or mergers.

3.1.2   The WTO Working Group on the Interaction between Trade and Competition Policy

At the first Ministerial Conference of the WTO in Singapore in December 1996, it was agreed to set up a Working Group to study issues relating to the interaction between trade and competition policy, including anti-competitive business practices. The Ministerial Declaration states clearly that any future negotiations regarding multilateral disciplines in this area would take place only after an 'explicit consensus decision' is reached by the WTO. In the Working Group, the European Union (EU), the USA and Japan have exhibited fundamentally different perspectives on the scope and approach of international 'competition policy' issues. The Working Group represents the current debate about competition policy.

The Working Group has a mandate 'to study issues raised by Members relating to the interaction between trade and competition policy, including anti-competitive business practices, in order to identify any areas that may merit further consideration in the WTO framework'.

3.1.3   Work Programme

For its first two-year work programme members suggested a number of issues for study:

1.   the relationship between the objectives, principles, concepts, scope and instruments of trade and competition policy; and the relationship of trade and competition policy to development and economic growth.
2.   stocktaking and analysis of existing instruments, standards and activities regarding trade and competition policy, including stocktaking and analysis of experiences with their application, specifically:

    • national competition policies, laws and instruments as they relate to trade;
    • existing WTO provisions;
    • bilateral, regional, plurilateral and multilateral agreements and initiatives.

3.   the interaction between trade and competition policy:

- the impact of anti-competitive practices (of enterprises and associations) on international trade;
- the impact on competition and international trade of
  -   state monopolies;
  -   exclusive rights;
  -   regulatory policies;
- the impact of trade policy on competition;
- the relationship between competition policy; and
  -   the trade-related aspects of intellectual property rights;
  -   investment.

The Working Group made frequent references to the relevance of the WTO disciplines of *transparency* and *national treatment* and suggested that there was already a degree of consensus on the 'core principles of competition policy'. But one has to distinguish between a market access framework (based on country access and international trade) and a competition framework (based on efficiency in globalising markets and competition from all modes of supply).

Business practices and government actions
There is obviously a strong interest among Working Group participants in competition law and in remedies for anti-competitive business practices that affect/distort/restrain *international trade*. The implication is that bringing these practices within WTO rules would serve trade objectives. This raises the question as to whether practices might be deemed anti-competitive because they distort trade. The correct question – for competition analysis – is whether an allegedly anti-competitive practice distorts competition and efficiency in a relevant market to such an extent that it fails an agreed *competition* standard.

The Group's interest in private business practices is balanced to some extent by the view that government policies and measures can also be anti-competitive and can themselves facilitate anti-competitive private conduct. As Section 1 established, and as Section 4 confirms, a wide range of government policies (including deregulation, regulatory reform and mutually reinforcing trade policies) are relevant to the promotion of competitive behaviour. This is consistent with the major shift over the past decade in domestic policy orientation.

The Working Group appears comfortable with specific competition advocacy activities aimed at fostering a national competition culture, procompetitive regulations and the removal of specific impediments to competition. But the stronger focus is on trade impediments and, implicitly, the interests of national producers and exporters.

There is interest in looking at the impact of trade policy, and trade remedies in particular, on competition and in promoting policy coherence and procompetitive policies throughout the WTO itself. But there is clearly tension on how anti-dumping should be treated in future. The US view, which supports the status quo, is that anti-dumping and competition laws should maintain their different objectives and that anti-dumping laws should neither be replaced by competition laws nor modified to reflect competition policy and principles. A modest departure from this stance would be to incorporate 'competition policy thinking ... into trade policy formulation'.

Categories of business practices

The Working Group has assembled much material on both the theoretical and practical risks of 'anti-competitive' business behaviour. In looking at anti-competitive practices, the Working Group adopted three 'broad analytical categories', while noting:

- that the impacts of the examples provided would depend on the particular surrounding circumstances and case-by-case analyses; and
- that a flexible approach might be appropriate in relation to 'non-conventional horizontal arrangements' such as strategic alliances and certain arrangements involving small- and medium-sized enterprises.

The three categories were:

1.   practices affecting market access for imports (for example, domestic import cartels; market allocations within international cartels; 'unreasonable obstruction' of parallel imports; exclusionary abuses of a 'dominant position'; vertical restraints that 'foreclosed markets to competitors'[5]);
2.   practices affecting international markets, where different countries were affected in largely the same way (for example, price and output policies of international cartels, including in service sectors such as maritime shipping and financial); and
3.   practices having a differential impact on the national markets of countries (for example, export cartels).

Competition law considerations

But it was far from clear how members' interests could be protected against such restrictive business practices. As already alluded to, the positioning of competition law is a matter of debate. A 'cautious and gradual approach was warranted'; 'basic standards' could be considered. Particular aspects raised in relation to competition law include:

- consistency with the WTO principles of non-discrimination and national treatment;

- the fact that multiple goals are often assigned to competition law, including the preservation of opportunities for small- and medium-sized businesses;
- whether there is sufficient regard to the effects in relatively small countries of multinational enterprise mergers;
- the increased use of a 'rule of reason' approach as distinct from *per se* competition rules;
- access to adjudicating authorities, and the importance of their transparency; and
- the benefits of strengthening international cooperation mechanisms for competition law enforcement.

The interface between competition law and intellectual property protection is an issue of relevance to both developed and developing economy participants.

Convergence and divergence of views

The Working Group Reports do not set out to establish consensus views although areas of convergence and divergence are discernible. On the convergence side: the issues are complex in conceptual and analytical terms, the multilateral role is not clear-cut, and the Group's focus should remain on the *interaction* between trade and competition policy (although this appears open to the interpretation of trade policy and competition policy). There is some concern about inconsistency between WTO rules and a competition objective, some interest in looking at those government as well as private measures that have the greatest negative impact on trade and competition, some focus on the welfare-reducing effects of trade restrictions and of exemptions from national competition rules, and some reference to the notion of global economic welfare and to the desirability of greater policy coherence to that end.

On the divergence side: there are fundamental differences of view as to the appropriate scope of competition issues for the WTO, as to where anti-dumping fits within international approaches to 'competition policy' and on whether or not countries (and developing countries in particular) should have a general competition law. The general concern here (not just in developing countries) is about a WTO 'competition framework' constraining the discretion of national competition authorities in respect of investigation, enforcement and remedies, and creating difficulties in domestic policy balance and objectives.

There are sharp divergences among the major members of the WTO. The EU considers that the WTO should develop competition disciplines and instruments to deal with anti-competitive practices with a significant international dimension. At the same time, WTO members should commit to adopting effective domestic competition policies, that is, including but not confined to competition law. Japan favours the WTO introducing a procompetitive dimension into its trade measures (notably anti-dumping and safeguard) together with the voluntary adoption of national competition law and enforcement regimes. The US is resisting any multilateral competition disciplines. It considers that the Working Group should focus on the role of competition policy in enhancing trade liberalisation, with implementation based on domestic competition laws coupled with bilateral cooperation agreements to deal with cross-border issues.

An important theme of this chapter is that underlying the divergent views is the tension (although not explicit) between a *national market access* approach to 'competition policy' and a *global market competition* approach. This is notwithstanding the apparent agreement (at least amongst the EU, Japan and the US) that the overriding aim of both trade policy and competition policy should be the promotion of economic efficiency and consumer or economic welfare. A market (= country) access approach targets any policy or practice that affects/distorts/restrains/harms international trade between two countries or that is seen to negate the benefits from negotiated trade concessions. The interest here is *trade maximisation.* A competition approach targets government or private conduct that adversely affects the competitive process in globalising markets (defined in economic not geographic terms). The interest here is efficient resource allocations and *welfare maximisation.*

The development dimension

The Working Group's mandate requires it to take 'the development dimension fully into account'. In broad terms, 'competition policy' is seen as a building block for economic development, while recognising the public education required to develop a competition culture.

There has been cooperation with UNCTAD (United Nations Conference on Trade and Development) and, amongst others, the World Bank and APEC have alerted the Group to issues and practices (for example, export cartels) of particular relevance to developing countries; to the incidence of anti-competitive enterprise practices between developing countries; and to the importance of flexibility in dealing with different stages of economic development and transitional issues as economies become more market oriented. Exclusions, exemptions and other temporary measures from competition disciplines are seen as important features for developing and transition economies. The same is true of technical cooperation for effective implementation of competition law and policy. The WTO might enhance voluntary cooperation through, for example, technical assistance and capacity building, and promulgating guidelines for regular review of national regulatory policies (relative to competition principles) and for cooperation agreements.

In ASEAN's view, as expressed to the Working Group, competition-restricting trade measures may be justified if they are a means of achieving national objectives, for instance, capital intensive development or national exploitation of natural resources. National competition laws are not essential.

Considering international competition law disciplines is premature. A first step should be to ascertain the conflicts between trade and competition policy.

Following a review by the Working Group at the end of 1998, the General Council agreed with the Working Group's recommendations that it continue its education work with a focus during 1999 on:

- the relevance of fundamental WTO principles of national treatment, transparency, and most-favoured-nation treatment to competition policy and *vice versa*;
- approaches to promoting cooperation and communication among Members, including in the field of technical cooperation; and
- the contribution of competition policy to achieving the objectives of the WTO, including the promotion of international trade.

The proposed work thus covers three important elements:

- the relevance of general principles to 'competition policy';
- international cooperation; and
- the link between competition policy and WTO objectives.

Determining the linkages between WTO principles and 'competition policy' would be a useful bridge to core Competition Principles and to the building of a more comprehensive and coherent approach to competition issues within the WTO. As reflected in Section 1, *non-discrimination* in the sense of *competitive neutrality* is a core element. And greater clarity of objectives is centrally important, as is intergovernment cooperation for building a competition framework to guide both government and business behaviour.

The current work programme makes no reference to specific topics previously discussed in the Working Group, such as cartel rules, strengthening of national competition laws, exclusions, minimum standards, convergence in merger or takeover procedures and policy inconsistencies. But neither are such topics expressly excluded from future deliberations. Given the Group's terms of reference, it would be especially difficult to exclude the trade-related instruments of anti-dumping and export and import cartels from future discussions.

3.2   COMPETITION POLICY IN APEC AND ASEAN

3.2.1   Competition Policy in APEC

At their Osaka Meeting in December 1995, APEC's Economic Leaders adopted an Action Plan. This included action in 15 specific areas, of which 'Competition

Policy' was one. The objective of this policy area is given as:

> APEC economies will enhance the competitive environment in the Asia–Pacific region by introducing or maintaining effective and adequate competition policy and/or laws and associated enforcement policies, ensuring the transparency of the above and promoting cooperation among the APEC economies, thereby maximising, *inter alia*, the efficient operation of markets, competition among producers and consumer benefits (APEC 1995).

To make these plans operational, APEC members develop both a Collective Action Plan (CAPs) and Individual Action Plan (IAPs) in the area of competition policy.

The Collective Plan states that APEC members will gather information, promote dialogue, develop the understanding of competition policy, encourage cooperation among the competition authorities and consider developing non-binding principles on competition policy and law in the APEC.

The Individual Action Plans are ongoing and reported by member economies each year. The Guidelines for the Individual Action Plans require each APEC economy to review its competition policy and/or laws, implement as appropriate technical assistance in regard to policy development of the powers and functions of enforcement agencies and the enforcement thereof in terms of transparency, and to establish appropriate cooperation arrangements among APEC economies.

Thus, the Osaka Action Plan does not require member economies to develop national competition policies and laws in the manner of NAFTA (North America Free Trade Agreement) and some other RTAs (Regional Trade Agreements). But it requires each member to review its competition policy and laws and takes a strong stand on competition advocacy. It also adopts the principles of transparency and bilateral cooperation where national laws exist.

The Committee on Trade and Investment of APEC agreed in 1996 to merge the areas of competition with that of deregulation, which was another of the 15 policy areas nominated in the Osaka Action Plan. This is a further indication of the broad view of competition taken in APEC.

The construction of the APEC Database on Competition Policy and Law received its mandate from the Collective Plan. This alone has made a major contribution to the promulgation and understanding of competition policy and law in the region. The Individual Action Plans (IAPs) report actions in the individual member economies. These IAPs show a wide range of view on the role of competition policy and competition law and its enforcement, as noted in Section 2 above.

APEC has drawn up non-binding principles of competition policy and law, as envisaged in the CAPs. The process began when the Pacific Economic Cooperation Council (PECC) set up the Competition Principles Project in 1993.

PECC is a tripartite body in the region and it is the only non-governmental official observer at APEC meetings. This Project culminated in the PECC Competition Principles (PECC 1999). These were completed in 1999 and forwarded to the APEC Committee on Trade and Investment. They emphasise principles of competition policy as distinct from rules or minimum standards. They enunciated four core principles: comprehensiveness, transparency in policies and processes, accountability and non-discrimination. The last is interpreted as 'competitive neutrality in respect of the different modes of domestic and international supply'. These Principles are notable for the broad view of competition policy and the emphasis on strong principles underlying the construction of policies and laws.

The 1999 APEC Leaders' Meeting in Auckland adopted APEC Principles to Enhance Competition and Regulatory Reform. 'These principles provide a core part of the framework for strengthening markets which will better integrate individual and collective actions by APEC economies to achieve those goals' (APEC 2000). The goals mentioned are the goals of 'free and open trade and investment' which were adopted at the Bogor Meeting of APEC Leaders in 1995. The APEC Principles draw very heavily on the PECC Principles. They have the same four core principles of non-discrimination, comprehensiveness, transparency and accountability. Non-discrimination is taken to be 'application of competition and regulatory principles in a manner that does not discriminate between or among economic entities in like circumstances, whether these entities are foreign or domestic'. The Principles also include a commitment to review regulations and policies to ensure they comply with the principles, technical assistance and capacity building, and to develop effective means of cooperation between APEC economy regulatory agencies including competition authorities.

These APEC Principles are non-binding and based on the recognition of differences among the countries in their economic circumstances and institutions. Thus, they have no legal force and continue the APEC practice of voluntary implementation. Overall, the main contributions of the APEC activities have been the development of a form of competition advocacy that is taken seriously by the member countries because it is voluntary and cooperative, and the development of core principles to underlie policies relating to competition. It has significantly aided the strengthening of competition policies in those APEC countries that do not have competition policies and/or laws.

3.2.2   Competition Policy in ASEAN

ASEAN which has not developed a region-wide competition law. The 1999 Hanoi Plan of Action, which is the latest statement of ASEAN direction, refers to cooperation to 'explore the merits of common competition policy' as a possible area of future integration (ASEAN 1999).

The absence of development of regional competition law in ASEAN reflects the general underdevelopment of competition law among the ASEAN countries, as noted in the earlier paper 'Competition Policy Principles and a Review of the Asia–Pacific Region'. This lack of development in ASEAN contrasts with the development of competition policy and law in some other regional trading arrangements, notably the EU and the CER (Closer Economic Relations between Australia and New Zealand). Competition policy and law in these two regional trading arrangements is discussed in Lloyd and Vautier 1999, Chapters 4 and 5.

3.3   CONCLUSION

The approaches to competition policy in these three domains differ considerably. This is a reflection of differences among nations with respect to competition policy issues and the uneven development of competition policy and law in the global economy. Yet, there is agreement on basic principles. The discussions in all three domains emphasise the importance of promoting competition in all markets, the necessity of observing the basic principles of neutrality, transparency and accountability and the necessity of all national governments to review their trade and industrial policies in order to ensure that markets are contestable and do not discriminate in favour of particular domestic or international producers.

REFERENCES

Asia–Pacific Economic Cooperation Forum (APEC) (1995), *Osaka Action Plan*, Singapore: APEC Secretariat.
APEC (1999), 'APEC Principles to Enhance Competition and Regulatory Reform', Attachment to *Leaders' Declaration – New Zealand*, Singapore: APEC Secretariat.
APEC (2000), 'Competition Policy and Law Database', <www.apecccp.org.tw/doc/>.
ASEAN (1999), *Hanoi Plan of Action*, ASEAN Secretariat, Jakarta.
Asian Development Bank (1999), *Asian Development Outlook 1999*, Manila: Asian Development Bank.
Lloyd, P.J. and K.M. Vautier (1999), *Promoting Competition in Global Markets: A Multi-National Approach*, Cheltenham, UK: Edward Elgar.
Pacific Economic Cooperation Council (PECC) (1999), *PECC Competition Principles: PECC Principles for Guiding the Development of a Competition-Driven Policy Framework for APEC Economies*, Singapore: PECC.
World Trade Organisation (WTO) (1996), 'Negotiating Group on Basic Telecommunications', *Reference Paper*, Geneva: WTO.

4. Competition Law in APEC Economies and in Vietnam

P.J. Lloyd

4.1 INTRODUCTION

Most nations, both developed and developing alike, now recognise that the promotion of competition among producers is an important objective of economic policies. There has been a profound change from the views that predominated a decade or more ago when competition was not a widely held objective. This change is reflected in the multilateral organisations such as the OECD, the WTO and the World Bank, all of which have introduced programmes to assist countries that do not have competition policies. In the Asia–Pacific region, the 1999 APEC Leaders' meeting in Auckland adopted APEC Principles to Enhance Competition and Regulatory Reform (APEC 2000) that are recommended but are not binding on member economies. (For a review of the reasons why competition is important and the development of new policies of competition promotion in the WTO, APEC and ASEAN, see Lloyd 2001.) Countries that do not have competition policies are now introducing them. Vietnam, a major economy in the APEC region, is one of these countries.

4.2 COMPETITION POLICY AND LAW

The term competition policy encompasses all government policies that promote competition among producers. These include policies relating to increased freedom of international trade in goods and services and foreign direct investment and labour. It also includes deregulation of previously regulated industries and the privatisation of previously government-owned enterprises. Privatisation and deregulation are especially important in countries that are making the transition from communist or socialist regimes in which the state owned or controlled most enterprises to a market-based economy. All of these are market opening or competition-promoting policies.

In this broad context competition law is one component of competition policies. It should be viewed a part of a more general set of policies to promote competition. It is the last resort, the method of enforcing competition when other policies have not succeeded in making markets competitive. (In the US this area is referred to as anti-trust law but the term competition law is the term used in the OECD, WTO and APEC.)

In short, the fundamental belief that underlies competition policy is that a competitive economy is the most efficient way of satisfying consumer demands but a competitive capitalist system does not mean laissez-faire capitalism. The role of a government competition policy is to constrain the behaviour of private producers so that they act competitively. Perhaps the most explicit statement of this belief is the concept of a 'social market economy' developed in the EU (see Monti 2001).

Section 4.3 reviews the state of competition policies in general and competition law in particular in the East Asian region. Section 4.4 discusses some aspects of competition law in transition economies. Section 4.5 comments on the coverage of the draft Vietnamese anti-trust laws compared to the coverage of competition laws in the five East Asian economies that already have comprehensive competition laws.

4.3   NATIONAL COMPETITION POLICIES AND LAW IN EAST ASIA

APEC is the major source of information on competition policies and competition law for the East Asian economies. All APEC member economies are required to report annually in their Individual Action Plans (IAPs) on major developments in the area of competition policy and deregulation. APEC also maintains a Database on Competition Policy and Law. These are the sources of the information reported in Tables 4.1 and 4.2 below.

The 12 East Asian economies which are members of APEC represent different forms of market systems. Some have a long history of free trade and claim to have practised liberal economic policies while others were fully regulated socialist states less than a decade ago. These historical circumstances have an obvious effect on the stage of implementation of competition policy and laws. Some of the economies have comprehensive competition policies and laws in place; this is true of Chinese Taipei, Indonesia, Japan, Korea and Thailand, though one should note that the extent and strength of these policies varies within the group. Some have sector-specific competition regulations; for example Hong Kong. Some have indicated that they do not have comprehensive or sector-specific competition policies; China, Indonesia, Malaysia, the Philippines, Singapore and Vietnam. (One should distinguish between Hong Kong and Singapore and the other economies. These two economies claim that they have small and very open economies that trade freely with the rest of the world in goods, services and capital and they do not, therefore, require comprehensive competition policies as their markets are contestable.) Of this last group, China and Vietnam have indicated that they plan to introduce new comprehensive competition laws.

Table 4.1 reviews the state of development of the competition law of the 12 East Asian economies the APEC member economies as reported in their 2000 IAPs. Of the five economies that have a comprehensive anti-trust law, only three can support a claim to have an operational and efficient enforcement mechanism; Chinese Taipei, Japan and Korea. The competition laws of Thailand and Indonesia are relatively new and the operation of these laws has not been developed.

For countries that do have comprehensive competition laws, it is not a simple matter to compare them. There are many elements of competition. In terms of the coverage of the laws, it is usual to break them down into three areas in terms of the type of business conduct: unilateral conduct, collusive conduct and mergers and acquisitions. For each area of business conduct, a distinction is made between legal actions which prohibit the conduct *per se* and the Rule of Reason. A *per se* prohibition declares that a type of conduct is always illegal; for example, price fixing and resale price maintenance are *per se* prohibited in many jurisdictions. The Rule of Reason applies where a type of conduct is subject to determination rather than *per se* illegal. The competition authority or court evaluates the pro-competitive and the anti-competitive effects of the conduct in order to decide whether or not the conduct on balance should be prohibited.

In addition to the coverage of conduct, one must also consider the objectives of the laws, the methods of analysis, exemptions or exclusions (such as government enterprises), the nature of remedies imposed on those considered to have breached the laws, and the rights of individuals to bring actions. In particular, the objectives of the laws are crucial as they determine the direction of change in the economy that results from the application of competition law.

Table 4.2 lists the main areas of business conduct which are regulated by national competition laws in the economies that do have comprehensive national competition laws. The first column lists the coverage and the targeted activity. The next three list the unilateral and collusive conduct that is prohibited *per se* and the coverage of mergers and acquisitions.

In all five countries, there is conduct that is prohibited in each of the three areas but the extent of the coverage differs. As a general rule, the laws of these countries are not as comprehensive in their coverage as those of the OECD countries. For example, the Thai anti-monopoly law is confined to price-fixing and collusive behaviour.

Table 4.1
Competition Laws – A Functional Overview

	Criterion	Brunei Darussalam	The PR of China	Taipei, China	Hong Kong, China	Indonesia	Japan	Korea	Malaysia	The Philippines	Singapore	Thailand	Vietnam
General/comprehensive competition law	Introduction of a general/comprehensive competition law	N	N	Y	N	Y	Y	Y	N	N	N	Y	N
	Intention of introduction of general competition law	?	Y	–	N	–	–	–	?	–	N	–	Y
	Single enforcement mechanism (in place or proposed)	N	Y	Y	N	Y	Y	Y	N	N	N	Y	N
	Evidence of operation of the competition law enforcement mechanism	N	?	Y	N	?	Y	Y	N	?	N	?	N
	Competition issues addressed in various laws	N	Y	–	Y	–	–	–	N	Y	N	–	N

Table 4.2 (a)
Main Conduct Regulated: Japan

Law	Coverage and targeted activity	Prohibited unilateral conduct	Prohibited collusive conduct	Mergers and acquisitions
Japan Act Concerning Prohibition of Private Monopolisation and Maintenance of Fair Trade 1947	• Comprehensive • Monopolisation	• *Private monopolisation** *exclusion or controlling the business activities of other entrepreneurs, thereby causing, (…) a substantial restraint of competition	• *Private monopolisation by combination or conspiracy with other entrepreneurs causing, (…) a substantial restraint of competition]* • *Unfair trade practices (vertical restraints)* and • *Unreasonable restraint of trade (horizontal agreements)* by which (…) entrepreneurs, mutually restrict or conduct their business activities in such a manner as to fix, maintain, or increase prices, or to limit production, technology, products, facilities, or customers or suppliers, (…) causing (….) a substantial restraint of competition (…).	• Prior notification • Threshold: substantial restraint of competition

Table 4.2 (b)
Main Conduct Regulated: Korea

Law	Coverage and targeted activity	Prohibited unilateral conduct	Prohibited collusive conduct	Mergers and acquisitions
Korea Monopoly Regulation and Fair Trade Act 1980	Corporations engaging in a financial or an insurance business have been excluded from the definition of the dominant market power	• *Abuse of market-dominant position* (by unreasonable price fixing, maintaining or altering the prices; unreasonable control of the sale of goods or services; unreasonable interfering with other enterprises; unreasonable hindering of competition; other threats) which substantially restrain competition	• Business combinations to acquire shares of the competitors, interlocking directorate, mergers between companies, take-overs of business, compulsion in business dealings, establishment of new corporations) which substantially restrict competition, unless acknowledged by the Fair Trade Commission	• Prior notification • Threshold – substantial restriction of competition

34

Table 4.2 (c)
Main Conduct Regulated: Chinese Taipei

Law	Coverage and targeted activity	Prohibited unilateral conduct	Prohibited collusive conduct	Mergers and acquisitions
Chinese Taipei Fair Trade Law 1991, (revised 1999, s.9 amended 2000)	Comprehensive • Prohibits specific types of anti-competitive conduct of the monopolistic enterprises • Monopolistic enterprise: defined as facing no competition or having a dominant position sufficient to enable it to exclude competition in relevant market	To: 1. directly or indirectly prevent any other enterprises from competing by unfair means; 2. improperly set, maintain or change the price for goods or the remuneration for services; 3. make a trading counter-part give preferential treatment without justification; or 4. otherwise abuse its market power. (Art.10)	No enterprise shall have any concerted action; unless the concerted action meets the requirements under one of the following circumstances: it is beneficial to the economy as a whole and in the public interest, and the central competent authority has approved such concerted action (Art.14)	Application for approval, when: 1. as a result of the merger the enterprise(s) will have one third of the market share; 2. one of the enterprises in the merger has one-fourth of the market share; or 3. sales for the preceding fiscal year of one of the enterprises in the merger exceeds the threshold amount publicly announced by the central competent authority. (Art.11) Threshold: size limit, but authorisable.

Table 4.2 (d)
Main Conduct Regulated: Indonesia

Law	Coverage and targeted activity	Prohibited unilateral conduct	Prohibited collusive conduct	Mergers and acquisitions
Indonesia Law No. 5/1999 on the Prohibition of Monopolistic Practices and Unfair Business Competition *No text available*	?	• Monopolistic practices • Dominant position abuse	• Price-fixing • Price discrimination • Vertical integration forbidden business agreements/arrangements and activities	?

Table 4.2 (e)

Main Conduct Regulated: Thailand

Law	Coverage and targeted activity	Prohibited unilateral conduct	Prohibited collusive conduct	Mergers and acquisitions
Thailand Competition Act 1999 (text not available at the APEC database – of 29 March 2001)	SOEs are excluded from its application (central, provincial and local government agencies, state-owned enterprises, agricultural operatives established by law, some other businesses as prescribed by means of Ministerial Regulations. (s.4).	*Abuse of a dominant position by (s.25)* 1 Price-fixing or maintaining unfair price levels; 2 Imposing unfair conditions, directly or indirectly (to limit their services, manufacture, etc.; 3 Ceasing, reducing or limiting services or imports so that they fall short of market demand; 4 Interfering with the business operations of others without reasonable cause.	*Practices leading to monopoly or reducing, limiting competition (s.27)* 1 Price-fixing agreements; 2 Quantitative limitations; 3 Joint agreements to manipulate or control the market; 4 Collusion in fixing an agreement or a condition to enable one party to succeed in a bid or auction or allow one party not to compete in a bid or auction. Restrictive practices undertaken jointly with overseas operators (s.28).	Merger and acquisitions need to be filed with the Board for prior permission when the merger may result in unfair competition or create a monopoly position. (S.26, 35).

However, the laws of these countries differ in terms of the language, tests and the admissible discretion of the enforcement bodies (in the authorisation of activities which fall under the definitions of prohibited anti-competitive behaviour). In regard to language, Japan uses the terminology of monopolisation whereas the other four countries use the more modern concept of abuse of a dominant market position. In regard to tests, each country uses its own threshold tests for the approval of mergers and acquisitions that may lessen competition or result in a substantial restraint of competition. In regard to admissible discretion, there is a great variety among the areas of conduct and the countries.

There is also considerable variation in terms of the objectives of the laws. For example, Section 1 of Chapter 1 of the Japan's Anti-monopoly Act declares its purpose in the following manner:

> This Act, by prohibiting private monopolisation, unreasonable restraint of trade and unfair trade practices, by preventing excessive concentration of economic power and by eliminating unreasonable restraint of production, sale, price, technology and the like, and all other unjust restriction of business activities through combinations, agreements and otherwise, [aims] to promote free and fair competition, to stimulate the creative initiative of entrepreneurs, to encourage business activities of enterprises, to heighten the level of employment and people's real income, and thereby to promote the democratic and wholesome development of the national economy as well as to assure the interests of consumers in general.

In Korea, the main act is the Monopoly Regulation and Fair Trade Act. Article 1 of Chapter 1 declares:

> The purpose of this Act is to encourage fair and free economic competition by prohibiting the abuse of market-dominant positions and the excessive concentration of economic power and by regulating improper concerted acts and unfair business practices, thereby stimulating creative business activities, protecting consumers, and promoting the balanced development of the national economy.

In Chinese Taipei, Article 1 of the Fair Trade Law 200 declares:

> This Law is enacted for the purposes of maintaining trading order, protecting consumers' interests, ensuring fair competition, and promoting economic stability and prosperity. Unless otherwise provided for in this Law the provisions of other relevant laws shall apply.

All of these have multiple objectives, including some provision relating to the 'wholesome [or balanced] development of the national economy' or 'economic stability and prosperity'. These acts are less focused on protecting the interests of the consumers and/or buyers, which is the ultimate justification of competition policy, than the acts of the OECD countries.

In Thailand, the Price-Fixing and Monopoly Act has no general purpose clause.

Similarly, the extent of exemptions of government-owned enterprises differs greatly among the countries. For example, the Anti-monopoly Act of Japan exempts '... railway, electricity, gas, or any other business constituting a monopoly by the inherent nature of the said business', special laws concerning a specific industry, cooperatives, depression and rationalisation cartels and resale price maintenance contracts. This is a major list of exclusions. In Korea, the exemptions are '... the acts of an Enterprise or Trade Association conducted in accordance with any Act or any decree to such Act.' and cooperatives, which is a large set of exclusions though smaller than that of Japan.

4.4   COMPETITION LAW IN TRANSITION ECONOMIES

Economies in transition from a past system in which many or all enterprises were publicly owned and heavily regulated pose special problems for the introduction of comprehensive competition policies.

The first and most fundamental point is that these economies should develop comprehensive competition policies and a national competition law. The same economic principles that lead to the advantages of competition in all markets in developed economies also apply to all markets in all developing economies. The advantages of competition in producing lower prices and meeting the demands of consumers are universal.

Yet, there are special circumstances in transition economies which merit special attention. Public ownership by itself is no obstacle to the application of competition law. Increasingly in the last decade competition laws in developed countries have been applied to government enterprises. Exemptions for government enterprises were once widespread in the OECD countries but most OECD countries have moved in recent years to extend the reach of national competition laws to enterprises owned wholly or substantially by governments. This includes access regimes for natural monopolies in industries such telecommunications, electricity generation and distribution, and gas and water distribution where the service provider is a government-owned enterprise. In some developed countries, some of these services are still provided by government-owned enterprises but they are subject to the national competition laws. This is true of most European economies, Australia, New Zealand and Canada (but not Japan).

The essential concept of competition in relation to government-owned enterprises is *neutrality*, that is, neutrality of market access and treatment between government-owned enterprises and privately-owned enterprises. Government should give no advantages to government-owned enterprises. Neutrality is one of the four principles enshrined in the APEC Principles to Enhance Competition and Regulatory Reform.

In practice, the major problem is that many state-owned enterprises (SOEs) are less efficient than non-state-owned enterprises in the same industries. For China, this has been verified by a number of empirical studies of the efficiency of different types of enterprises in Chinese industries, using stochastic production frontier techniques (for example, Kong, Marks and Wan 2000; and Zhang and Zhang 2001) or data envelopment analysis (Hirschberg and Lloyd 2001). These are alternative techniques for estimating the efficiency of state-owned enterprises relative to the efficiency of non-state-owned enterprises. These studies have confirmed that the SOEs are the least efficient form of enterprise in China, ranking below other Chinese-owned private enterprises as well as foreign-invested enterprises. Many of these state-owned enterprises are also burdened by debt (see Yuan 2001).

In these circumstances, a combination of market reforms and competition law is required. Reforms may include conversion of SOEs to shareholding companies and sales to other private enterprises. For those SOEs that remain state-owned, at least for the foreseeable future, other measures should be adopted to give managers the incentives to raise the productivity of these enterprises. Measures may also be needed to reduce non-performing debts of SOEs.

In this context, a competition policy can play a major role in guiding the nature of regulatory reform and other reforms to improve the efficiency of SOEs. Competition policy emphasises the importance of entry conditions and of competition between several actual or potential rivals. Monopolies are lazy and inefficient. Privatisation and deregulation may be necessary to establish conditions of competition. Reform of the law may be necessary to establish clear property rights and intellectual property rights.

Privatisation and deregulation of industries with previous state-owned enterprises should be accompanied by the introduction of firm principles of competition law and adequate means of enforcing these laws. Privatisation and deregulation without the introduction of competition law may allow the operation of private monopolies and other collusive business conduct that leads to excessive prices and poor customer service. The principle of neutrality between enterprises in an industry is fundamental to competition among enterprises.

Market reforms and privatisation may be accompanied by relaxation of the restrictions on foreign direct investment. In this circumstance, competition law should apply to foreign investors. There is no reason to shelter them from competition from domestic enterprises or from other actual or potential foreign investors.

There are a number of precedents for reform in transition economies in East Europe. After the demise of the USSR, ten East European states have become Associate Members of the EU and have applied for full membership of the EU. They were obliged to accept the *acquis communautaire* of the EU, that is, all of the accepted practices and rules of the Community. These include the EU competition policies as competition policy has been one of the area of common (completely harmonised) policies of the European Community since the signing of the Treaty of Rome in 1956. These countries have signed Europe Agreements which include provisions that require them to introduce competition laws and, moreover, for these laws to converge with those of the EU. This has taken place while these countries have struggled with the process of transforming their economies from models based on public ownership and central planning to some form of Western-type capitalism.

This process is described in Estrin and Holmes (1998). While the process has been difficult, it has guided the transformation of these economies. In particular, it has created a culture of competition and a commitment to competition law that are essential components of successful capitalism.

In the case of the East European states, one of the major difficulties – the choice of national competition policies – was determined by their having to adopt the EU model of competition law. This is an advanced model of competition policy in terms of the comprehensiveness of the policies and their effective enforcement. Yet, the success to date shows that it is possible for transition economies to make this policy transition to advanced national competition policies. Indeed, the adoption of an external model may be easier than the development of an internal model.

4.5   THE DRAFT VIETNAM COMPETITION LAW

This section makes some comments on the Draft Competition Law in the light of the principles of competition policy and competition law developed above and the survey of practice in those five East Asian countries that currently have comprehensive competition law.

Table 4.3 presents a brief summary of the major provisions, along the lines of the summaries of the five East Asian countries in Table 4.2. There are provisions under each of the three headings. Chapters of the draft law deal with anti-competitive agreements, abuse of dominant position, merger or consolidation and acquisition of enterprises, and unfair competition. There is, however, no provision for access regimes in natural monopoly industries. In Chapters 2 and 3 dealing with Anti-competitive Agreements and Abuse of Dominant Position respectively, the prohibitions are *per se* prohibitions with the criteria for determining the prohibited conduct specified in each case.

Table 4.3

Main Conduct Regulated: Vietnam Draft Law

Law	Coverage and targeted activity	Prohibited unilateral conduct	Prohibited collusive conduct	Mergers and acquisitions
Vietnam Draft Competition Law	• Comprehensive • Unfair competition laws Exemptions for practices of individuals and organisation under the decisions of Government	• Anti-competitive agreements (tied sales, price discrimination) • Abuse of dominant position (predatory pricing, price discrimination, tied sales, etc.)	• Anti-competitive agreements (price-fixing, market-sharing, etc.) • Abuse of dominant position	• Prior registration • Threshold: creating or strengthening market dominance or resulting in considerable competition restraint

One unusual feature of these provisions is that in several cases the same behaviour is listed under both Chapter 2 and Chapter 3. Thus, Article 9.1.d and Article 17.4 both prohibit in identical language 'Conditioning the closing of contracts with the purchase of goods and services, or accepting of other obligations which are not directly related to the object of the contract'. Similarly, Article 19.1.dd and Articles 17.3 both prohibit 'Applying dissimilar conditions to identical or equivalent transactions with different business person thereby placing them at a competitive disadvantage in the market'. Predatory pricing is explicitly prohibited in Chapter 5 (Unfair Competition) and appears to be prohibited also in Article 17.1 of Chapter 3.

The Foreword states the purpose of the Act as:

> To protect and promote fair and equal competition in the market; to ensure the right to equality before the law in competition activities of all individuals and organizations conducting business in goods and services; to protect the legitimate rights and interests of the State, consumers, individuals and organizations with the aim of developing production and business, promoting the economic reform,...

This enshrines the principle of neutrality. However, it does not state a clear objective. Article 6 states 'Any competition practice causing harm to the national interest shall be prohibited'. This does not clarify the objective as the concept of national interest is undefined and can therefore be defined to mean whatever is wished.

Article 3 is the exemption clause. It states 'This law shall not apply to practices of individuals and organisations under the decisions of Government, of local governments within its tasks and duties for national and/or public interest'. This appears to exempt all state-owned enterprises which is a far-reaching exemption in an economy with a large number of state-owned enterprises.

Chapter 5 provides for the establishment of the 'Competition Agency' on proposal of the Minister of Trade. There are two alternatives. It shall be a department under the Ministry of Trade or national committee under the government. Neither is an independent authority.

The remedies include criminal prosecution for anti-competitive agreements or abuse of dominant position where the breach has serious consequences. Under Article 57, individuals or organisations harmed by breaches of the law have the right to lodge complaints in order to recover compensation for damages caused by the breach with the relevant body or court.

REFERENCES

Asia–Pacific Economic Council (APEC) (1999), 'APEC Principles to Enhance Competition and Regulatory Reform', Attachment to leaders' Declaration – New Zealand, APEC Secretariat, Singapore.

Estrin, S. and P. Holmes (1998), *Competition and Economic Integration in Europe,* Cheltenham, UK: Edward Elgar.

Hirschberg, J. and P.J. Lloyd (2001), 'Does the Technology of Foreign-invested Enterprises Spill over to Other Enteprises in China? An Application of Post-DEA Bootstrap Regression Analysis', in P.J. Lloyd and X. Zhang (eds), *Models of the Chinese Economy*, Cheltenham, UK: Edward Elgar.

Kong, X., R.E. Marks and G. Wan (2000), 'Productivity Performance of Chinese State-owned Enterprises in the early 1990s: A Stochastic Production Frontier and Malmquist Productivity Index Analysis', in P.J. Lloyd and X. Zhang (eds), *China in the Global Economy*, Cheltenham, UK: Edward Elgar.

Lloyd, P.J. (2001), 'Competition Policy in the WTO, APEC and ASEAN', *First APEC Workshop on Anti-trust law and Competition Policy*, Hanoi, Vietnam, 17–18 January.

Monti, M. (2001), 'Competition in a Social Market Economy', *EU Competition Policy Newsletter,* 2–7 February.

Yuan, G. (2001), 'Non-performing Debts in SOEs and the Effect of Policies Aimed at their Solution', in P.J. Lloyd and X. Zhang (eds), *China in the Global Economy*, Cheltenham, UK: Edward Elgar.

Zhang, X. and S. Zhang (2001), 'Technical Efficiency of Foreign-invested Enterprises : The Case of the Iron and Steel Industry', in P.J. Lloyd and X. Zhang (eds), *Models of the Chinese Economy*, Cheltenham, UK: Edward Elgar.

5. Competition Policy and SMEs in Asian Transition Economies: The Experience of China

Charles Harvie

5.1 INTRODUCTION

China has experienced a prolonged and impressive period of economic growth and development during its 20 years of economic reform. The most fundamental change that this reform has brought about has been the development of the non-state sector, which has resulted in multiple types of ownership including urban and rural private businesses, township enterprises, foreign-invested enterprises and joint stock companies. The non-state sector is increasingly replacing the state sector in the supply and distribution of goods and services. In view of this contribution to rising living standards in China, the status of the sector was recognised politically and legally as a significant component of the 'socialist market system' in the March 1999 amendment to the constitution. With this recognition the authorities indicated a readiness to accept a renewed phase of further reducing the role of state-owned enterprises in the economy, and to accept a further significant expansion, in particular, of the role of the private sector. The country's membership of the WTO in December 2001 will result in the entry of foreign firms and intense competition in those industries that are currently dominated by state-owned enterprises. This will contribute to a further reduction in the role of the state in the economy and provide sustained impetus to the development of the domestic private sector and fundamental changes in China's ownership landscape.

Compared with the state sector, the non-state sector is primarily composed of SMEs engaged in labour intensive lower-value-added activities. The domestic private sector has insufficient access to financial resources to make the large scale investments required to become established in capital-intensive industries. The underdeveloped banking sector, dominated by the four state-owned banks, with its traditional focus upon providing credit to the state sector, has become a bottleneck to continued high growth as it fails to channel resources to the most productive sectors in the economy – the private and so-called township and village enterprises (TVEs). The extent of the distortion of resource allocation is exemplified by the fact that the non-state sector contributes more than 70 per cent of output but uses less than 30 per cent of total bank credits. This severe misallocation of investment resources across different ownership groups and across industries is making the prospects of China's economic growth unclear. A serious policy mistake during the period of reform has been the lack of development of non-state financial institutions that would more adequately serve the growth of the non-state sector. The fundamental process of replacing SOEs with enterprises of other types of ownership and reforming the banking system by introducing competition, can lead to better utilisation of economic resources in China and therefore lead to higher economic growth. Introducing competition into the banking industry is particularly important so that resources are channelled to the most productive sectors of the economy. With foreign banks handling renminbi (RMB) business soon after China's membership of the WTO, there is greater potential for private enterprises in China to obtain finance from the banking sector.

The remainder of this chapter proceeds as follows. Section 5.2 focuses upon the importance of the market mechanism, liberalisation and competition in the process of transition, and the significance of ownership diversification and the contribution of an indigenous private sector. Section 5.3 identifies the significant contribution to transition in terms of restructuring, generating competition and sustaining growth that can be made by small- and medium-sized enterprises (SME). Section 5.4 focuses upon China's economic transition and the growing significance during this period of the non-state sector. Section 5.5 identifies the specific contribution of China's rural enterprises, the so-called township and village enterprises (TVEs) to the marketisation and development of the economy. Section 5.6 looks at some of the factors which have contributed to their rapid growth and success over the period 1980–95, as well as the key difficulties they are now experiencing in China's rapidly evolving market economy. Section 5.7 identifies possible strategies essential for the survival of the TVEs, emphasising the need for organisational change, the development of business alliances and the likelihood of change of ownership form from collective to private. Section 5.8 conducts of review of China's rapidly developing private sector and the particularly significant contribution of private SMEs. Policies for the further development of the private sector are discussed in Section 5.9. Section 5.10 conducts a brief comparison of market liberalisation, competition, and private sector developments in China with that of Vietnam. Finally, Section 5.11 presents a summary of the major conclusions from this chapter.

5.2 ECONOMIC TRANSITION – THE ROLE OF THE MARKET, COMPETITION AND THE PRIVATE SECTOR

A common thread amongst the economies in transition has been the movement away from a centrally determined allocation of resources to one in which markets play the key role in allocating resources and determining what will actually be produced. The centrally planned system contained a number of deficiencies: the planning process became more difficult as the complexity of economies increased; SOEs had little incentive to use resources efficiently; major resource misallocations occurred, with heavy industry favoured at the expense of light industry and services; prices did not reflect scarcity values; there were continual supply shortages primarily for consumer goods; in Eastern Europe and in Vietnam these deficiencies contributed to economic stagnation. As a consequence the model was rejected in Eastern Europe in the late 1980s and early 1990s, gradually in China from 1978, and gradually in Vietnam from 1986.

Each of these countries intended using the market as the primary means for allocating resources, with the potential for improved efficiency in resource allocation, higher productivity, production based on comparative advantage, faster economic growth and rapid integration into the global economy. Commensurate with this movement the transition economies have engaged, at a varying pace, in the liberalisation and deregulation of markets and sectors and stabilisation of the economy, to take full advantage of their more market-oriented systems. Liberalisation has involved freeing prices, trade and entry from state controls, and stabilisation has involved reducing inflation and containing domestic and external imbalances. Over the longer term, institutional reforms – establishing clear property rights, sound legal and financial infrastructure, and effective government – will be needed to make markets work efficiently and support growth. Markets work at their best where there is freedom of entry and exit and there is intense competition.

Market liberalisation is important for the transition economies as it enables the decentralisation of production and trading decisions to enterprises and households and addresses the two fundamental weaknesses of central planning: poor incentives and poor information. Liberalisation exposes enterprises to customer demands, the profit motive, and competition, and it lets relative prices adjust in line with true scarcities. In most cases the outcome is greater efficiency, although market failure is still possible. Combined with supporting institutions, competitive markets force technological and organisational change. Evidence from many of the transition economies suggest that there is a strong relationship between liberalisation, stabilisation and economic growth. Growth can result from the lifting of restrictions on new entry and from lifting restrictions on previously repressed activities, especially services, export industries and agriculture in the Asian transition economies. Liberalisation also means freeing entry into production, services, and trade, including the freedom to open a new business, to expand or break up an existing business, and to change product mix, suppliers, customers, or geographical base.

Transition requires changes that introduce financial discipline and increase the entry of new firms, exit of unviable firms, and competition. These spur needed restructuring, even in state-owned enterprises. Ownership change, say to private ownership, for a large proportion of the economy is also important. Once markets have been liberalised, governments cannot indefinitely control large parts of a dynamic, changing economy. Decentralising ownership is the best way to increase competition and improve performance. This is the approach adopted by the transition economies in both Europe and Asia. The economies in transition have increasingly experienced an expansion in private sector ownership as well as private sector contribution to overall GDP. By the second half of the 1990s this had expanded to over 50 per cent of GDP in Albania, Croatia, Czech Republic, Estonia, Hungary, Latvia, Lithuania, Poland, Russia and the Slovak Republic. A remarkable transformation in a short period of time. Vietnam and China similarly had 50 per cent of their GDP accounted for by the private sector during the period of the 1990s.

There are two ways to move to an economy dominated by the private sector: through privatisation (equitisation) of existing state assets and through the entry of new private businesses. The two are equally important. New private firms, spurred by liberalisation, give quick returns and can accomplish a great deal by themselves; but the mass of state assets in transition economies makes some degree of privatisation unavoidable. The question is not merely how much to privatise but how and when. Considerable problems have been encountered in practice in privatising large enterprises. A number of options exist for doing so: sales to outside owners; management-employee buyout; equal access voucher privatisation; restitution; spontaneous privatisation and equitisation. The major obstacles involved in privatisation relate to the high capital requirements, major restructuring needs, and regulatory and governance weaknesses. The privatisation of small-scale enterprises do not contain such obstacles.

Liberalisation and competition are therefore key ingredients in the process of economic growth and development. A key related question is whether it matters if property is publicly, privately, or somewhere in between owned. The World Bank (1996) argues that, for industrial market economies, empirical literature from the 1980s indicates clearly that private firms exhibit higher productivity and better performance than public enterprises. More recent evidence suggests a similar outcome in developing economies. The type of private ownership can also exert an important influence. Sales to outsiders produced better performance than sales, at bargain prices, to insider buyers.

In China, widespread privatisation of the so-called pillar industries has not, and will not, take place any time soon. However, much of the Chinese economy has moved away from state ownership, some in to private hands and others into intermediate forms of ownership. The non-state sector has grown much faster than China's state enterprises despite an imprecise property rights framework. Ownership does, therefore, matter, but the need to privatise is not equally urgent in all settings. Slower privatisation is viable, although not necessarily optimal, if the government, or workers themselves, are strong enough to assert control over enterprises and prevent managers from stealing assets, and if saving and growth in the non-state sector are high. But where governments are weak and enterprise managers strong, or where the needs of restructuring dwarf available funds, privatisation is urgent.

Development of the private sector, through privatisation of existing state-owned assets or through the establishment of new privately owned enterprises, can, therefore, make a significant contribution to economic growth and development. Figure 5.1 summarises some of the measures for promoting, and outcomes derivable, from the development of the private sector in a transition economy. The key ingredients for encouraging the development of the private sector are: ownership reform; official recognition of the role and significance of the private sector, most important of which being recognition of property rights; opening up of markets previously prohibited to private sector enterprises and competition; explicit incentives for private sector investment including protection of property and intellectual property rights; a legal framework for the proper functioning of a market economy with substantial private sector involvement; accessibility of private enterprises to land, and land use rights; reform SOEs including that of privatisation, selling to the highest bidder; bank reforms enabling the private sector to gain greater access to credit and other bank services; open up the economy to expanded trade, enabling private firms to import and export without the need for licences or being subject to quotas and permits; and finally to develop essential business support services, provided by the private sector itself, in such areas as accounting, legal services, insurance, marketing, and transport and distribution to enable private enterprises to access such essential services without having to conduct these, at a higher cost, in-house.

While the development of the private sector can play an important role in economic growth and development for a transition economy, the private sector for such economies tends to be characterised, particularly for developing transition economies, by a large number of household microenterprises, as in the case of Vietnam, and a smaller number of large enterprises. Consequently, the enterprises between these extremes, that is small and medium enterprises, have not been sufficiently developed, and signify a poorly structured private sector. Hence there is considerable scope in transition economies for the development of SMEs. The advantages deriving from SMEs is now widely recognised in the region, particularly after the Asian financial and economic crisis of 1997–98. This is now discussed further in the following section.

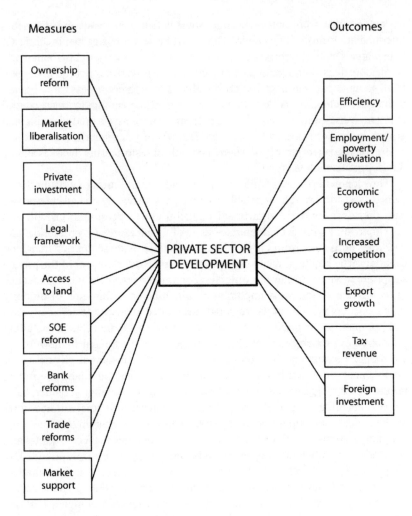

Measures   Outcomes

Figure 5.1   Promoting the Private Sector

5.3   IMPORTANCE OF THE SME SECTOR FOR RESTRUCTURING, COMPETITION, EXPORTING AND SUSTAINING ECONOMIC GROWTH

The development of private SMEs is largely recognised as being of primary importance for the generation of economic growth, export growth, the alleviation of poverty, the promotion of more pluralist societies, employment growth and the generation of competition in domestic and international markets (see Hallberg

2000). In market economies SMEs are the engine of economic development, and in the context of a transition economy have substantial potential to play a similar role. Due to their private ownership, entrepreneurial spirit, their flexibility and adaptability as well as their potential to react to challenges and changing environments, SMEs can contribute to sustainable growth and employment generation in a significant manner. In Asia, with the liberalisation of economies, the restructuring of industries and, in some economies, the process of change of ownership, have resulted in governments facing difficulties due to the growing number of unemployed. Many of the crisis afflicted countries in Asia are recognising that SME development will be a crucial factor in the process of industrial restructuring, employment growth, export growth, and providing the basis for a sustained recovery of regional economies. Parallel with ownership reform and privatisation, the number of SMEs is increasing.

SMEs occupy an important and strategic place in APEC. They contribute significantly to the region's wealth and employment, as intermediate and final producers as well as consumers of goods and services. They are the primary vehicles by which new entrepreneurs provide the economy a continuous supply of ideas, skills and innovation. Strong SME sectors attract and enable foreign investors to establish and expand domestic linkages. SMEs thus play a critical role in creating opportunities that make the attainment of equitable and sustainable growth possible.

The strategic importance of SMEs today is recognised for a number of reasons, including the following (see Figure 5.2):

- In market economies SMEs are the engine of economic development, arising from their private ownership, and the entrepreneurial spirit of their owners. A structural shift from large enterprises, privately and state-owned, to smaller privately owned SMEs will increase the number of owners, a group that represents responsibility and commitment to meeting changing market demands.

- Support for SMEs will help the restructuring of large enterprises by streamlining manufacturing complexes, as units with no direct relation to the primary activity are sold off separately. Through this process the efficiency of the remaining enterprise might be increased as well. SMEs are flexible and able to adapt to challenges and changing environments.

- SMEs are contributing to employment growth at a higher rate than larger firms. The private sector, and in particular SMEs, form the backbone of a market economy, and in the long term are likely to provide most of the employment. SMEs tend to be concentrated in relatively labour intensive activities, consequently playing an important role in employing the growing labour force in developing countries and alleviating the severe unemployment that threatens the survival of

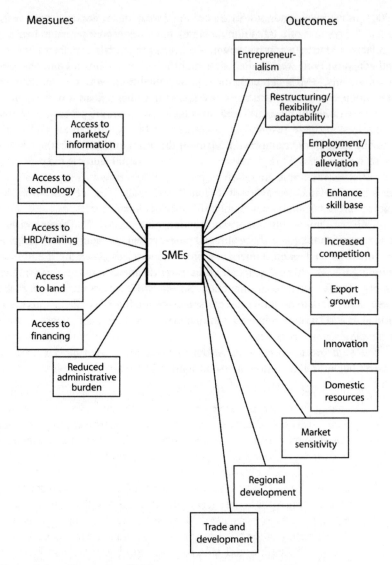

Figure 5.2   Promoting SMEs

the poor. A recent World Bank sector policy paper showed that labour intensity is from 4 to 10 times higher for small enterprises. Their ability to generate employment can therefore make an important contribution to poverty alleviation in developing transition economies.

•   Through interenterprise cooperation, they raise the level of skills with their flexible and innovative nature. Thus SMEs can generate important benefits in terms of creating a skilled industrial base and industries and developing a well prepared service sector capable of contributing to GDP through higher value added.

- SMEs curb the monopoly power of large enterprises, and offer them complementary services and absorb the fluctuation of a modern economy. They therefore represent an important source of competition in markets, improving the overall efficiency of the economy.
- SMEs not only play a key role in the economic development of individual economies, but, according to APEC, are also instrumental in promoting trade and investment activities among different economies. They are therefore instrumental in promoting the facilitation of a more open investment environment in the APEC region.
- An increased number of SMEs will bring more flexibility to society and the economy and might facilitate technological innovation, as well as provide significant opportunities for the development of new ideas and skills.
- A characteristic of small industrial enterprises is that they produce predominantly for the domestic market, drawing in general upon national resources and use and develop predominantly domestic technologies and skills.
- SMEs are sensitive to the needs of the market. If they are not they will not remain in business for long.
- New business development is a key factor for the success of regional development, particularly given the need to restructure and reconstruct many existing businesses and industries in the crisis afflicted economies.

Because of this strategic importance a number of measures have been used to promote the development of SMEs in both developing and developed economies. These include (see again Figure 5.2):

- Improvement of management training for SME managers. There is a general recognition that SME managers, especially in small firms in the start up phase, have to carry an enormous burden, as they have to perform various functions simultaneously.
- Reduction of administrative burdens for SMEs. Such firms have special difficulties in complying with too many regulations and procedures, especially in the start-up phase. SME managers have little time for this, and cannot afford consultants and lawyers to help them with advice and administrative requirements. There is a need for one-stop shopping.
- Facilitate financing for SMEs. This is an important and sensitive issue, as many SMEs have continuous cash-flow problems even outwith a financial and economic crisis. As practice shows, large banks are much more ready to give loans to larger enterprises than to small enterprises.

Often SMEs have to pay a 2–6 per cent higher interest rate for bank credits than larger firms.

- Stimulate industrial research and development activities in SMEs. Many SMEs perform little or no R&D, partly because they have no tradition of it, and partly because they cannot afford it. Measures to increase industrial R&D in SMEs have to be created, especially if the SME is a supplier to a larger firm.

The Ottawa meeting of APEC, concerned with SMEs and their development, in September 1997, focused upon five key areas of importance to SMEs. These are access to: markets; technology; human resources; financing; and information.

- *Access to markets*. SMEs are recognised as facing special problems relating to their size and that, in the context of rapid trade liberalisation, they need to develop capacities to take advantage of opportunities arising from a more open regional trading system. The internet is regarded as being of particular importance, as is the need to identify appropriate partners for joint ventures, to harmonise standards and professional qualifications, including investment laws and taxation procedures, and the protection of intellectual property rights.
- *Access to technology*. In a knowledge-based economy, applications of information and communications technology can be a great leveller for SMEs. However, when SMEs have limited access or understanding of these technologies, their prospects of acquiring and utilising these for their benefit is reduced.
- *Access to human resources*. Human resource development for SMEs requires a comprehensive approach including: social structures and systems such as broad educational reforms; encouragement of entrepreneurship, business skills acquisition and innovation in society; mechanisms for self learning and ongoing training and enhancement of human resources; and appropriate governmental support programmes.
- *Access to financing*. Many SMEs lack awareness of financing resources and programmes available from commercial banks and other private sector and government sources, and that they have difficulty defining and articulating their financing needs. Financial institutions need to be responsive to their needs and for continuing simplification of trade documentation.
- *Access to information*. Accurate and timely information is crucial for SMEs to compete and grow in a global market environment.

An emerging consensus appears to have emerged relating to new approaches needed to improve the effectiveness of government strategies and programs supporting SMEs in market economies. In the field of microfinance new approaches have emerged with the need to establish good practices for SME financing and for the provision of non-financial services to SMEs.

While government strategies to assist SMEs vary, depending upon the country's stage of development, there are some basic principles of successful SME development strategies. Firstly, the creation of a level playing field. The fundamental key to a successful SME development strategy is the establishment of a business environment that helps SMEs compete on a more equal basis. To establish a level playing field, governments need to re-evaluate the costs and benefits of regulations that place a disproportionate burden on SMEs, implement regulations with the flexibility needed by SMEs, and place greater emphasis on competition and procurement policies to open SME access to markets. This issue is of particular significance in the context of developing transition economies. Secondly, to carefully target public expenditure to use scarce public resources effectively. Governments need to design a clear, coordinated strategy for SME development that carefully separates equity and efficiency objectives. Public expenditure should be confined to those services and target groups that are under-served by the market and for which there is a clear justification based on public goods or equity considerations. Using the methodology of microfinance, good practice in the delivery of services to SMEs can be judged according to the performance criteria of coverage, cost effectiveness, financial sustainability and impact. Finally, encourage the private provision of a wide array of financial and non-financial services. In most developing countries, SMEs do not have access to institutions and instruments appropriate to their needs. To ensure SME access to a diverse range of financial and non-financial services, governments should strive to develop private markets for services suitable for SMEs, stimulating market development on both the demand and supply side.

5.4   CHINA'S TRANSITION AND THE DEVELOPMENT OF THE NON-STATE SECTOR

One of the most striking outcomes during China's period of economic reform since 1978 has been the rapid growth of the non-state sector. This consists of four broad types of business entities: township and village enterprises (TVEs); urban collectives; private and individual enterprises; and joint ventures and wholly foreign-owned enterprises, which together are called foreign-funded enterprises (FFEs). The sector has attained major outcomes in terms of output, employment and export growth as well as in technology upgrading, profitability and gains in total factor productivity. By 1998 the non-state sector produced 72 per cent of the gross value of industry output, which compared with 24 per cent in 1980 and 45 per cent in 1990 (China Statistical Yearbook 1999).[1] The industrial output share of state-owned enterprises (SOEs) and urban collectives dropped, while that of the more dynamic TVEs and local private and foreign enterprises has grown rapidly. Indeed the highest growth rates during the 1990s have been recorded by the privately owned enterprises and FFEs. A similarly radical shift has occurred in industrial employment patterns. While in 1980 SOEs employed more people than all other ownership forms of industrial enterprises combined,[2] by the late 1990s the non-state sector's contribution had increased substantially, to 43 per cent of the urban population, and the TVEs had become the single largest source of employment for industrial workers. TVE employment, overall, more than quadrupled between 1980 and 1996.[3]

The non-state sector dominates light industry and has generated about three-quarters of total export growth since 1978. It also produces over 80 per cent of industrial output in the coastal provinces. In fact the pre-eminence of the non-state sector in these provinces is one of the main sources of dynamism of the coastal region. In the past the non-state sector confronted discriminatory tax and other policies, and, until recent developments in the late 1990s,[4] still had some concerns regarding security of property rights. Difficulties remain in accessing bank finance, upgrading technology, obtaining access to skilled labour and management personnel, dealing with government interference in the management of some enterprises and securing product transport and distribution. However, legal and regulatory reforms and political developments in the 1990s have greatly improved the position of non-state sector firms, contributing to the sector's dramatic growth.

The dynamism of the industrial sector during the latter half of the 1980s was primarily provided by the TVEs. Their output increased by 25 per cent a year from the mid 1980s to the mid 1990s, resulting in their share of GDP increasing from 13 per cent in 1985 to over 30 per cent by the mid 1990s (World Bank 1996, p. 51). During the period from 1980 to 1995 they created over 100 million new rural jobs. A comparison of their performance with that of the SOEs is also remarkable. Although the capital–output ratio in collective industry, of which the TVEs are a crucial component, in China is only 25 per cent of that in the state sector, labour productivity (output per capita) is close to 80 per cent of that in state enterprises and rising at more than 10 per cent a year (World Bank 1996, p. 51). Total factor productivity in TVEs was also considerably higher than in the state sector, growing at 5 per cent a year, more than twice the rate in state enterprises (World Bank 1996, p. 51). Since 1996, however, the major momentum for growth has increasingly shifted towards the private sector.[5]

During the period of economic reform the non-state sector has made major strides. A small proportion of the labour force in 1980, some 6 per cent, was employed by urban collectively owned factories at the beginning of the reform programme. Only a negligible percentage of people were engaged in self-employed business, such as bicycle and shoe repairs.[6] In 1980 the state sector employed 19 per cent of the working population, while the non-state sector, including agriculture, accounted for the remaining 81 per cent. By 1998, in the urban sector, the contribution of the non-state sector to employment stood at

43 per cent. Hence, the state sector still dominates in the towns and cities. In the rural area private and township enterprises developed into a major source of employment, contributing nearly 34 per cent of total rural employment in 1998, with the remainder working in agriculture. The growth of non-state-owned businesses, plus the dissolution of the commune system in the rural sector, reduced the overall employment contribution of the state sector to 13 per cent by 1998. In addition to expanded employment in the non-state sector, this sector has also seen an expansion in its share of total fixed assets to 45 per cent by 1998 in comparison to the state's share of 55 per cent.

The performance of the non-state sector in manufacturing industries is most noteworthy. The share of the non-state sector in manufacturing increased from 25 per cent in 1980 to 72 per cent in 1998 in terms of total output, from 43 per cent in 1993 to 53 per cent in 1997 in terms of value added, from 34 per cent in 1986 to 43 per cent in 1998 in terms of employment, and from 28 per cent in 1993 to 37 per cent in 1997 in terms of total fixed assets (China Statistical Yearbook 1999). While the non-state sector has assumed an increasingly important role in the production of manufactured goods, SOEs are still major players. Contributing some 47 per cent of manufacturing value added in 1997. This higher share of SOEs in industrial value added than in output suggests that the non-state sector is composed of SMEs engaged in lower value added activities. SOEs dominate the more capital-intensive industries, since the domestic private sector has insufficient access to financial resources to make the large-scale investment in capital intensive industries. The under-developed banking sector, dominated by the state-owned banks, favours the SOEs and therefore fails to channel resources to the most productive sectors, the private and township enterprises, of the economy. This contributed to the recent growth slowdown of the economy.

A similar pattern of ownership structure can be observed in the services industries as for the manufacturing industries. There has been increasing significance of the non-state sector in the smaller services industries, with the dominance of SOEs in key and more capital-intensive services sectors. In catering, leasing, recreation, information and consulting, computer application, tourism and commercial brokerage the non-state sector has started to play an important role alongside SOEs. In three of the largest service industries, hotel, construction and retail services, the non-state sector has also taken a considerable share. In the retail industry, SOEs accounted for only 21 per cent of retail sales of consumer goods in 1998. However, SOEs dominate in other large services sectors, such as electricity, gas and water, transport and storage, post and telecommunications and wholesale (see China Statistical Yearbook 1999). Such is also the case in the banking industry. About 85 per cent of the total assets of the banking sector are in the hands of the four large state-owned commercial banks and the three state policy banks. Another 13 per cent are joint stock banks with SOEs as major shareholders. Less than 2 per cent of banking sector assets are held by foreign-invested banks and private individuals are not allowed to start a banking business (see Mai 2000).

5.5   TVES' PERFORMANCE AND CONTRIBUTION TO THE ECONOMY

Greater autonomy, financial support, freedom from bureaucracy and entrepreneurial drive resulted in a stunning rate of growth for the TVEs during the period of economic reform, which contributed significantly to the rapid growth of the Chinese economy. The TVEs made major progress on a number of fronts including that of output, employment, export growth, as well as improvements in efficiency as measured by both labour productivity and total factor productivity, an upgrading of technology, and sustained profitability.

Table 5.1
Basic Statistics of China's TVEs, 1978–98

Year	Number of Enterprises (Million)	Workers Employed (Million)	Gross Output Value (Billion Yuan)
1978	1.52	28.27	49.3
1980	1.43	30.00	65.7
1984	6.07	52.08	171.0
1985	12.23	69.79	272.8
1986	15.15	79.37	345.1
1987	17.50	88.05	476.4
1988	18.88	95.45	649.6
1989	18.68	93.66	742.8
1990	18.50	92.65	846.2
1991	19.09	96.09	1162.2
1992	20.79	105.81	1797.5
1993	24.53	123.45	3154.1
1994	24.95	120.18	4258.9
1995	22.03	128.62	6891.5
1996	–	135.08	–
1997	20.15	130.50	–
1998	20.04	125.37	–

Source: State Statistical Bureau, *China Statistical Yearbook 1996*, Tables 11-29, 11-30, 11-31, pp. 387–9; State Statistical Bureau, *China Statistical Yearbook 1999*.

5.5.1 Output

Table 5.1 shows the output value, number of establishments and employment level of the TVEs during the period of economic reform. The output value of TVEs increased from 49.3 to 6891.5 billion yuan over the period from 1978 to 1995. In line with this rapid expansion in output, TVE numbers also increased rapidly from over 1.5 million in 1978 to 22 million by 1995, almost 3 million less than for 1994, declining to 20 million by 1998. By the mid 1990s TVEs accounted for 25.5 per cent of GDP and over 30 per cent of gross industrial output, or close to 40 per cent if urban collectives are included (Table 5.2), which compares with a figure of 22 per cent in 1978. In conjunction with these developments the SOE share of industrial production fell steadily during the period of reform, from 78 per cent in 1978 to less than 30 per cent by 1998 (see Table 5.2). There has also been a rapid expansion in the contribution of privately owned and foreign-funded enterprises, whose joint share of industrial production increased from being negligible in 1978 to over 25 per cent by the mid 1990s. The latter represents a rise almost as spectacular as that of the TVEs themselves, and has important implications for the future evolution of the TVEs in terms of their organisational as well as ownership form. Although growth

Table 5.2
Gross Industrial Output by Business Type 1990–98 (million yuan)

Year	1990	1991	1992	1993	1994	1995	1996	1997	1998
Total	23 924	26 625	34 599	48 402	70 176	91 894	99 595	113 733	119 048
SOEs	13 064	14 955	17 824	22 725	26 201	31 220	36 173	35 968	33 621
Per cent	54.6	56.1	51.5	47.0	37.3	34.0	36.3	31.6	28.2
Collectives	8523	8783	12 135	16 464	26 472	33 623	39 232	43 347	45 730
Per cent	35.6	33.0	35.1	34.0	37.7	36.6	39.4	38.1	38.4
Individual-owned enterprises*	1290	1287	2006	3861	7082	11 821	15 420	20 376	20 372
Per cent	5.4	4.8	5.8	8.0	10.1	12.9	15.5	17.9	17.1
Other**	1047	1600	2634	5352	10 421	15 231	16 582	20 982	27 270
Per cent	4.4	6.0	7.6	11.1	14.8	16.6	16.6	18.4	22.9

Notes:
*   In both the urban and rural areas.
** Mainly foreign-funded enterprises.
Source: State Statistical Bureau, *Chinese Statistical Yearbook, 1999*, Table 13.

of the TVEs continued apace during the 1990s (see Table 5.1), developments during the latter half of the 1990s indicated a slowdown in their growth. The reasons for this are discussed in more detail below.

5.5.2   Employment

In terms of employment creation the contribution of TVEs to the rural economy has been truly spectacular. They employed some 28.3 million workers in 1978, rising to a peak of 135 million by 1996 (see Table 5.1). This made a major contribution to the employment of surplus labour in rural China, in a cost-efficient way, as well as raising rural incomes. These are two essential tasks in the development of China's rural economy. Table 5.3 indicates that the TVEs are the largest employers of industrial labour. Indeed over the period 1978–96 they provided an additional 100 million jobs in the rural sector.

While the output growth of TVEs has remained at a high rate concern has, more recently, arisen from the fact that expanded TVE employment has increased at a much slower rate (see Table 5.4). For example, the net output of TVEs increased by 125 per cent at fixed prices from 1991 to 1995 but employment expanded by only 27 per cent. There is a general concern by the authorities that the TVEs alone may not be able to expand sufficiently to absorb unemployed labour in both the rural and urban economies. Hence the increasing importance of the private sector is recognised in this regard. As Table 5.4 indicates, the major source of recent employment growth has come from the private sector. The major shedding of jobs has occurred in the state sector and from the urban collectives.

Table 5.3
Employees by Business Type ('000 persons)

Year	SOEs	Urban collectives	FFEs	TVEs	Private*	Individual#
1980	80 190	24 250	–	30 000	–	810
1985	89 900	33 240	60	69 790	–	4500
1990	103 460	35 490	620	92 650	1700	21 050
1995	112 610	31 470	2410	128 620	9560	46 140
1998	90 580	19 630	2930	125 370	17 100	61 140

Notes:
* Urban and rural sectors.
\# Self employed in the urban and rural sectors.

Source: State Statistical Bureau, *China Statistical Yearbook, 1999*, Table 5.5, pp. 136–7.

Table 5.4
Employment Growth by Business Type 1990–98 (per cent)

Year	SOEs	Urban collectives	FFEs	TVEs	Private*	Individual#
1990	2.4	1.4	50.0	−1.1	na	na
1991	3.0	3.3	66.7	3.7	11.8	10.0
1992	2.2	−0.3	40.0	10.6	21.1	6.9
1993	0.3	−6.3	−7.1	6.8	65.2	19.0
1994	2.7	−2.9	53.8	−2.7	71.1	28.6
1995	0.4	−4.3	20.0	7.0	47.7	22.0
1996	−0.2	−4.1	16.7	5.1	21.9	8.9
1997	−1.8	−4.6	7.1	−3.4	15.4	8.4
1998	−17.9	−32.6	−3.1	−3.9	26.7	12.5

Notes:
  * Urban and rural sectors.
  # Self employed in the urban and rural sectors.

Source: State Statistical Bureau, *China Statistical Yearbook, 1999*, Table 5.5, pp. 136–7.

5.5.3 Exports

Until 1984 exports from TVEs were negligible, but starting from 1985 they increased rapidly. In 1986 TVEs' exports of US$5 billion accounted for one-sixth of China's total exports. In the same year about 20 000 TVEs specialised in production for export, 2400 TVEs were involved in equity and cooperative joint ventures, and about 10 000 were engaged in compensation trade and production according to clients' requirements or samples. In 1987 China's new policy of accelerating the economic development of coastal regions gave 14 cities the status of coastal open cities, with extra freedoms and tax breaks for foreign trade and investment and gave a further impetus to the development of TVEs. In this year, TVEs were allowed to participate directly in international trade, rather than just indirectly as subcontractors to state trading companies and SOEs, and the result was a dramatic increase in TVE exports (Sachs and Woo 1997). From the second half of 1988 to 1991, both central and local governments put great emphasis on the development of export oriented businesses to acquire capital, technology, and raw materials from western companies and international markets. Although during the same period the central government was tightening money supply and controlling investment in domestic markets, export oriented TVEs began to take off. They succeeded because of their operating flexibility and customer oriented approach. The position of TVEs in China's foreign trade became increasingly important thereafter (see Table 5.5). From 1987 through

Table 5.5
Share of TVEs in Total Exports

Year	Total exports billion yuan	TVEs' exports % of total exports	Total exports % of GDP
1987	147	10.9	12
1988	177	15.3	13
1989	196	18.9	12
1990	299	16.4	17
1991	383	17.5	19
1992	468	25.4	19
1993	529	44.4	17
1994	1042	32.6	23

Source: Sachs and Woo 1997, Table 5.

1992 TVEs' exports and imports grew by an average of 60 per cent per year. Their exports of 468 billion yuan (US$20 billion) in 1992 accounted for a quarter of China's total exports (US$85 billion). By the mid 1990s about 80 000 TVEs were engaged in export-oriented production, accounting for over 30 per cent of China's total exports and over 25 per cent of China's GDP. The share of overall exports accounted for by TVEs increased from 9.2 per cent in 1986 to more than 40 per cent, at its peak, in 1996.

5.5.4   Profitability

Table 5.6 compares the profit rates between TVEs and state-owned industrial enterprises (SOIEs) during the period of economic reform. This suggests that for most of the years from 1978 to 1994 the pre-tax and after-tax profit rates of the TVEs have been higher than those of the SOIEs, except for the years from 1986 to 1989. However, to obtain a more accurate picture of their respective performances, the profit rates of the SOIEs must be discounted by the subsidies provided by the central government. These budget subsidies increased from 11.7 billion yuan in 1978 to 36.6 billion yuan in 1994, and for most of the years this accounted for a share of more than 10 per cent of total government revenue. Therefore, if the profit rates of the SOIEs recorded in Table 5.6 are discounted by this factor, their performance has lagged considerably further behind that of the TVEs which operate in the absence of government subsidy.

5.5.5   Upgrading of Technology

During the period 1991 to 1995 the capital stock of TVEs increased by 142 per cent, and was the primary factor behind the rapid growth in TVE output during

Table 5.6
Profit Rates of TVEs and SOIEs, 1978–94 (%)

Year	TVE		SOIE	
	Pre-tax	After-tax	Pre-tax	After-tax
1978	39.8	31.8	24.2	15.5
1979	35.4	29.1	24.8	16.1
1980	32.5	26.7	24.8	16.0
1981	29.1	22.3	23.8	15.0
1982	28.0	20.2	23.4	14.4
1983	27.8	18.5	23.2	14.4
1984	24.6	15.2	24.2	14.9
1985	23.7	14.5	23.8	13.2
1986	19.7	10.6	20.7	10.6
1987	17.0	9.0	20.3	10.6
1988	17.9	9.3	20.6	10.4
1989	15.2	7.1	17.2	7.2
1990	13.0	5.9	12.4	3.2
1991	12.7	5.8	11.8	2.9
1992	14.3	4.8	9.7	2.7
1993	19.0	11.6	9.7	3.2
1994	14.8	9.0	9.8	2.8

Note: Profit Rate = Pre or After-tax Profit/(Fixed Capital + Working Capital).
Source: ZGTJNJ 1992: 391, 431; 1993: 436–7; 1994: 366; 1995: 403–6.

this period. This expansion of capital intensity of TVE production is confirmed from Table 5.7, which clearly indicates an upgrading of the technology employed by TVEs. The vast majority of the funds for which came from bank loans and retained earnings, with the latter becoming of increasing significance during the period of the 1990s (see Table 5.8). While this is of benefit to some TVEs, as they move to increasingly higher value products, it does present a strange paradox in a labour-surplus economy, and explains the slowdown in labour absorption in rural China as previously indicated. Why has labour been substituted for capital in this way? Recent research (see Liu 1997) suggests that in the coastal provinces the reason for this is that most of the surplus labour has already been absorbed, and that further production is being achieved by increasing relatively cheap capital for increasingly costly labour. In the poorer inland provinces with surplus labour, the marginal productivity of labour is already low, and hence expanded production could come about more easily through an expansion of capital rather than labour. This, Liu concludes, has important policy implications for labour migration and training, and for the allocation of capital, to improve labour

Table 5.7
Capital Intensity of TVEs and SOEs

Year	TVEs' capital-to-labour ratio	SOEs' capital-to-labour ratio
1985	1362.8	10 434.6
1986	1636.5	11 488.7
1987	2034.2	12 830.2
1988	2522.5	14 283.3
1989	3148.6	16 459.6
1990	3633.6	18 529.9
1991	4110.1	21 259.4
1992	5022.3	24 292.6
1993	6532.9	29 571.9
1994	8808.9	35 867.1
1995	11 780.9	39 741.0
1985–95 % p.a. (nominal)	24.1	14.3
1985–95 % p.a. (deflated)	12.2	2.4

Source: TVE *Statistical Yearbook* 1995 and previous years.

absorption in rural China across its provinces. Labour should be encouraged to move to the coastal provinces, and capital to the poorer inland provinces.

5.5.6 Efficiency

Strong empirical evidence exists supporting the proposition that TVEs have been successful in closing the efficiency gap relative to SOEs. For example, Weitzman and Xu (1994) compared the growth rates of output, capital, labour and total factor productivity (TFP) of the SOIEs and the TVEs from 1979 to 1991. They found that the growth rates associated with the TVEs was much higher than that of the SOIEs. It is particularly evident for the growth of TFP, which grew three times faster for the TVEs in comparison to that of the SOIEs. Similar results were derived by Jefferson and Rawski (1994), who found that the collective form of enterprise performed better than that of the state sector both in terms of labour productivity and more importantly in terms of TFP. These results reflect the fact that TVEs achieved considerable technological progress as previously mentioned, and particularly relative to both the SOIEs and collective industries in urban areas.

The reasons behind the phenomenal success of the TVEs during the period of the late 1980s and early 1990s, as well as outstanding problems, are discussed in the following section.

Table 5.8
Sources of Enterprises' Investment Finance, 1980–93

	SOEs	Urban collectives	TVEs	Joint ventures	WFOEs
Plan allocation					
1980–84	12	0	0	0	0
1985–89	9	0	0	0	0
1990–93	12	0	0	0	0
Bank loans					
1980–84	82	80	na	25	na
1985–89	72	67	81	24	37
1990–93	76	78	53	47	27
Retained earnings					
1980–84	6	20	na	75	na
1985–89	18	33	19	74	63
1990–93	9	22	47	47	73
Share/bond issues					
1980–84	0	0	na	0	na
1985–89	1	0	0	0	0
1990–93	3	0	0	6	0

Source: Perkins and Raiser 1994, Table 12 from a survey of 300 coastal province enterprises.

5.6   REASONS FOR THE SUCCESS OF THE TVES

A number of reasons have been advanced in the literature (see, for example, Harvie and Turpin 1997; Kwong 1997; Sachs and Woo 1997, p. 39; and World Bank 1996, p. 51) to explain the phenomenal growth and impressive efficiency record of TVEs relative to that of the SOEs in particular. The major ones include the following:

- *Small, flexible and market driven.* From the outset TVEs had to rely on markets for sourcing supplies and selling products. Many TVEs positioned their business in areas where there were severe shortages, or where SOEs were weak. Most were small and autonomous compared with SOEs, and thus had flexibility to respond to market changes quickly. Their management was also more market-oriented.

- *Appropriate production technology.* The TVEs faced cheap labour and expensive capital and natural resources, causing them to choose appropriate production technologies. As the reform process progressed and prices were gradually liberalised to reflect relative scarcity values, the SOEs found themselves at a competitive disadvantage because of inappropriate capital and resource intensive technologies.
- *Distortions, market opportunities and rural saving.* The TVEs were highly profitable because of the distortions carried over from the formerly planned system. At the beginning of the reform process in 1978, the average rate of profit on TVE capital was 32 per cent.[7] Most of the new TVEs were in manufacturing where initial state price controls kept profitability high so that the state could obtain high revenues from the SOEs. In addition, due to past biases in the planned system against light industry and services, the TVEs could enter market niches for which the SOEs had either failed to produce or failed to innovate and improve quality control. The resulting high profits achieved by TVEs attracted further investment and rapid growth. This was further strengthened by high rural saving and demand, following the agricultural reforms of 1978, in conjunction with the limited scope for emigration from rural areas.
- *Low taxation.* Taxes on TVEs were low, requiring them to pay only 6 per cent of profits as tax in 1980, climbing to 20 per cent after 1985. Such low tax rates in China were primarily due to a policy driven desire to foster rural industrialisation.
- *Decision-making.* Information channels between the TVE managers and local government authorities tended to be both shorter and simpler compared to those for the SOEs, encouraging greater efficiency. Further, this greater flexibility and autonomy in management has meant that inter-firm alliances and technological alliances with universities and research institutes have produced a 'networked' approach to innovation and industrial production. Such institutional innovations could be implemented without the approval of the central government. Recent locally initiated transformation of TVEs into 'shareholding cooperatives' is a case in point. This feature has enabled the TVEs to move closer to best international practices in corporate governance.
- *Decentralisation plus financial discipline.* In 1984 a decentralisation of fiscal power took place in China which allowed lower levels of government to retain locally generated revenues, creating a strong incentive for the development of local industry. A non-performing TVE in this system would become a drain on limited resources. Local government officials and TVE managers, therefore, had to focus more upon financial objectives, profit plus local tax revenues, since local governments lacked the borrowing capacity of higher levels

of government and TVEs could not automatically turn to banks for a bail-out. Hence the TVE enterprises under their jurisdiction faced harder budget constraints than SOEs, and were more likely to fall into bankruptcy if persistent losses were made. This focused upon the need for TVEs to be efficient, competitive and profitable in a period of a rapid opening up of markets. Meanwhile managers of SOEs, having responsibility for housing and other social services as well as industrial operations, faced a more complex set of objectives and state obligations.

* *Kinship and implicit property rights.* A number of researchers have suggested that, despite the absence of well defined property rights, the demographic stability of China's rural communities promoted the emergence of 'invisible institutions' to provide a 'moral framework for rights' or a 'cooperative culture' that served to reduce problems of shirking and monitoring found in most public enterprises (see Byrd and Lin 1990; Yusuf 1993a, 1993b; and Weitzman and Xu 1994). The incentives facing TVEs are similar to those facing private firms in that residual profits are dispersed among a small group, consisting of a stable local community and in particular its local government and TVE manager. Studies have shown the importance of TVE profits in local government budgets and the close links between local economic performance and the status, income and career prospects of local officials.

* *Links with the state enterprise sector.* The state sector also represented an important, and not sufficiently recognised, component in the successful development of TVEs and other non-state firms. The TVEs and collectives in general relied on the state sector as a source of capital, materials, equipment, specialised personnel, technology, subcontracting arrangements and sales revenue. For example, in southern Jiangsu province more than two-thirds of TVEs established various forms of economic and technical cooperation arrangements with industrial enterprises, research units, and higher educational institutions in larger cities. Local government officials attempting to develop industry in poor localities are encouraged to pursue joint operations with scientific research organisations or large and medium scale state enterprises.

* *Market entry and competition.* The continual reduction of entry barriers associated with China's industrial reform created a domestic product cycle in which new products, materials and processes introduced by innovative state firms were adopted by TVEs and other non-state enterprises.[8] They could then use their cost advantages to erode state sector profits and force state industry toward fresh innovations. In addition there was intense competition for investment, including that

for foreign investment, among communities with TVEs. The ability to attract such investment is strongly influenced by the reputation of the TVEs, as well as local economic performance. TVEs themselves are being increasingly subject to competition from the even more dynamic but smaller private and foreign invested sectors. An issue discussed further in a later section of this chapter.

• *Improvement in human resources, innovation and quality.* Many TVEs put special emphasis on human resources, innovation and product quality. With their autonomous and flexible systems it is their usual practice to recruit highly competent engineers and technicians from SOEs, to pay them attractive salaries and actively pursue innovation. At the beginning of the 1980s they mainly targeted and sought retired technicians and engineers from urban areas. Since the mid 1980s their attention shifted to scientists and technicians working in research institutes and SOEs, who were discontented with their working conditions. More recently they have been competing with large- and medium-sized SOEs for talented staff and trying to attract foreign experts. TVEs maintain close links with research institutes. About 60 per cent of inventions and innovations developed by China's scientific and technological institutions have been put into production by TVEs.

• *International orientation.* Many TVEs, particularly those in coastal provinces, actively pursued cooperation and joint ventures with SOEs, with other TVEs, and with foreign companies. Joint ventures between TVEs and foreign companies having grown rapidly during the 1990s. By developing joint ventures and sub contracts with foreign firms, TVEs gradually upgraded their technology, became involved in foreign direct investment (FDI), and expanded the quality of their produce for overseas markets.

• *Lower cost structure.* TVEs possessed lower cost structures than SOEs, and paid less tax. Because their managers historically had to rely on retained earnings and loans instead of government grants, they constantly pressured local authorities to give them tax breaks. Wages in rural areas are also significantly lower than in cities where most SOEs are found. They do not have thousands of retirees for whom they are liable for pension payments, they do not have to offer welfare benefits like healthcare and social security insurance to their workforce, and they do not have to provide housing for their workers. TVE workers work long hours, and the quality of their production has improved. Where simple technology is required this represents a big advantage, particularly in light industries like textiles and electrical appliances.

Despite these favourable characteristics, many TVEs still suffer from a number of difficulties, including the following:

- *Limited funds and supplies.* Although the Chinese government implemented favourable loan and taxation policies to support TVEs, it did not directly invest in TVEs as it did with SOEs. The growth of TVE investment to sustain their rapid development during the latter half of the 1980s depended primarily upon bank loans, and increasingly upon retained earnings during the early part of the 1990s (Table 5.8). Another difference between TVEs and SOEs is that the former never benefited from supplies, at low cost, through the central plan.
- *Obsolete technology.* Many TVEs are still using obsolete technology, partly because their businesses are small and newly established and partly because their managers and employees have only recently stopped working on the land. In fact, some worked part time as employees and part time as farmers. Hence, they are incapable of pursuing R&D activities and developing new products. Apart from some TVEs in the southern coastal provinces, most relied on mechanical or semi-mechanical technology and quite a few on manual work. Many are too small to invest in R&D and keep up with the latest technology, making them vulnerable to competition from financially stronger foreign invested ventures.
- *Low level of employees' education.* One of the major problems in TVEs is their employees' very low level of education. In the early 1990s only about 200 000 employees in TVEs had a degree or higher education, and only 420 000 held a medium level technical qualification. These two figures come to less than 1 per cent of their employees.
- *Profitability not clear.* Many foreign investors partnering TVEs sometimes discovered that much of their profitability was based purely on preferential tax policies.
- *Vague property rights.* Growing conflicts of interest may arise from their historically vague ownership status. Because employees theoretically own everything collectively and nothing individually, they often act more like employees than owners seeking to increase their salaries rather than cut costs and maximise company profit. Vague ownership rights and reliance on special privileges have clouded their future. In response to this the authorities passed the Law of Township and Village Owned Enterprises in October 1996 with the objective of clarifying TVE property rights.

5.7   TVE PROSPECTS

For the TVEs to maintain their remarkable performance they will be required to evolve into enterprises capable of being competitive within the context of China's increasingly market oriented economy. This will require making further advances in a number of key areas, including: management control; clarification of property rights; expanding access to finance; gaining access to developments in science and technology; enhancing the human capital of its employees and managers; ensuring access to input supply; and improving the efficiency of their distribution and marketing systems. Those TVEs unable to make such advances are unlikely to survive within the new economic environment rapidly evolving in China. This has been given further impetus with China's membership of the WTO. Successful TVEs are likely to be those able to develop into new organisational forms based upon business alliances with other enterprises, involving cooperation and joint ventures between TVEs, SOEs, private domestic and foreign enterprises, and also with research institutes and universities in order to gain access to advances in science and technology. This will enable them to compete in both domestic and international markets, as well as to invest overseas.

The gap between the developed coastal and backward inland regions is likely to widen since TVEs in the coastal region attract and introduce far more FDI than inland regions. This process will encourage more and more TVEs to turn to exports, including processing and manufacturing based on clients' samples and specifications, processing clients' raw materials and direct export. Joint ventures between TVEs and foreign firms will increase. TVEs in the coastal region will gradually develop their own R&D capacity. More and more capable technicians will be attracted to TVEs in the coastal region, where they enjoy a higher living standard than inland areas and have autonomy and funds to pursue research. Additionally, the intensification of competition, particularly from the rapidly developing private sector and foreign enterprises, is likely to result in the traditional collective ownership structure of the TVEs no longer being viable.

5.8   GROWTH OF CHINA'S PRIVATE SECTOR

5.8.1   Rapid Growth of Private Enterprises

The private sector in China was suppressed during the period of central planning, but re-emerged with the initiation of reforms in 1978.[9] The sector grew rapidly over the next 20 years and by 1998, including household agricultural production, accounted for approximately 50 per cent of GDP,[10] although there is no clear dividing line between genuinely private and collective enterprises. A recently more favourable attitude by the authorities towards private ownership in China contributed to growth in the number of registered private firms, employment in these firms and increased share in total GDP.

Individual private enterprises, in particular, developed rapidly during the 1980s. From 1981 to 1988, the gross industrial output value of the individual sector grew at an average annual growth rate of 87 per cent. The growth trend

Table 5.9
Growth Trend of Private and Other Categories of Enterprise in China
(Average growth rate, %, 1989–98)

	Average	State	Collective	FDI	*Getithu*	Private[a]
Number of firms	na	5.37	0.27	34.4	8.48	33.27
Employment	2.64	–0.01	–0.06	22.55	13.6	29.76
Registered capital	na	12.89	11.56	36.94	27.64	63.97
Tax revenue	17.55	14.83	11.8	30.37[b]	60.79	73.15
Fixed capital investment[c]	24.2	21.6	28.2	11.73[d]	16.0	33.8
Gross value of output (industrial)	16.61	5.39	18.3	27.84[c]	32.95	51.85
Retail sales	13.2	5.32	4.64	na	22.35	57.24

Notes: na = not available;
a   'Private' refers to formally registered private enterprises
b   1994–97
c   1990–98
d   1994–98.

Source: Garnaut and Song 2000, p. 3.

of formally registered private enterprises, including single industrial and commercial proprietor enterprises called *getihu*, can be seen from Table 5.9. The average growth rate of formally registered private enterprises far exceeded that of both state and collective enterprises over 1989–98 in all measurements listed, most noticeably employment, registered capital, tax revenue, gross value of industrial output and retail sales. From the early 1990s many small- and medium-sized SOEs were taken over by, or merged with, private enterprises.

Most individual businesses are located in industrial retail sectors and in service industries. The fast development of individual enterprises provided an outlet of self-employment for people who could not get into the SOEs and the collectives, or who were not satisfied with their situation in the SOEs or the collectives. However, rural private enterprises have not been overshadowed by urban private enterprises. There appears to be a division of labour between the urban and the rural private sectors. The rural private sector concentrates upon the primary and the secondary sectors,[11] while the urban private sector is dominant in the tertiary sector.[12] Because both types are subject to capital constraints these individual enterprises tend to be small in size.

The success of the private sector in a regulatory environment overwhelmingly geared to the requirements of the state-owned enterprises is remarkable. The recent reform of the regulatory and institutional framework provides more beneficial conditions for the private sector, which is the most dynamic, and now the larger, part of the Chinese economy. This has the potential to provide new impetus for economic growth. In particular, the component of the collective sector that is in reality private will now grow rapidly, as the regulatory and ideological advantages of a real or nominal 'red hat' disappear. This will be beneficial to the economy overall as this sector is likely to use resources more effectively than the state sector.

5.8.2   Contribution of the Private Sector to the Economy

The growth of the private sector has played an important role in the development of the economy, particularly during the period of the 1990s, in a number of areas. Its contribution in terms of growth of employment, tax revenue, fixed capital investment, industrial output and retail sales for the period 1989–98 is summarised in Table 5.9. Its contribution to increased employment has enhanced labour productivity, by recruiting new workers into the non-farm economy as well as absorbing laid-off workers from reformed SOEs.[13] The private sector has increased competition in those sectors where it has been allowed to compete, as well as nurturing competition and initiating innovation. It has helped to channel an increasing part of investment into more efficient uses and hence increased the overall efficiency of the economy. In meeting the demands of the private sector a regulatory and institutional framework more compatible with a market system can be established, which will also assist in improving the performance of state-owned and collective enterprises. An expanding private sector can also accelerate growth with less risk to macro-economic stability than the expansion of state-owned enterprises, since private firms are subject to a hard budget constraint.

Before 1985 the share of formally registered private enterprises in national industrial output was negligible, although its share of employment was already around 2 per cent of the national non-agricultural labour force in 1981. By 1997, the sector's share in national industrial employment reached more than 18 per cent. Its share of national industrial output rose from below 2 per cent in 1985 to 12.2 per cent in 1993 and 34.3 per cent in 1997. In absolute terms, formally registered private enterprises' industrial output has experienced substantial and rapid growth in the last 20 years to reach 3.8 trillion yuan in 1997. Employment expansion in the private industrial sector experienced a major downturn from 1989 to 1991,[14] but thereafter recovered rapidly (see Table 5.10). By 1998, the total number of workers employed in the private sector had reached 78.3 million.

The private sector's share in GDP, outside agriculture, reached 33 per cent in 1998, which was still smaller than the state sector's share of 37 per cent. If agriculture, a sector comprising mainly individual farmers, is regarded as mainly private, the share of the private sector rises to 50 per cent (Garnaut and

Table 5.10
Employment in the Private Sector, 1990–98 (million)

Year	Urban		Rural		Total private sector#	% of total employ- ment
	Private	Individual*	Private	Individual		
1990	0.6	6.1	1.1	14.9	22.7	4.0
1991	0.7	6.9	1.2	16.2	25.0	4.3
1992	1.0	7.4	1.3	17.3	26.7	4.5
1993	1.9	9.3	1.9	20.1	33.2	5.5
1994	3.3	12.3	3.2	25.5	44.3	6.6
1995	4.9	15.6	4.7	30.5	55.7	8.5
1996	6.2	17.1	5.5	33.1	61.9	9.0
1997	7.5	19.2	6.0	35.2	67.9	9.8
1998	9.7	22.6	7.4	38.2	78.3	11.2

Notes: * Self employed individuals.
            # Urban and rural sectors.

Source: State Statistical Bureau, *China Statistical Yearbook, 1999*, Table 5.5, pp. 136–7.

Song 2000). The true private sector and true collectives together contribute a non-state sector share of 62 per cent in 1998. The fast growth of the private sector in the 1990s was mainly within the formally registered private firms, as distinct from non-incorporated enterprises. The disproportion between its performance and resource shares is a major feature of China's private sector development in the 1990s.

5.8.3   Major Constraints

The extraordinary growth of the private sector occurred despite an initially highly unfavourable environment. In a country whose production and commercial activities have been dominated by large state-owned enterprises for decades, there is still much discrimination against smaller and private enterprises in areas such as business registration, taxation, financing and foreign trading rights. It therefore remains a big task to develop the regulatory framework to allow a wider and more direct participation by private firms in developing China's economy (Garnaut and Song 2000).

Amongst the most important areas where reform is required are: improving the operation of markets for goods, services and factors of production; strengthening the rule of law, specifically in relation to property and contract rights; streamlining and raising the efficiency of government; removal of rent-seeking behaviour by government in its dealings with business; and the development of fiscal and other measures by government to alleviate unfavourable income distribution effects that may be associated with sustained, rapid private sector development. Measures aimed at encouraging private sector development have been gradually introduced. Of these, the most important has been the recognition of the sector in the constitution and state policy at the March 1999 meeting of the National People's Congress. Within this context a large number of small- and medium-sized SOEs are currently being restructured based on market conditions in which private firms are allowed to play an important role.

State commercial banks have been asked to assist in the development of small firms, including private enterprises, by charging flexible interest rates, capable of being varied in response to market conditions including perceptions of risk on loans made to these firms. From the beginning of 1999, for the first time since 1957, a number of private enterprises were granted licenses to conduct foreign trade on their own, and more sectors, including infrastructure and financial services, have been opened to foreign competition.

The private sector faces a number of constraints that require urgent attention if it is to face a level playing field with state-owned and collective enterprises. These include the following: the imposition of arbitrary fees and taxes on private enterprises by local governments; unequal access to business finance particularly from state financial institutions; the absence of efficient and transparent bank lending systems to small- and medium-sized enterprises in general, and more particularly to private enterprises; a weak skill base at both the managerial and employee levels, and particularly that facing small- and medium-sized enterprises; weak and non transparent accounting and auditing practices; insufficient support to private enterprises by different levels of government in registration, land use, finance, market entry and law enforcement; a weak legal and regulatory environment; weak markets particularly in the financial and labour markets; and the absence of a competitive environment in which all types of firms are competing on an equal footing.

5.9   POLICIES FOR FURTHER DEVELOPMENT OF THE PRIVATE SECTOR

If the private sector, and small businesses in particular, are to be further developed, a number of areas, therefore, still require urgent further reform. These include: reform of the financial system; reforming the government tax and revenue system; enhancing the technical innovation system; improved legal protection of property rights; improved education and training; and opening up more sectors for private investment and competition.

5.9.1 Financial System

An uneven distribution of bank loans between the state and non-state sectors represents a major constraint on the further development of the non-state sector, particularly for small-sized private enterprises. The result has also been an inefficient use of bank funds. In 1998, the non-state sector contributed 71 per cent of industrial gross output value but its share of total bank loans was only 30 per cent. Small private enterprises in particular find it difficult to get a bank loan. It may be that loans extended to small enterprises are perceived as being more risky than those to larger enterprises. This financial constraint on small private enterprises seriously restricts their development and growth and requires urgent attention from the authorities.

A number of policy changes will be required if these problems are to be overcome. First, a more even-handed treatment of state and non-state enterprises by the state banks is required. Second, there is also the need to develop non-state financial institutions that would more adequately serve the growth of the non-state sector. China's membership of the WTO will eventually offer opportunities for foreign banks based in China to engage in domestic currency lending, and this will have an important impact upon the further development of the private sector. Third, the current policy of zero risk lending by state banks, applied mainly to non-state enterprises, should be replaced by portfolio management. With this a bank branch or an employee would be evaluated by the profitability of the resources allocated to them over a certain period, not simply by whether one or two loans had been lost. They would not be evaluated differently according to whether the borrower was a state or a private enterprise. This outcome would be achieved naturally by requiring state banks to operate competitively and profitably within a rational system of prudential supervision, which systematically discounted non-performing assets independently of the identity of the borrower, and which required maintenance of minimum ratios of capital to assets, all within a transparent accounting framework.

To give incentives to banks to extend loans to small enterprises, to cover their perceived risk of losses, and to eliminate rent seeking behaviour, a flexible interest rate is needed. As a first step, controls on lending rates can be eased to allow banks to charge different rates according to different risks of loans. To finance small- and medium-sized enterprises, there is a need to develop new non-state financial institutions. A new policy should allow non-state financial institutions to grow, but under the supervision of the state. A total ban on all new financial institutions is inappropriate. Small business would also potentially benefit from the removal of current impediments to the provision of venture capital. Carefully designed loan guarantee funds or systems could usefully be used to resolve financing problems facing private enterprise at the moment. From this perspective, it seems that firm-managed guarantee funds may be a solution to small- and medium-sized firms' financing problems (Garnaut and Song 2000).

5.9.2   Government Taxation and Revenue System

Although the tax burden on private enterprises is relatively low compared with other countries, there are considerable irregular fees, fines, involuntary 'donations' collected by various government departments at the different administrative levels. In addition, the actual tax burden among firms is uneven. Small firms have been known to pay a higher proportion of their sales revenue in the form of taxation. This reflects the fact that large firms have more opportunity for tax privileges.

The current tax system discourages investment and technical innovation by enterprises. This is mainly because investment in capital assets and R&D does not attract deductions in assessment of value-added tax and income tax. The tax system therefore needs to be made more transparent and more equitable in its application across firms. For fairness and equity in tax collection, efforts are required to help small enterprises to improve management and accounting systems. Accounting and auditing services are also required to meet the increasing needs of private firms, especially small-sized firms.

5.9.3   Technical Innovation, Property Rights and Human Capital

Although private enterprises are found to be very active in technical innovation, there have been several major constraints to their investment in R&D and other activities conducive to development of technological capabilities. These constraints include shortages and weaknesses in human capital, financial resources, information and effective protection of intellectual property rights.

China also lacks financial institutions dealing with investments in R&D and venture capital more generally, which have high risk but high potential returns. The government intends establishing various kinds of funds for the purpose of research and development. Again, non-government institutions should also be allowed and encouraged to participate in these efforts. It is important that information services systems of importance to private and especially small business be improved, in order to effectively provide information on international and domestic goods, services and factor markets as well as technology and management. This can be best achieved by facilitating the emergence of new businesses providing these services on a market basis. It would be helped by a more competitive telecommunications system, providing basic services at international prices.

An important measure for technical innovation is to improve and strengthen the system of legal protection for intellectual property rights. This will give more incentive to enterprises for increased R&D expenditures and other innovation activities. Protection of property rights should be legislated more clearly and should be protected more effectively. The legal system needs to be further improved and law enforcement to be strengthened to curb irregularities and to reduce transaction costs.

During the past two decades of economic growth the government and business sectors alike have paid insufficient attention to education and other investments in human capital, partly due to the lack of funds. Based upon the experiences of other countries it can be suggested that rapid economic growth is unlikely to be sustainable without a significant improvement in the rate of investment in human capital. Consequently, the government needs to invest heavily in education as well as expenditure on R&D. The government could also reduce its financial burden on developing a sound education system by allowing private investors, including overseas investors, to invest in education. Of particular importance currently to the private sector is investment in education in relevant business skills including: business law; accounting; auditing; business and public administration; as well as specialised areas including finance and economics.

5.9.4   Opening Up More Sectors for Private Investment

China's accession to the WTO will require rapid liberalisation and opening of its economy to foreign traders and investors, and consequently will require considerable adjustments to its regulatory framework. However, such changes and adjustments are quite consistent with the current policy shift towards accommodating the development of the private sector in the economy. One area that needs further action by government is the opening of more areas for private investment and trade. All sectors, except the small number in which the state has indicated an intention to maintain predominant control, should be open to private investment. The Law on Protection Against Unfair Competition, enacted in December 1993, to create a fair and competitive business and investment environment needs to be strictly implemented. Preferential policies towards SOEs and foreign investments need to be gradually phased out and a policy of national treatment to enable domestic private enterprises to compete with SOEs and foreign firms, on an equal footing, needs to be adopted. Foreign trading rights for all qualified private enterprises need to be extended to allow direct and wider participation by private enterprises in China's foreign trade.

5.10   A COMPARISON OF CHINA AND VIETNAM

This section presents a brief review of the progress made in Asia's two major transition economies in terms of: market liberalisation; encouragement of competition; and the development of the private sector. Table 5.11 summarises these developments on the basis of a number of criteria consisting of: market liberalisation; encouragement of different ownership forms; legal framework;

contribution and development of the private sector; the significance and role of SMEs; access to land and land use rights; market support institutions; regulation of natural monopolies; trade reform, SOE reform, bank reform; establishing a conducive environment for FDI; extent of integration with the regional and global economies; and overall reform progress in these areas.

China has seen considerable liberalisation of its markets since the 1980s, with the growth of the TVEs and their ability to compete with the SOEs. During the 1990s markets have been further liberalised with the development and growth of private SMEs. The authorities in China recognise the important contribution of ownership forms other than that of state and collective, specifically that of the private sector, to the future growth and development of the economy. The private sector has flourished during the period of the 1990s, providing the major engine of growth of output and employment. With the liberalisation of domestic markets to both domestic and foreign private enterprises, this trend can only continue. The development of the private sector has been primarily in the form of individual and private enterprises (mainly SMEs). As a consequence the private sector is developing in a balanced manner, with microenterprises at the household level, then SMEs and then larger private enterprises. The development of SMEs is important, as it is from these enterprises that the larger enterprises of the future will develop. Those enterprises that will remain owned by the state and which dominate markets will need to be regulated to ensure that they do not abuse their market position. The necessary regulations, in the context of a market-oriented economy, will need to be put in place. China has made major advances in terms of its trade reform, opening up its markets to foreign competitors and enabling more domestic enterprises to trade freely in terms of imports. SOE reform has proceeded slowly, with many large SOEs operating inefficiently and making losses. Reform in this area slowed considerably with the recent slowdown of the economy and concerns over rising unemployment. Linked to this is bank reform. This will be essential to bring about reform of the SOEs as well as to bring about further development of the private sector. Again, reform is proceeding slowly in this area. China has been a major recipient of FDI since 1992. During the period of the Asian crisis FDI was adversely affected, but with the recovery in the region FDI has once again started to increase. The Chinese economy has become increasingly integrated with both the regional and global economies. Export growth from the early 1990s has been rapid. The country is a member of APEC, and it became a member of the WTO in December 2001. The latter will have a profound impact upon the economy, opening its domestic markets further to foreign trade and investment. It will give further impetus to reform and the development of the country's market economy, its domestic private sector, liberalisation of markets, foreign direct investment and exports.

Vietnam's transition economy has also experienced successful growth with the adoption of 'Doi Moi' in 1986 and the speeding up of further reform measures in 1989.[15] The period of the 1990s saw impressive GDP growth rates that only faltered in 1998 and 1999 as a consequence of the regional crisis. This recent decline in economic growth has provided further impetus to the reform process.

In terms of market liberalisation, Vietnam is lagging developments in China. However, approval and implementation of the new Enterprise Law (effective January 2000) to improve the climate for private sector investment, by simplifying requirements for entry registration of firms, will encourage private entry. The initial response to the Enterprise Law was to encourage 10 000 new SMEs to register during the first nine months of 2000, with an average registered capital of around VND800 million per enterprise. This growth rate was exceptional relative to earlier years. The Competition Law, currently being formulated, if properly implemented will also be of considerable importance. The revision to the 1996 Law on Foreign Investment will encourage foreign investment. However, there still appears to be only grudging official recognition of the importance of private ownership forms of enterprises, and the private sector remains more constrained than in other countries of the region. However, the Prime Minister's opening address to the National Assembly in November 1999 emphasised the priority of creating a climate conducive for private sector development. In particular, tapping into the potential of the private non farm sector, to produce and to export, can play a key role in restoring higher growth of income and employment in the foreseeable future. Recently, the government has also developed the Private Sector Promotion Action Plan under the Miyazawa initiative, to establish a more favourable environment for the private sector.

The private sector,[16] in 1998, accounted for 51 per cent of GDP (see Table 5.12), as in China, a share that has remained stagnant over the past five years. The bulk of this is accounted for by the household, mainly farm-based, and services sector (34 per cent of GDP), and foreign invested businesses (10 per cent of GDP). The domestic non-household private sector, still mainly in the form of SMEs, only accounts for 7 per cent of GDP. Important trends are developing which suggest the important contribution that the private sector can bring to the future growth of the economy. While less than half of manufacturing GDP is produced by private firms, the domestic private sector dominates this share. Private SMEs in manufacturing, especially the larger ones, are highly export-oriented, and operate in labour intensive sectors like garments, footwear, plastic products and seafood. Currently, household enterprises and private SMEs employ more than 64 per cent of industrial workers, while SOEs, producing the bulk of industrial output, employ only 24 per cent. On average, private SMEs export around three-quarters of their production implying greater export orientation than SOEs. Foreign-invested enterprises are also playing an increasingly important role in the economy: contributing 18 per cent of manufacturing output; employing 300 000 workers; and exporting around half of their output.

Reform of the trade, SOE and banking sectors remain top priorities for the authorities, if the private sector is to develop further and to be internationally

Table 5.11
Market Liberalisation, Competition and Private Sector Development
– A Comparison between China and Vietnam

Criteria	China	Vietnam
1. Market liberalisation	Improving – Protection against Unfair Competition Law (1993) Constitution March 1999	Lagging – Competition Law (in process) Enterprise Law (2000)
2. Different ownership forms	Accepted – seen as important for the future development of the economy	Ambiguous – importance has not been given official recognition
3. Legal frame-work	Still being developed	Still being developed
4. Private sector development	50% of GDP Advanced and developing rapidly	50% of GDP Restricted, lagging in development
5. Role of private SMEs	Significant in rural and urban sectors. Developing rapidly. Major source of employment and export expansion	Lagging, only contribute 7% of GDP. Considerable room for development. Has major output, employment and export potential
6. Access to land	Restricted	Restricted
7. Market support institutions	Still evolving and developing	Still evolving and developing
8. Natural monopoly regulation	To be developed	To be developed

Criteria	China	Vietnam
9. Trade reform	Advanced	Restricted – inadequate access to imports and export outlets
10. SOE reform	Slow – more urgency required; divestitures, equitisation, mergers and bankruptcy	Slow – more urgency required; divestitures, equitisation, mergers and bankruptcy
11. Bank reform	Slow – recapitalisation, non-performing loans, SOEs still priority, commercial orientation; inadequate access to finance (private sector and SMEs in particular)	Slow – recapitalisation, non-performing loans, SOEs still priority, commercial orientation; inadequate access to finance (private sector and SMEs in particular)
12. Foreign direct investment	Increasing; important for growth and exports; encourage labour-intensive, exporting investment	Decreasing; essential for growth and exports; encourage labour-intensive, exporting investment
13. Economic integration	APEC member, PNTR with USA, WTO membership imminent	ASEAN member, APEC member, US bilateral trade agreement July 2000, WTO membership a long way off
14. Overall reform progress	WTO membership will considerably speed up reform, particularly essential for SOEs and the banking system	More urgency required if Vietnam is to benefit from the regional recovery after the Asian crisis. Delay will only increase further the costs of reform

Table 5.12
Private Sector's Share in 1998 GDP (per cent)

	Total GDP	Manufacturing GDP
State sector	49	54
State-owned enterprises	na	na
Private	51	46
Foreign-invested sector	10	18
Domestic private sector	41	28
Of which		
Household enterprises/farmers	34	18
Private SMEs		

Source: GSO, *Statistical Year Book.*

competitive. Foreign investment has been slowing, with many investors waiting to see further reform development before committing to further investment in Vietnam. Much of this FDI was adversely affected by the economic downturn in the region, plus many of the sectors in receipt of much of the early FDI are now saturated (real estate, and hotel and tourist developments). It will be essential for the country to attract more FDI to achieve faster economic and export growth. However, instead of this being primarily capital intensive in nature, it would be desirable to attract more FDI in line with the country's comparative advantage – labour and resource intensive, light-manufactured goods production.

Vietnam is integrating its economy increasingly within the regional and global economies. As a member of ASEAN and APEC, Vietnam can benefit from increased trade and investment flows within this region. The recent bilateral trade agreement with the US in July 2000 has been forecast to lead to a doubling of Vietnam's exports to the US. This agreement could also be a precursor to the country's membership of the WTO, and its full integration into the global economy. The overall reform process has proceeded much slower in Vietnam than in China. In the latter's case, its membership of the WTO will further intensify the need to engage in more rapid reform of the SOE and banking sectors in particular. There is also a need for Vietnam to speed up its reform process if it is to fully benefit from the economic recovery now underway across the region. Many of its regional neighbours, including that of China, have engaged in considerable economic restructuring and reform, and are in a good position to benefit from the regional recovery. Vietnam will be in a relatively weak position, and fall further behind, unless it speeds up its reform process. The costs of such reform will increase the longer it is delayed. Reform momentum must, therefore, remain a priority for the authorities.

5.11   SUMMARY AND CONCLUSIONS

The success of China's rural small businesses, the TVEs, was largely an unanticipated outcome from the process of economic reform. They were able to attain a major market niche in the production of consumer goods for both domestic and international markets, a legacy of the central planning system and the SOEs' lack of consumer goods production. Their rapid rate of growth during the reform era contributed significantly to: the absorption of surplus rural labour; higher labour productivity; the generation of higher rural incomes and saving; the economic development of local rural communities; and the generation of revenue for local governments. These developments contributed to reducing the extent of migration to urban areas.

While there are many aspects of the TVEs that are specific to China, they can still provide important lessons for other economies in transition. These include, most notably, the significance of liberal market entry, the benefits of competition, the need for enterprises to operate under a hard budget constraint, the benefits of appropriate fiscal incentives for local governments, and the gains to be had from access to science and technology. However, to maintain competitiveness in China's rapidly developing market economy will require changes in their organisational form, through the development of both business and scientific alliances. The rapid rise of China's privately-owned and foreign-funded enterprises suggests that the major source of future competition will no longer simply be with the SOEs, over which the TVEs' relative performance has been impressive, but rather with these alternative forms of business entities. The pressure for change on TVEs will be intense, and even more so with greater openness of the economy arising from membership of the WTO, and may ultimately require a change of ownership form of the TVEs themselves as well as their location. The former has already been underway since the mid 1990s.

While the literature in general suggests that the longer-term growth of TVEs in their present form is unsustainable, there is much evidence to suggest that many TVEs are already transforming themselves into complex interconnected networks involving science, industry and local government. The status of firms in China is highly dynamic in the present environment. Hence the key issue is not whether the TVEs will be able to maintain their industrial momentum, in the light of deepening reforms, but rather whether they will be able to develop appropriate organisational and ownership forms that will enable them to do so.

The development of small private enterprises in China was steady during the early years of the reform and rapid since the early 1990s. Private firms have made, and will increasingly make, a significant contribution to the growth of the economy. True private businesses already account for half of total output and will account for a much higher proportion a decade hence. Further liberalisation and institutional reform hold the key for producing a vibrant and dynamic private sector in the economy. The construction of the right policy, legal and regulatory framework will have a large pay-off in terms of more rapid development of the private sector. SMEs will be required to absorb new and modern managerial practices, focus more on the market rather than government bureaucracies, pay more attention to technological innovation and development of new products, upgrade the human capital of their workers, and rely more on external sources of financing.

There is growing demand by the private sector for specialised expertise and training to develop the necessary skills. The skill requirements include that of financing, corporate planning and governance, management skills, business strategy, marketing and technological know-how. Competitive firms in these areas, especially those from overseas, will be well placed to provide such services to domestic enterprises.

A recent significant development was the constitutional amendment acknowledging the importance of the private sector, adopted during the March 1999 sessions of the National People's Congress. It provides a legal basis to embrace private enterprise in the Chinese economy, gives official recognition that the growth in non-farm employment and output is in the private sector despite the continued tendencies for capital to be allocated disproportionately to SOEs, allows individual enterprises to take off their 'red hats', reduces uncertainty in the business environment, and allows the official policy and regulatory environment to be refocused to remove impediments to continued dynamism in this major part of the economy. This will provide the momentum necessary for this sector to make an even more important contribution to the growth and reform of the Chinese economy.

NOTES

1   Garnaut and Song 2000, estimated that the non-state sector's contribution to GDP, which includes the agriculture sector, reached 62 per cent in 1998.
2   Some 68 per cent of total employment was in agriculture.
3   TVE employment peaked in 1996 at 135.1 million. Since this time the numbers employed have declined.
4   In 1997 official acceptance of different ownership forms and the importance of the private sector occurred. In March 1999, this recognition was included in the country's constitution.
5   In the case of TVEs there was increased blurring between what were effectively private TVEs (so called 'red hat enterprises') and true collective TVEs.
6   There were about 810 000 self-employed persons in 1980 in urban China (*China Statistical Yearbook* 1987, p. 115).

7 Capital being defined as depreciated fixed capital plus all inventories.

8 However, competition in many key sectors of the economy was not permitted, and remained dominated by SOEs.

9 Individual private enterprises never disappeared from China's economy in reality. They were not recorded in Chinese industrial statistics in 1978 due to their small size and lack of legitimacy in the constitution compared with the SOEs and collectives.

10 See Garnaut and Song 2000, p. 2.

11 Essentially, the agriculture/resources sector and industrial sector respectively.

12 The services sector.

13 Since 1995 over 15 million state employees have been laid-off and at an accelerating rate. Many of whom have been re-employed in the private sector.

14 This was a period in which a 'rectification programme' was implemented by the authorities, with the objective of slowing down economic reform and growth of the overheated economy (see for example Bell et al. 1993, p. 3).

15 See Chapter 9 of this volume for a more detailed discussion of economic reform and its outcomes in Vietnam.

16 This consists of farmers, household microenterprises, private SMEs and relatively large foreign-invested enterprises.

REFERENCES

Alchian, A.A. and H. Demsetz (1972), 'Production, Information Costs, and Economic Organisation', *American Economic Review*, **62** (5), 777–95.

Asian Development Bank (2000), 'Country Economic Review: Socialist Republic of Vietnam', Asian Development Bank, Manila, November.

Bell, M.W., H.E. Khor and K. Kochhar (1993), 'China at the Threshold of a Market Economy', IMF Occasional Paper 107, IMF, Washington, September.

Byrd, W.A. and Lin, Q. (1990), 'China's Rural Industry: An Introduction', in W.A. Byrd and Q-S. Lin (eds), *China's Rural Industry: Structure, Development, and Reform*, New York: Oxford University Press.

Cheung, S.N.S. (1982), 'Will China go "Capitalist"?', Hobart Paper 94, Institute of Economic Affairs, London.

China State Science and Technology Commission (1991), *White Paper on Science and Technology No. 4*, Beijing: International Academic Publishers.

China State Science and Technology Commission (1993), *China S&T Newsletter*, No.13, December.

Christerson, B. and C. Lever-Tracy (1996), 'The Third China? China's Rural Enterprises as Dependent Subcontractors or as Dynamic Autonomous Firms?', paper presented to The Asia–Pacific Regional Conference of Sociology, Manila, 28–31 May.

Demsetz, H. (1967), 'Towards a Theory of Property Rights', *American Economic Review,* **57** (2), 347–59.

Fischer, S. and A. Gelb (1991), 'The Process of Socialist Economic Transformation', *Journal of Economic Perspectives*, **5** (4), 91–106.

Furubotn, E.G. and S. Pejovich (1974), 'Introduction: the New Property Rights Structure:1-9', in E.G. Furubotn and S. Pejovich (eds), *The Economics of Property Rights*, Cambridge: Ballinger.

Garnaut, R. and L. Song (2000), 'Private Enterprise in China', paper presented at the *China: Growth Sustainability in the 21st Century* conference, ANU, Canberra, Australia, September.

Hallberg, K. (2000), 'A Market-Oriented Strategy for Small and Medium-Scale Enterprises', IFC Discussion Paper No. 40, World Bank, Washington, DC.

Harvie, C. (1998), 'The Transition of the Centrally Planned Economies in Eastern Europe to Market Economies: the Cases of the Czech Republic, Hungary and Poland', in A. Levy-Livermore (ed.), *Handbook on the Globalization of the World Economy*, Cheltenham, UK: Edward Elgar.

Harvie, C. and T. Turpin (1997), 'China's Market Reforms and its New Forms of Scientific and Business Alliances', in C.A. Tisdell and J.C.H. Chai (eds), *China's Economic Growth and Transition: Macroeconomic, Environmental and Social/Regional Dimensions,* New York: Nova Science Publishers.

International Finance Corporation (2000), China's Emerging Private Enterprises: Prospects for the New Century, IFC, World Bank, Washington, DC.

Jefferson, G.H., T.G. Rawski and Y. Zheng (1992a), 'Growth, Efficiency, and Convergence in China's State and Collective Industry', *Economic Development and Cultural Change*, **20** (2), 239–66.

Jefferson, G.H., T.G. Rawski and Y. Zheng (1992b), 'Innovation and Reform in Chinese Industry: A Preliminary Analysis of Survey Data (1)', paper presented at the annual meeting of the Association for Asian Studies, Washington, DC, April.

Jefferson, G.H., and T.G. Rawski (1994), 'Enterprise Reform in Chinese Industry', *Journal of Economic Perspectives*, **8** (2), 47–70, Spring.

Kwong, C.C.L. (1997), 'Property Rights and Performance of China's Township-Village Enterprises', in C.A. Tisdell and J.C.H. Chai (eds), *China's Economic Growth and Transition: Macroeconomic, Environmental and Social/Regional Dimensions,* Commack, USA: Nova Science Publishers.

Liao S-L. (1995), 'The Development of Township Enterprises in Rural Fujian Since the Early 1980s', paper presented to the International Workshop on South China, Nanyang Research Institute, Xiamen University, PRC, 22–24 May.

Liu, Y. (1997), 'Labour Absorption in China's Township and Village Enterprises', paper presented at the *International Conference on the Economies of Greater China*, Perth, Australia, July.

Mai, Y.H. (2000), 'China's Marketisation Process and the WTO', paper presented at the *China: Growth Sustainability in the 21st Century* conference, ANU, Canberra, Australia, September.

Naughton, B. (1994), 'Chinese Institutional Innovation and Privatization from Below', American Economics Association, *Papers and Proceedings*, **84** (2), 266–70, May.

Oi, J. (1992), 'Fiscal Reform and the Economic Foundations of Local State Corporations in China', *World Politics*, **45** (1), 99–126, October.

Oi, J. (1995), 'The Role of Local Government in China's Transitional Economy', *The China Quarterly*, 144, 1132–49, December.

Perkins, D. (1994), 'Completing China's Move to the Market', *Journal of Economic Perspectives*, **8** (2), 23–46, Spring.

Perkins, F.C. and M. Raiser (1994), 'State Enterprise Reform and Macroeconomic Stability in Transition Economies', Kiel Working Paper, No. 665, Kiel University, Kiel.

Pitt, M. and L. Putterman (1992), 'Employment and Wages in Township, Village, and other Rural Enterprises', mimeo, Brown University.

Putterman, L. (1995), 'The Role of Ownership and Property Rights in China's Economic Transition', *The China Quarterly*, 144, 1047–64, December.

Rawski, T.G. (1994), 'Chinese Industrial Reform: Accomplishments, Prospects, and Implications', American Economics Association, *Papers and Proceedings*, **84** (2), 271–5, May.

Research Centre for Rural Economics (1995), 'Case Study on Technology Transfer and Development of Township and Village Enterprises (TVEs)', Report to UNESCO, Beijing.

Sachs, J.D. and W.T. Woo (1997), 'Understanding China's Economic Performance', NBER Working Paper, No. 5935, Cambridge, USA.

So, B.W.Y. (2000), 'Development Trends of Indigenous Private Enterprises in the 1990s', paper presented at the *China: Growth Sustainability in the 21st Century* conference, ANU, Canberra, Australia, September.

Sun, L., E.X. Gu and R.J. McIntyre (1999), 'The Evolutionary Dynamics of China's Small-and Medium-Sized Enterprises in the 1990s', United Nations University/World Institute for Development Economics Research, World Development Studies 14, Helsinki, Finland, October.

Svejnar, J. (1990), 'Productive Efficiency and Employment', in W.W. Byrd and Q. Lin (eds), in *China's Rural Industry: Structure, Development, and Reform*, New York: Oxford University Press.

Tisdell, C.A. and J.C.H. Chai (1997), 'China's Economic Growth and Transition – Macroeconomic, Environmental and Social/Regional Dimensions', Commack, USA: Nova Science Publishers.

Tseng, W., H.E. Khor, K. Kocharm, D. Mihajek and D. Burton (1994), 'Economic Reform in China: A New Phase', IMF Occasional Paper 114, IMF, Washington, November.

Wen, M. (2000), 'Can China Sustain Fast Economic Growth? – a Perspective from Transition and Development', paper presented at the *China: Growth Sustainability in the 21st Century* conference, ANU, Canberra, Australia, September.

Wietzman, M. and C. Xu (1994), 'Chinese Township Village Enterprises as Vaguely Defined Cooperatives', *Journal of Comparative Economics,* **18** (2), 121–45.

World Bank (1996), *From Plan to Market – World Development Report*, New York: Oxford University Press.

World Bank (1999), 'Vietnam – Preparing for Take-off? – How Vietnam can Participate Fully in the East Asian Recovery', an informal report of the World Bank Consultative Group Meeting for Vietnam, Hanoi, December.

World Bank (2000), 'Vietnam – Taking Stock', an informal stocktaking of Vietnam's economic reforms prepared for the mid-year Consultative Group Meeting, Dalat City, June.

Yusuf, S. (1993a), 'The Rise of China's Non-State Sector', unpublished manuscript, World Bank.

Yusuf, S. (1993b), 'Property Rights and Non-State Sector Development in China', unpublished manuscript.

Zweig, D. (1991), 'Rural Industry: Constraining the Leading Growth Sector in China's Economy', Joint Economic Committee, US Congress, China's Economics Dilemmas in the 1990s: The Problems of Reforms, Modernisation and Interdependence, April.

6. Korea's Competition Policy and Its Applications to Other Asian Economies

Hyun-Hoon Lee

6.1 INTRODUCTION

Korea's competition laws and policies have evolved gradually since the Monopoly Regulation and Fair Trade Act (MRTFA) was enacted in 1980. In recent years in Korea, competition policy has been central to economic reform, because its principles provide a benchmark for assessing the degree of efficiency.

Section 6.2 first reviews the evolving process of Korea's competition laws and then discusses the objective of, major content of, and exemptions from, the MRTFA. Section 6.3 deals with the aspects of enforcement of Korea's competition laws and policies. In particular, discussions are centered on organisation and authority of the Korea Fair Trade Commission (KFTA) and actions taken by the KFTA before and after the 1997 financial crisis in Korea. Section 6.4 attempts to draw some lessons from the Korean experience and their possible applications to other Asian economies.

6.2 KOREA'S COMPETITION LAWS

6.2.1 Evolution of Korea's Competition Laws

Korea was one of the poorest countries in the world when it was liberated in 1945 from the Japanese colonial rule of 36 years (1910–45). The Korean War (1950–53) left the country in ruins. In 1962, for example, Korea's per capita GNP (gross national product) was only US$80 in current prices. With the beginning of the first five-year plan (1962–66) under the rule of the Park Chung Hee administration, a remarkable transformation of the economy took place. The national goal was rapid economic development, on the basis of the so-called state-led export-oriented industrialisation. Markets were controlled, directed and protected. The government assigned top priority to industrial and trade policies that were intended to maximise investment and market shares, and hence, without doubt, competition policy played hardly any role in the 1960s.

During the 1970s, a very premature form of competition laws and policies was formulated. With the first oil shock in 1972, Korea had to deal with surging prices. The Price Stabilisation Act was enacted in 1973 to establish a fair trade order by banning refusal to sell, and to attain price stability by placing price ceilings on goods and services.

By overhauling the Price Stabilisation Act, the Monopoly Regulation and Price Stability Act was enacted in 1975. The new Act stipulated the prohibition of unfair trade practices and laid the legal groundwork for issuing corrective orders against enterprises that breached the law with the purpose of establishing a fair trade order. This statute provided for the setting of the maximum prices, the authorisation of the prices of monopolistic or oligopolistic products and utility prices, the issuing of directions for the supply and delivery of goods and the implementation of measures for coordinating supply and demand in emergency.

The Monopoly Regulation and Price Stability Act produced side effects such as restricting the proper functioning of the price mechanism, because the focus of the law enforcement was primarily on achieving price stability. The price authorisation by the government distorted the market function and prompted the public to expect inflation in the future, resulting in the avoidance of production, creation of double prices and hoarding.

The 1975 Act was replaced by the Monopoly Regulation and Fair Trade Act (MRFTA) enacted on 31 December 1980 (and took effect on 1 April 1981). The MRFTA is a comprehensive anti-monopoly law, centring on fair trade practices. That is, the MRFTA covers most of the key competition policy issues including collusion, abuse of dominance, monopoly, M&As (mergers and acquisitions) and unfair practices. The MRFTA also created Korea's authority of competition policy, named Korea Fair Trade Commission (KFTC). The MRFTA marked a significant departure from the tradition of a government-led economy to a market-oriented economy. But the price-control tradition coloured the early application of the MRFTA (OECD, 2000). The MRFTA prohibited undue pricing by monopolies and parallel price increases by oligopolies. The MRFTA has undergone nine revisions in 1986, 1990, 1992, 1994, 1996, 1998, February 1999, December 1999 and January 2001.

In addition, the Fair Subcontract Transactions Act and the Adhesion Contract Regulations Act were enacted in 1984 and 1986 respectively, in order to protect subcontractors and consumers. In 1999, the Fair Labelling and Advertising Act (FLAA) came into force. It aims to promote the provision of correct and useful information, thereby to enable consumers an easier access to information necessary for making choices. The Act provides that trade associations must not restrict labelling or advertising activities of the enterprises belong to the association.

In addition, the Omnibus Cartel Repeal Act was enacted in 1999, in order to regulate undue concerted activities being exempt from the MRFTA. The enforcement of this Act led to the elimination or improvement of 20 cartels under 18 different laws. In particular, this Act limited or eliminated the exemptions for some professions from the MRFTA. That is, statutory authority to approve price agreement was repealed for lawyers, customs brokers, licensed tax accountants, accountants, administrative scriveners, patent lawyers, certified labour services, veterinarians and architects.[1] Under the new Act, each insurance company must now determine independently its loading premium based on the net premium set out by the Insurance Development Institute.[2] The new Act repealed the authority of the Minister of Construction and Transportation to handpick a bidder for an offshore construction project.

6.2.2   The Objective of the MRFTA

The MRFTA's stated purpose is 'to encourage fair and free competition by prohibiting the abuse of market-dominant positions, the excessive concentration of economic power, and by regulating undue concerted acts and unfair business practices, thereby stimulating creative business activities, protecting consumers and promoting the balanced development of the national economy'. Figure 6.1 summarises the objective and purpose of the Act.

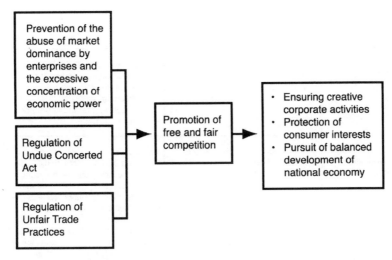

Figure 6.1   The Objective of the MRFTA

Table 6.1
Amendments of the MRFTA

	Chaebol regulation	Competition rules
Original MRFTA (Dec. 1980)	None	• Prohibits abuse of dominance, anticompetitive merger, unfair business practices, anticompetitive trade association activity, resale price maintenance, unfair int'l contracts • Requires registration of collaborative acts

1st amendment (Dec. 1986)	• Prohibits holding company
	• Designation of 'large business groups'
	  · bans cross-shareholdings
	  · limits equity investments in other domestic companies to 40% of net assets
	  · bans finance companies from voting their shares in other members
		• Prohibits undue collaborative acts
		  · maximum surcharge of 1% of sales volume
		  · cartel can be inferred from parallel behaviour

2nd amendment (Jan. 1990)	• Exempts financial companies from investment limits, merger control, and prohibition of abuse of dominance and resale price maintenance	• Maximum surcharge of 1% of sales volume for cartel by trade association
3rd amendment (Dec. 1992)	• Limits loan guarantees for affiliates to 200% of equity capital	• Implementation of collusive agreement is not required for illegal cartel • Maximum surcharge of 30 million won for unfair business practices
4th amendment (Dec. 1994)	• Lowers investment ceiling to 25% of net assets	• Rule against cartels is expanded from sales to transactions • Raise maximum surcharge for cartels (1–5% of sales volume) and unfair business practices (30 million won – 2% of sales volume) • Introduce surcharges for abuse of dominance (3% of sales volume) and resale price maintenance (2% of sales volume)

	Chaebol regulation	**Competition rules**
5th amendment (Dec. 1996)	• Lowers the ceiling of loan guarantees to 100% of equity capital • Prohibits undue assistance of specially related persons or other companies by providing loans, assets and manpower	• Repeals exemption for financial companies in merger control • Adopts market share criteria for presumption of illegality of a merger • Adopts leniency programme for cartel • Requires KFTC to ask indictment for serious violations
6th amendment (Feb. 1998)	• Eliminates investment limits • Bans intragroup cross debt guarantees	• Introduces efficiency defence and failing firm doctrine in merger control
7th amendment (Feb. 1999)	• Allows holding company under restrictive conditions • Gives KFTC special power for 2 years to investigate bank accounts of the top 30 chaebols	
8th amendment (Dec. 1999)	• Re-introduces 25% investment ceiling • Raises maximum surcharge for undue assistance to 5% of sales volume • Requires top ten chaebols to obtain prior approval of the board of directors and to issue a public notice before engaging in large-scale intragroup transactions	
9th amendment (Jan. 2001)	• Gives KFTC special power for 3 years to investigate bank accounts of the top 30 chaebols • Relax requirements for holding companies	• Expands leniency programme for colluders • Allows maximum rpm

Source: Shin and Seong 2001.

The stated purpose implies that competition policy in Korea has the three immediate goals: prohibiting abuse of market-dominant positions, preventing excessive concentration of economic power, and regulating undue concerted acts and unfair business practices. And it further implies that competition policy is to promote both 'free' and 'fair' competition to accomplish the three ultimate goals: innovation and dynamic efficiency; consumer protection; and balanced economic development.

Lee (1998) contends that 'fair' competition must be understood as a moral conception that all economic actors should abide by the same set of rules, whereas 'free' competition is a mode of conduct, the pursuit of individual, private interest, made possible by protecting rights of property and freedom of contract. The goal of balanced economic development is taken to be the basis for the KFTC's concentration on aspects of *chaebol* behavior and protection of the interests of small- and medium-sized enterprises against 'unfair' competition from larger firms (OECD 2000).

Table 6.1 summarises the major distinctions of the Act, as it has undergone nine revisions to date. As shown in the table, the Act has been more than a conventional competition law since it was substantially revised in 1986 to provide a legal basis for direct control on the *chaebols*.[3] The chaebols have been criticised that they monopolise the factor market through circular investments, cross-debt guarantees and undue subsidisations within the group, resulting in the distorted allocation of resources. These are monopoly problems at the national economy level, obstructing the proper functioning of the market mechanism. Thus competitive market conditions cannot be created without solving chaebol problems. (OECD 1999)

In general, MRFTA closely resembles the competition laws of other OECD countries. But its extensive regulations of corporate and financial structures, which have played a central role in *chaebol* control, are unusual and different in these respects from the competition laws of OECD countries (OECD 2000).

6.2.3   Main Contents of the MRFTA[4]

The MRFTA is a sound substantive foundation for reform based on market principles. The legal criteria and available sanctions under the MRTFA are generally adequate to cover competition problems (OECD 2000). These are discussed below.

Horizontal agreements
The basic prohibition against agreements restricting competition is in Article 19 of the MRFTA. Eight types of restrictive agreement are specified, from fixing prices and terms, restricting production or trade, restricting territories, and forming joint ventures, to hindering other enterprises. Contracts to achieve these ends are null and void. Sanctions include orders to cease the offending act and take corrective measures, and surcharges of up to 5 per cent of sales revenue during the period of violation. Criminal fines up to W200 million or imprisonment for up to three years can be imposed. Korea's rule about restrictive agreements has recently been strengthened. After the February 1999 amendment, the legal standard changed from a general 'rule of reason' to

something approaching *per se* treatment. Under the previous rule, it was possible to defend an agreement on the grounds that it had relative little actual effect, but now it is no longer possible.

Vertical agreements

Some vertical restraints are covered by Article 19's prohibition of restrictive agreements, and most others are covered by Article 23's prohibition of unfair business practices. Unfair business practices are described generally as those that may undermine fair trade. They are detailed both in the statute and in implementing regulations. Particular rules address tying arrangements, exclusive dealing agreements and territorial or customer restraints. A separate section of the law, Article 29, expressly prohibits resale price maintenance, thus appearing to treat it as illegal *per se*.

Abuse of dominance

Korea uses the concept of abuse of dominance, (whereas Japan has rules about 'private monopolisation' and 'monopolistic situations'). The prohibition against abuse of market-dominating positions is the first substantive provision in the statute. Its form displays the law's origin in price-control measures, as the listing of prohibited types of abuse begins with unreasonable pricing, followed by unreasonable control of sales or services, interference with other enterprises, hindering entry of new competition and otherwise threatening substantially to restrain competition or harm consumer interests (Article 3-2). The statutory definition of 'market-dominating enterprise' no longer solely depends on market shares and structure. 'Market-dominant enterprise' is now defined to mean a supplier (or buyer) that has the power to determine, maintain, or alter price, volume, quality or other terms in a relevant market, either on its own or with others. The definition itself provides that determining whether a firm is market-dominant calls for assessing its market share, the existence and scope of entry barriers and the comparative size of competing enterprises.

Merger control

The MRFTA covers horizontal, vertical, and conglomerate combinations, the last category being particularly significant in the context of *chaebol* regulation. A merger is presumed to violate the law if it creates a firm that meets either of the tests for being a market-dominating enterprise, provided that two additional conditions are met. First, the combined firm must be the largest firm in an industry. Second, it must be significantly larger than the next largest firm. Efficiency and failing-firm provisions were added to the law in 1999. The KFTC may approve an otherwise anti-competitive combination if the benefits of efficiency outweigh the harm from reduced competition, or if the combination involves a firm that is otherwise non-viable.

Unfair competition

Among the subjects of the MRFTA's general prohibition of 'unfair practices' are: false or misleading advertising, unfair practices, predatory pricing, and abuse of economic dominance. For the most part, the detailed rules about unfair business practices are all subject to the standard of 'unreasonableness'.

6.2.4   Exemptions from the MRFTA

Whether competition laws and competition policies can provide a suitable framework for a 'fair and free competition among enterprises' and for a consumer protection is partly determined by the extent of general exemptions from the statutes.

Small- and Medium-Sized Enterprises (SMEs)

The most important general exemptions from competition laws in Korea are designed to promote and protect the interests of SMEs. Indeed, a justification offered for the controls on the *chaebols* is to protect SMEs against competition from the chaebols. There are two kinds of exemptions that were specifically drafted to protect SMEs. First, case-by-case exemptions may be granted from the MRFTA's prohibition of unfair collaboration activities, provided that all parties are SMEs and they show that, without the proposed agreement, it would difficult for them to compete efficiently with large enterprises. Second, cooperatives composed of SMEs may enjoy what appears to be a statutory exemption. The purpose of the cooperative must be to provide mutual aid among small businesses or consumers. Members must have equal voting rights, and limits on profit distribution must be set in the by-laws. In addition, there are several programmes to promote and protect the interests of SMEs. The Fair Subcontract Transactions Act is also intended to assist SMEs in their position as subcontractors to prime contractors with economic power. However, there is concern that some of these programmes erect potentially damaging barriers to competition (OECD 2000).

Public enterprises

In principle, activities of enterprises, both public and private, are subject to the MRFTA. However, its application to public enterprises is limited, because they are regulated utility monopolies in electric power, telecommunications and gas. Their pricing would not lead to action under the MRFTA. But other anti-competitive conduct, such as exclusion or discrimination in favour of a subsidiary or partner firm, is subject to the enforcement of MRFTA.

Sector-specific exemptions

In principle, the MRFTA now applies to all industries, with no sector exceptions. The implicit exceptions for a few industries, such as agriculture, fisheries, forestry and mining, were abolished in February 1999. However some cartels remain protected by the operation of particular statutes. For example, joint sale and purchase by cooperative federations in the agricultural, fishery, forestry and livestock industries and contract farming among ginseng producers and processing businesses are exempt from the statute. Telecommunications (telecoms) and financial sectors are also exempt from the MRFTA. Other government agencies apply sectoral regulations that affect competition issues. The Korea Communications Commission is responsible for some issues in telecoms, and the Financial Supervisory Commission (FSC) is responsible for some in the financial sector. The justifications offered for separate responsibilities are the need for technical expertise in telecoms, and the concern for institutional soundness in finance. In each sector, the KFTC retains a role, though. For example, the KFTC would address collusion about network prices or interest rates and commissions. Determining which agency has jurisdiction over a problem calls for continued *ad hoc* consultations between the KFTC and these two commissions. (OECD 2000, p. 193) Publications, construction, intellectual property, rice wine and ocean shipping have also been exempt from the competition laws.

Professions

Fees for many professional occupations had been determined by agreement of the associations and then approved by the relevant ministries. Ministry approval conferred exemption from the MRTFA. The 1999 Omnibus Cartel Repeal Act has limited or eliminated the exemptions on some professions from the MRFTA. That is, statutory authority to approve price agreement were repealed for lawyers, customs brokers, licensed tax accountants, accountants, administrative scriveners, patent lawyers, certified labour services, veterinarians and architects.

6.3   ENFORCEMENT OF KOREA'S COMPETITION LAWS AND POLICIES

6.3.1   Organisation and Authority of the Korea Fair Trade Commission

As noted in the previous section, the Korea Fair Trade Commission (KFTC), Korea's main competition authority, was established under the Economic Planning Board (EPB) in 1980 by the Monopoly Regulation and Fair Trade Act (MRFTA). The MRFTA was revised in 1990 and the KFTC was entitled to pursue independently competition policy, even though it remained under the EPB. The 4th amendment of the MRFTA in 1994 separated the KFTC from the EPB, making the Commission an independent body.[5] That is, the KFTC is established under the jurisdiction of the Prime Minister. Further in 1996, the status of the KFTC Chairman was elevated to ministerial level.

The basic responsibilities of the KFTC are applying the provisions of the MRFTA and several other competition laws such as the Fair Subcontract Transactions Act, the Adhesion Contract Regulations Act, the Fair Labelling and Advertising Act, and the Omnibus Cartel Repeal Act. The KFTC is also responsible for consulting and coordinating about the actions and rules of other government bodies that relate to policies to promote competition or suppress competition.

The central administrative body of the KFTC is composed of nine commissioners, including the Chairman, Vice Chairman, three standing Commissioners and four non-standing Commissioners. The commissioners are appointed by the President upon the recommendation by the Chairman and are guaranteed a three-year term, which can be renewed once. Historically, the standing commissioners have all come from within the staff of the KFTC. Qualifications are set by statute: prior experience as a public official in monopoly and fair trade issues, or 15 years experience as a judge, lawyer or prosecutor, or 15 years academic experience in law, economics or business administration, or 15 years of business or consumer protection experience. The Chairman and Vice-Chairman are considered to be 'political appointees', and others have the status of government officials. Commissioners may be removed from office involuntarily only for incapacity or after criminal conviction for wrongdoing.

The Chairman has a seat on the Cabinet Meeting presided by the President and can voice his/her opinions. The Vice Chairman is also entitled to the same authority at the Vice Ministerial Meeting. This direct, face-to-face contact with other ministries and agencies has strengthened the advocacy role of the KFTC (OECD 2000).

As with any other government agencies in Korea, the KFTC must establish and report its major projects and plans to the President at the beginning of the year. This annual report to the President is not compulsory by law, yet it can still be seen as an established practice. And at the end of the year, its performance is inspected by the National Assembly.

As shown in Figure 6.2, the Secretariat of the KFTC has three Officers, six Bureaus and 29 Divisions under the headquarters, and has four regional offices. There were 402 staff members as of September 2000, about 70 were dealing with policy matters and about 300 with actual enforcement.

The KFTC may initiate an investigation if it believes that there has been a violation of the law, or in response to a complaint. In principle, the KFTC is required to respond to all complaints; all complaints must be investigated to determine whether there has been any violation of law. Complaints are subject to a preliminary review. If they fall under the jurisdiction of law, investigations are opened to look into the alleged law violations. The staff may close the matter if it finds no evidence of violation.

The KFTC can summon the parties concerned, interested parties, and

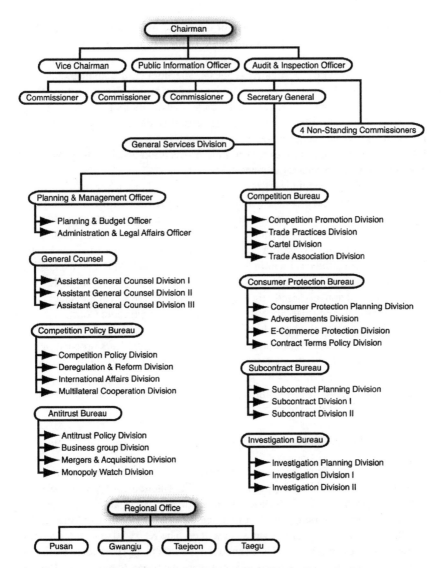

Figure 6.2 Organisation of the Korean Fair Trade Commission

witnesses to a hearing and elicit their testimony; designate expert appraisers and procure their opinions; require an enterprise, trade association or their officers and employees to submit related information; and carry out on-site investigations. The KFTC can look into the bank accounts of *chaebol* affiliates when it is deemed necessary for the probes into undue intra-group transactions.

The KFTC can seek the opinions of the heads of pertinent administrative agencies or groups. The KFTC can also call for the submissions of materials that are deemed necessary. However, administrative fines are the only sanction for failure to comply with investigative requests. The amounts are small enough that large firms may elect to pay the fines rather than give the KFTC the information (OECD 2000). It can also request necessary investigations from the heads of pertinent administrative agencies or groups if it deems such cooperation necessary to ensure compliance with a corrective measure. In particular, the KFTC sometimes refers cases for criminal prosecution because the prosecutor has more powers to obtain evidence.

In principle, proceedings are open to the public, although they may be closed if necessary to protect business confidentiality. If the KFTC finds a violation, it may issue a warning, a recommendation for correction, an order for correction, an order to pay a surcharge, or a request for indictment. Parties may file objections to the decision at the KFTC within 30 days. If such an objection is filed, the KFTC is to re-deliberate the case within 90 days. The General Council is responsible for conducting a re-investigation. The defendant need not object at the KFTC, but may instead appeal directly by filing an administrative suit at the Seoul High Court. A further, and final, appeal can be taken to the Supreme Court.

Financial and criminal penalties can be substantial. Surcharges are computed as a proportion of the average sales revenue for the three years proceeding the decision. Before 1997, they were based on total revenues during the period of violation. The law provides for several degrees of criminal penalty as well. Criminal fines up to W200 million can be imposed, and the law also provides for imprisonment for up to three years.

6.3.2   Actions Taken by the KFTC

The FKTC's decisions are made available on its Internet home page (http://www.ftc.go.kr). Table 6.2 presents the KFTC's action by type of violation during the period 1981–99. It should be noted that unfair business practices are the most common type of conduct handled by the KFTC: in 1999 the KFTC handled 514 cases of unfair business practices. The KFTC also handles a large number of cases under special laws about subcontracts. In 1999, there were 311 unfair subcontract matters. Most of these were payment disputes. In addition, the KFTC took corrective measures on a total of 255 unfair adhesion contracts under the Adhesion Contracts Act. Most were real estate contracts and insurance policies. It should also be noted that the KFTC has dealt with the increasing number of cases relating to a cartel. This implies that enforcement of the rule against undue collaborative acts has steadily been strengthened. The cases relating to unfair international contract has been decreasing in recent years, since the amendment of the MRFTA in 1995 replaced the reporting requirement with the voluntary review request.

Table 6.2
KFTC Actions by Type of Violation, 1981–99

Year	Chaebol Regulation	Abuse of Dominance	Merger	Cartel	Trade Assoc. Activity	Unfair Business Practice	Unfair Int'l Contract	Unfair Subcontract	Unfair Adhesion Contract	Total
1981–86	–	5	189	21	75	671	1210	383	–	2554
1987	1	4	35	6	16	240	242	141	2	687
1988	27	–	37	15	41	275	70	144	8	617
1989	11	–	32	11	24	320	39	144	7	588
1990	21	2	12	12	23	177	288	97	10	642
1991	3	–	22	20	31	336	235	199	8	854
1992	37	6	19	9	45	292	57	149	8	622
1993	5	2	24	16	58	320	113	218	27	783
1994	8	1	13	19	56	337	55	224	72	785
1995	3	3	23	26	40	353	40	387	51	926
1996	14	1	36	36	66	339	26	494	56	1068
1997	6	2	47	22	53	510	2	534	152	1328
1998	11	5	29	37	101	404	1	580	112	1280
1999	38	2	15	34	93	514	–	311	255	1262
Total	185	33	533	284	722	5088	2378	4005	768	13 996

Source: Shin and Seong 2001.

Table 6.3
KFTC Measures against Violations, 1981–99

Year	Request for indictment	Corrective order	Request for correction	Recommendation of correction	Warning	Total	Surcharge No. of cases	Surcharge No. of firms	Surcharge Amount (mill. won)	Criminal Penalty Fine	Criminal Penalty Imprison	Criminal Penalty Both
1981–86	6	358	–	234	1956	2554				4		
1987	4	76	–	109	498	687				4		
1988	5	114	2	85	411	617	1	6	2097	4		
1989	3	103	4	125	353	588				1		
1990	5	84	1	68	484	642				3		
1991	10	173	2	78	591	854	1	7	270	7		
1992	8	159	–	39	416	622	9	15	3375	7		
1993	7	219	3	58	496	783	24	64	1070	5		1
1994	13	207	5	108	452	785	68	104	2574	10	1	1
1995	33	199	3	119	572	926	51	64	4919	29		
1996	16	250	4	179	619	1068	22	65	16 275	10		
1997	35	221	10	329	733	1328	9	33	1191	27		
1998	37	533	5	57	648	1280	69	261	136 057	26		4
1999	11	617	4	149	481	1262	101	238	146 794	5		
Total	193	3313	43	1737	8710	13 996	355	857	314 622	142	1	6

Source: Shin and Seong 2001.

Table 6.3 summarises the KFTC measures taken against violations. As shown in the table, enforcement has gradually been strengthened from the early 1990s. In particular, surcharges have increased drastically in recent years. In 1999, measures taken by the KFTC consisted of 11 request for indictment, 617 corrective orders, four requests for correction, 149 recommendations for correction and 481 warnings.

6.3.3   The Role of KFTC in the Corporate Sector Reform after the 1997 Financial Crisis

The financial crisis erupted in Korea in 1997. Because the Korean crisis had its roots in the weakened fundamentals of the economy, an attempt at stabilising only the financial market without an emphasis on structural reforms would be like treating the symptoms without addressing the cause.[6] Accordingly, since the onset of the financial crisis, the Korean government has pursued structural reforms in the four identified sectors: the financial sector, the corporate sector, the labour market and the public sector. Principles of competition have been at the heart of the restructuring of the Korean economy. The KFTC has helped wrapping up corporate sector restructuring.

The very high leverage level of Korean firms played a crucial role in causing the 1997 financial crisis in Korea. In particular, the *chaebols* in Korea tended to borrow excessively through cross-payment guarantees among interlinked subsidiaries. By the end of 1997, the top 30 *chaebols* had debt–equity ratios of 519 per cent, in sharp contrast with 154 per cent in the United States and 193 per cent in Japan. Poor corporate practices and governance also contributed to the 1997 crisis in the form of inaccurate company financial information, no credible exit threat, insufficient financial institution monitoring, and few legal rights and forms of protection for minority shareholders. Hence, the priority in corporate sector reform has been to focus on achieving a major reduction in corporate indebtedness and bringing corporate practices into line with international standards.

In January 1998, the then President-elect Kim Dae-jung and the leaders of the five largest *chaebols* agreed on the five principles of corporate sector reform. The five principles were: (1) heightening of the transparency of corporate management, (2) prohibition of cross-guarantees between affiliates, (3) improvement of the corporate financial structure (by preventing undue subsidisation), (4) business concentration on core competence, and (5) responsibility reinforcement of governing shareholders and management.[7]

In August 1999, three additional tasks were identified. They were: (1) strengthening of taxation and tax collection regime to prevent inheritance and donation within *chaebol* families, (2) appointment of half of the board members from outside, in order to prevent *chaebol*'s monopoly of the financial market, and (3) a ceiling on the total amount of equity investment to prevent the distortion of corporate governance stemming from the complex web of share holding among *chaebol* affiliates.

Thus, corporate sector reform has proceeded under the 'five plus three formulas'. Among these measures, eliminating cross-debt guarantees among *chaebol* affiliates, preventing undue subsidisation and curbing cross equity investment have been planned and pursued by the KFTC. The amendment of the MRFTA in February 1998 banned cross-debt guarantees among affiliates of *chaebol*, and the February 1999 amendment of the MTFRA authorised the KFTC for two years to investigate bank accounts of the top 30 *chaebols*, The December 1999 amendment made it mandatory for large-scale intragroup transactions conducted by firms belonging to the top 10 *chaebols* to be subject to the resolution of the board of directors and to public disclosure. In addition, the ceiling on surcharges assessed against undue subsidisation was raised from 2 per cent to 5 per cent of sales volume. In January 2001, the MRFTA underwent the 9th amendment and gave the KFTC special powers for 3 more years to investigate the bank accounts of the top 30 *chaebols*.

In addition, the KFTC has been deeply involved in the process of public sector reform. Elimination of excessive regulation has been an important task in the process of public sector reform. From April 1997 to the end of 1998, the KFTC set up and operated the Economic Regulatory Reform Committee. Since April 1998, the KFTC has kept a cooperative relationship with this Committee under the Office of the Prime Minister. The KFTC Chairman takes part in the Economic Regulatory Reform Committee as a Commissioner. In order to assist the efforts of the Committee, the KFTC established in October 1999 a Task Force for the Deregulatory Reform.

6.4 LESSONS FROM KOREA'S EXPERIENCE

In spite of the success of the high rate of growth and low rate of unemployment for over 30 years or so, Korea came to acknowledge in 1997 that the state-led industrialisation was not sustainable in the long run. This is so mainly because the state-led growth resulted in a low level of domestic competition among others. Competition guides resources to their natural and most efficient use. Therefore the first lesson from Korea's experience during the 1997 economic crisis is that there must be a strong commitment to the market principle and a strong support for competition policies.

Second, even though the principles of market and competition should be at the heart of the reform of a transition economy like Vietnam, we must understand that there is no one-size-fits-all competition policy. In particular, one should not try to impose models that may be very well fitted for developed countries upon developing countries. One should be mindful of the local level of economic development and political and legal systems before advising on the issue of competition policy.

The second lesson leads to the third one. That is, adopting and incorporating competition laws and policies should be an ongoing agenda in the process of economic development. The competition laws and policies in Korea have evolved gradually over the past 20 years. Much has been done to remove the structure of anti-competitive regulations. But much remains to be done. It is to note that, in Korea, the promotion of competition laws and policies has had close links not only with the level of economic development but also with the level of political democracy.

Fourth, one should be aware that countries that pursue state-led economic development can breed anti-competitive governmental regulations and large conglomerates. These countries like Korea in the past and Vietnam in the present, thus, are required to make special efforts to prevent this from happening at their initial stages of development. In Korea, the anti-trust authority has pursued policies designed to control the activities of the *chaebols*. Therefore it is advised that the competition laws in Vietnam incorporate a special feature to deal with the governmental regulations and large conglomerates or even large state-owned enterprises.

Fifth, in order to help the new competition law take root in a short time period, it is pivotal to grant powerful authority and decision-making independence to the competition agency. This is so because the promotion and enforcement of the competition law always face a formidable resistance, and hence take a considerable amount of energy and commitment. The government should be careful not to undermine the independence of the competition agency.

NOTES

1   Before the 1999 Omnibus Cartel Repeal Act, fees for many professional occupations had been determined by agreement of the associations and then approved by the relevant ministries. For example, lawyers' fees had been set by rules of the Korea Bar Association, and had been endorsed by the Ministry of Justice.

2   Previously, insurance companies had customarily set premiums jointly, based on rates established by the Insurance Development Institute. The Institute's rates had incorporated both the net premium (to cover the risk) and the loading premiums (to cover operational costs and profits). The new Act still permits the Institute to set the risk premiums, and this still inhibits competition.

3   The *chaebols* are the large family-controlled conglomerates. The *chaebols* are historical products of the period of government-led economic growth. They expanded most rapidly during the period of the 'heavy and

chemical industry drive' of the 1970s. The *chaebol* structures offered some advantages, notably accumulation of capital for mediating resource transfers in the absence of development factor markets. (OECD 2000). As Korea's market opened more to foreign comptition in the 1980s, however, weaknesses in the *chaebol* became evident. For more discussions on the *chaebol*, see Yoo 1995, and Lee and Lee 1996.

4   This section is taken from OECD 2000, pp. 177–85.
5   In 1994, the Korean government abandoned the five-year plan system and abolished the Economic Planning Board that had been responsible for it. A new Ministry of Finance and Economy was created from the merger of the Board and the Ministry of Finance. As a result, the KFTC emerged as a separate body.
6   Drawing upon the analogy between a financial crisis and a human stroke, Lee 1999 shows how numerous factors, such as fundamental weaknesses, an unfriendly environment, policy mistakes and exogenous shocks, were systematically intertwined in causing the financial crisis.
7   Under these five principles, the top five *chaebols* and their creditors reached an agreement on debt reduction and other restructuring measures in early 1998. The agreement includes: (1) adoption of consolidated financial statements from fiscal year 1999; (2) compliance with international standards of accounting; (3) strengthening of voting rights of minority shareholders; (4) compulsory appointment of at least one outsider director from 1998; (5) establishment of an external auditors committee; (6) prohibition of cross-subsidiary debt guarantees from April 1998; and (7) resolution of all existing cross-debt guarantees by March 2000. In addition, the Korean government required the top five *chaebols* to reduce their debt–equity ratios to 200 per cent by the end of 1999 and improve their financial structure by asset sales, recapitalisation and foreign capital inducement.

REFERENCES

Korea Fair Trade Commission (KFTC) (2000), *White Paper on Monopoly Regulation and Fair Trade 2000*, Seoul: KFTC (in Korean).
Lee, H.-H. (1999), 'A "Stroke" Hypothesis of Korea's 1997 Financial Crisis: Causes, Consequences and Prospects', *University of Melbourne Research Paper* No. 696, <www.ecom.unimelb.edu.au/ecowww/research/696.pdf>.
Lee, K.-U. (1998), *Competition Policy, Deregulation and Economic Development: The Korean Experience*, Seoul: Korea Institute for Industrial Economics and Trade.
Lee, K.-U. and J.-H. Lee (1996), 'Business Groups (*Chaebols*) in Korea:

Characteristics and Government Policy,' *Occasional paper*, No.23, Seoul: Korea Institute for Industrial Economics and Trade.

Oh, J., H.-H. Lee and C. Harvie (2002), 'Financial Crisis Management in Korea: Its Processes and Consequences', in T. Van Hoa (ed.), Economic Crisis Management, Cheltenham, UK: Edward Elgar.

Shin, K.-S. and S. Seong (2001), '20 Years of Competition Policy in Korea: Evaluation and Prospect', paper presented at Seoul Competition Forum, April.

Yoo, S.M. (1995), 'Chaebol in Korea: Misconceptions, Realities, and Policies', *KDI Working Paper*, No. 9507, Seoul: Korea Development Institute.

OECD (2000), 'Chapter 3, The Role of Competition Policy in Regulatory Reform', *Regulatory Reform in Korea*, Paris: OECD.

OECD CLP (1999), 'Annual report on Competition Policy Developments in Korea', <www.oecd.org/daf/clp/Annual_reports/1999-00/korea.pdf>

7. Thailand's Global Competitiveness: Some Indicators

Chaiyuth Punyasavatsut

7.1   BACKGROUND

Post-analyses of the Thai crisis of 1997 have been largely focused on the financial sector, particularly the banking sector, thus ignoring other important sectors of the economy and, especially, their role in the face of increasing globalisation and international competitiveness or competition. In this chapter, we focus on tracking the performance of the real sector, the manufacturing sector in particular, and making some connection to the economic boom of the country before the crisis. We demonstrate the performance of the manufacturing sector through various economic indicators, covering the period 1991–2000. The complete story of the Thai manufacturing sector during both the pre- and post-crisis periods thus provides us a better understanding on Thai international competitiveness.

This chapter is in fact a summary of results of the first phase of the study that intends to gather and build the necessary information for the United Nations Industrial Development Organisation (UNIDO). The results presented below are still at a preliminary stage and would provide no policy recommendation.[1]

Competitiveness is defined here in its most popular form following Krugman (1994), that is, 'our ability to produce goods and services that meet the test of international competition while our citizens enjoy a standard of living that is both rising and sustainable'.[2] Since Thailand is a small open economy with the value share of manufactured exports to GDP being 48 per cent in 2000, Thai industry competitiveness at the international level can be shown by her trade performance. It should also be noted that this study is not designed to measure the competitiveness of the nations as defined by the World Economic Forum and the International Institute for Management Development (IMD).

The study identifies international competitiveness of the Thai industries using well-known economic indicators and analyses. In this study, we construct the Revealed Comparative Advantage (RCA) index, the Domestic Resource Cost

(DRC), the Nominal Rate of Protection (NRP), the Effective Rate of Protection (ERP), the Real Effective Exchange Rate (REER) index and the Total Factor Productivity (TFP) index.[3]

7.2   INDUSTRY CLASSIFICATION

Thai industrial data are, as in many other developing countries, plagued by the different systems of industry classification, making an international comparison a daunting task. One objective of this study is to build a comparable data based on the International Standard of Industrial Classification (ISIC), Revision 3.

Moreover, the poor quality of Thai statistics from industrial surveys makes it difficult for us to assign a good measure of soundness to our findings. As a result, a report on Thai TFP statistics by the industrial sector is rarely seen. Measuring the Thai TFP and comparing them with benchmarks and our competitors are thus extremely important.[4]

7.3   PRELIMINARY FINDINGS

7.3.1   Macroeconomic Environment: Pre-Crisis

An anatomy of the Thai and Asian crises in 1997 has been explored by numerous studies and their findings will be briefly noted here.[5] We can say many of these studies showed that not only short-term factors such as a cyclical slow-down in the demand for Thai exports can explain the abrupt decline in export growth in 1996,[6] but the long-term factors have also been at work dating back to the early 1990s. In the early 1990s, Thailand started to feel the pressure from its various domestic problems, ranging from rises in real wages to an appreciation of its real effective exchange rate. This is in addition to a decline in the quality of public infrastructure, rampant corruption, a lack of skilled labour and an inability to absorb foreign technology.

7.4   DOMESTIC FACTORS

7.4.1   Real Wage Rises

The increase in real wages has not been matched with an increase in labour productivity (Figure 7.1). Both demand and supply for labour played a role in this case. A boom in the service (non-traded) sector led to rises in real wages relative to both traded and non-traded good prices (Warr 1998, p. 58). Labour

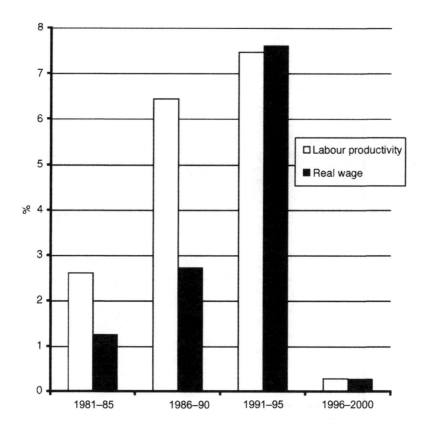

Source: Pranee and Chalongphob 1998, p. 44, Table 21 for 1980–95. Author's calculation for 1996–2000.

Figure 7.1   Growth in Real Wage and Labour Productivity

shortage was an alarming issue in the early 1990s, due to an earlier rapid expansion of the Thai economy.

7.4.2   Real Appreciation of Exchange Rate

The increase in real effective exchange rates indicated the loss of price competitiveness of Thai exports (Figure 7.2). The real appreciation was already evident by early 1995.[7] The real appreciation undermined the competitiveness of Thai export sectors in terms of their capacity to compete with the non-traded sectors over domestic resources.

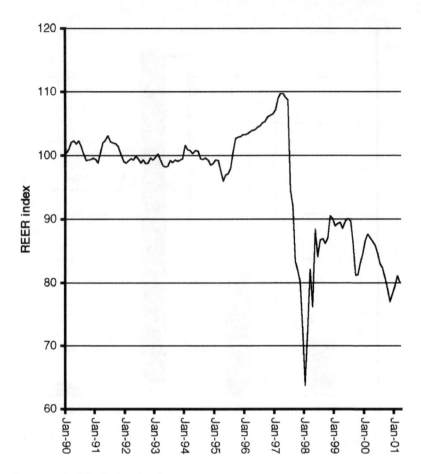

Source: Bank of Thailand, various issues.

Figure 7.2   Real Effective Exchange Rate

7.5   INTERNATIONAL FACTORS

The international factors include the new entrants in the world market, and these entrants have much lower wages than Thailand. These entrants include, for example, China, India, Indonesia and the Philippines. As a result, the gap between Thailand's unit labour cost (ULC) and that of competing countries has been widening (see Figure 7.3).

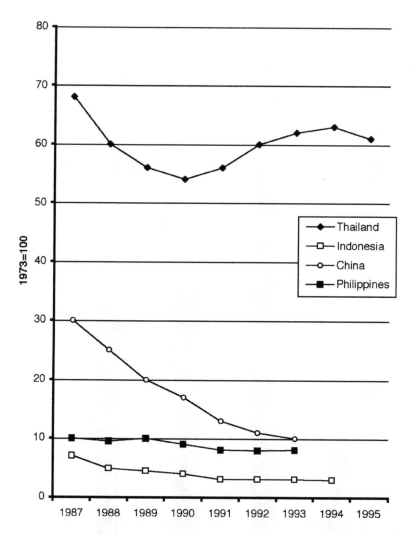

Source: Tzannatos 1997.

Figure 7.3   International Unit Labour for Selected Countries, 1987–95

The declining terms of trade for labour-intensive products, such as apparel, footwear and consumer electronics, caused slower export earnings. World prices for manufactured exports fell about 2 per cent in 1996, where as semiconductors prices fell almost 80 per cent in 1996.[8]

7.6   TOTAL FACTOR PRODUCTIVITY STILL LOW

Rises in real wages forces export industries (most are highly labour-intensive) to increase overall productivity since they are price-takers in international markets. However, the growth of total factor productivity of the manufacturing sector in Thailand during the period 1991–95 was somewhat unimpressive (Figure 7.4).

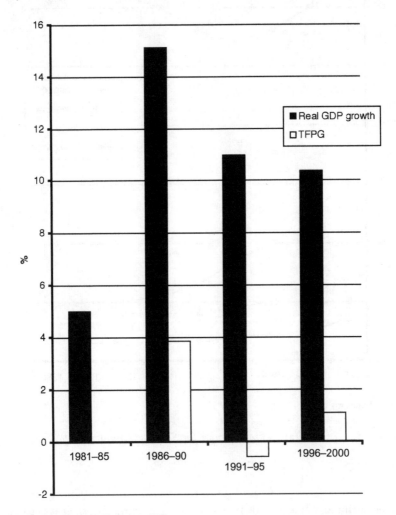

Source: Pranee and Chalongphob 1998.

Figure 7.4   Total Factor Productivity Growth in Thai Manufacturing, 1981–95

The collapse of Thailand's export growth in 1996 was evident in the slow-down in growth of labour-intensive industries (Figure 7.5).[9]

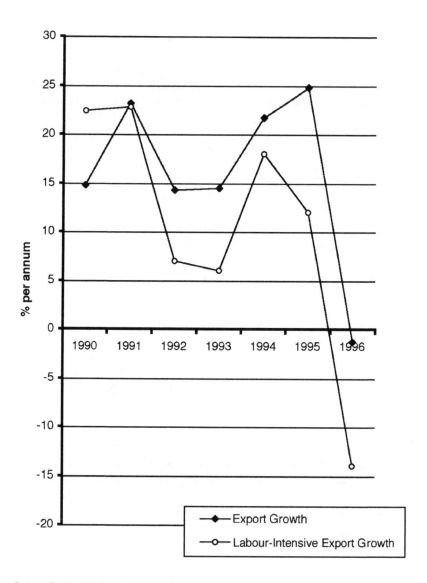

Source: Bank of Thailand.

Figure 7.5   *Thailand Export Growth: Total Manufacturing and Labour-Intensive Manufacturing, 1990–96*

7.7   QUANTITATIVE STUDY CONFIRMING LOSS OF COMPETITIVENESS OF THAI EXPORTS

The qualitative story of the pre-crisis competitiveness in Thailand is largely built on some economic indicators, notably the REER, TFPG, Real Wages and ULC. One quantitative study using the Constant Market Share (CMS) analysis showed that the loss of export competitiveness of Thai industry sectors during 1995–96 can be explained by their loss in competitiveness (see Table 7.1). This negative effect dominated the positive effects from the world trade and market-distribution. The same analysis was applied to the SITC 2 and 3 digits and compared to some other competitors. Table 7.2 showed some examples of the loss of competitiveness in the electronics industry (SITC 77).

In spite of other analyses on the causes of the economic turmoil in July 1997 in Thailand, in our view, the erosion of Thai export competitiveness, the inefficiency of investment, and the build-up financial vulnerability triggered this crisis.

The following section of this chapter will include analyses of labour skills development, and technology transfer supplementary with microevidence.

7.7.1   Post-Crisis

Real wages reconsidered. After the 1997 crisis and the subsequent Baht devaluation and despite a 35–40 per cent drop in the effective price of labour, labour costs were still high compared to those of the lower-income countries (see Figure 7.6). As we have already discussed, not only factor costs, but also productivity, determine our export competitiveness. Unfortunately, growth in real wages was still higher than that of labour productivity (Figure 7.1). As a

Table 7.1
Factors Contributing to Changes in Thai Exports
Using the Constant Market Share (CMS) Analysis (%)

	1990–95	1995–96
Change in export	100	−100
World trade effect	31	277
Market-distribution effect	6	57
Competitiveness effect	63	−434

Source: Samai Kothinthokom 2000, p. 57

Table 7.2
Factors Contributing to Changes in SITC-77 Exports for Selected Countries, 1995–96

Export growth (%)	Singa-pore	Korea	Malay-sia	Mexico	China	Thai-land	Indon-esia
World	3.4	5.3	3	2.4	2.9	3.6	2.96
Country	6	−28.5	7.8	22.8	8.2	1	34.4
Factor contribution (%)							
World trade effect	57	19	44	11	36	361	8
Market-distribution effect	41	9	8	−24	25	152	5
Competitiveness effect	2	−128	49	113	39	−413	86

Source: Samai Kothinthokom 2000, p. 75.

result, Thailand was still not competing well in labour-intensive industries such as apparel, wood working, footwear, textiles, leather and rubber goods. The downward trend of the RCA indexes shown below confirms this conclusion. The share of labour-intensive exports in manufactured exports declined from 23 to 13 per cent in 2000 (Figure 7.7).

REER reconsidered. After the Baht devaluation, the low level of price inflation was a big surprise. Unfortunately, this moderate inflation implied that the REER have increased concurrently. Ignoring the spikes at the end of 1997 and early in 1998, the REER against trading partners increased by 10 per cent after the crisis to the middle of 1999. More importantly, the REER against competitors had been appreciated to the pre-devaluation level, reducing the price competitiveness of Thai exports.[10] From the middle of 1999 to the end of 2000, the REER had depreciated back by 10 per cent. We note that Thai manufactured exports grew, during the post-crisis period, considerably in terms of the Baht, doubling its value posted in 1995. Thai manufactured exports in US dollars grew 19.5 per cent in 2000.[11]

TFPG reconsidered. The preliminary estimates of the TFPG of the country showed higher negative value in average between 1997 to 2000, relative to the pre-crisis. The result is not surprising due to the economic recession during the post-crisis and the past overinvestment in many industries. In 2000, overall manufacturing industries still had excess capacity. The average of the capacity utilisation rate was 56 per cent.[12]

Next in the chapter, we will report on an analysis of the impact of oil prices on Thailand's industrial competitiveness.

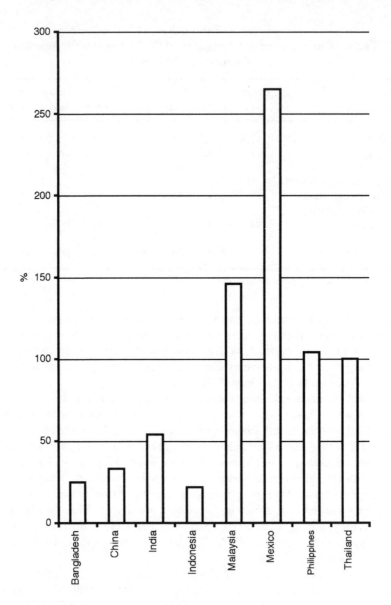

Note: All countries, wages in US dollars in 1998.

Source: UNIDO, ILO.

*Figure 7.6   Manufacturing Wage as a Percentage of the Thai
             Manufacturing Wage, 1998*

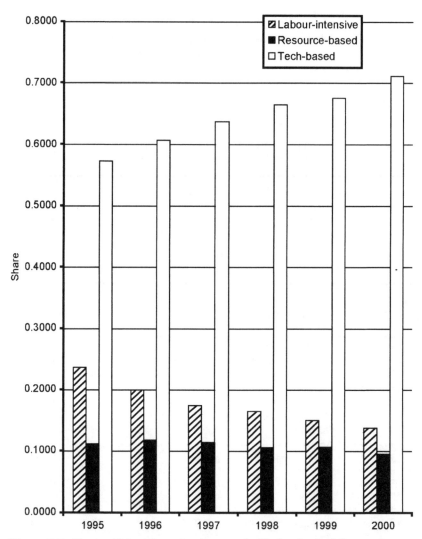

Figure 7.7 Share of Manufacturing Exports by Technological Categories

7.8 INDUSTRIAL COMPETITIVENESS: SOME INDICATORS

7.8.1 Revealed Comparative Advantages (RCA)

Thailand–RCA indexes by ISIC classification during 1995–98 can be summarised into four groups (Table 7.3).[13]

Table 7.3
Thai Industries Classified by RCA Indices
and its Trend during 1995–98

	Upward trend	Downward trend
RCA > 1	15, 30, 31, 32	01, 18. 19, 36
RCA < 1	11 ,17, 20, 21, 23, 24, 26, 27, 28, 29, 34	13, 22, 25, 33, 35

Note: Numbers in parentheses are the ISIC Code, Revision 3.
Source: Author's calculation.

Table 7.4
Domestic Resource Cost (DRC) Indices, 1997

ISIC Rev.3	I-O Code	I-O Description	DRC	
15	345	Canning and preservation of fruits/vegetables	0.82	(E)
15	346	Canning and preservation of fish and other seafoods	3.82	(E)
15	348	Animal oil, animal fat, vegetable oil and by-products	3.90	(M)
15	355	Sugar	1.02	(E)
15	356	Confectionery	1.94	(M)
15	358	Monosodium glutamate	3.76	(B)
15	360	Other food products	3.82	(B)
15	361	Animal feed	3.82	(B)
15	362	Distilling and spirits blending	1.60	(M)
17	367	Spinning	1.10	(M)
17	368	Weaving	2.01	(M)
17	370	Made-up textile goods	3.63	(B)
17	371	Knitting	3.71	(B)
18	372	Wearing apparel	3.57	(B)
19	373	Carpets and rugs	3.73	(E)
19	375	Tanneries and leather finishing	2.44	(M)
19	376	Leather finishing	3.74	(E)
19	377	Footwear except rubber	3.73	(E)
20	378	Saw mills	1.17	(M)
20	379	Wood and cork products	3.58	(B)
21	381	Pulp, paper and paperboard	1.05	(M)

ISIC Rev.3	I-O Code	1-O Description	DRC	
23	093	Petroleum refineries	2.92	(M)
23	094	Other petroleum products	1.07	(M)
24	084	Basic industrial chemicals	1.03	(M)
24	085	Fertiliser and pesticides	1.05	(M)
24	086	Synthetic resins, plastic and artificial fibre materials	1.37	(M)
24	088	Drugs and medicines	1.02	(M)
24	089	Soap and cleaning preparations	1.31	(M)
24	090	Cosmetics	1.58	(M)
24	092	Other chemical products	1.25	(M)
25	095	Rubber sheet and block rubber	0.84	(B)
25	096	Tyres and tubes	0.75	(B)
25	097	Other rubber products	0.77	(B)
25	098	Plastic wares	1.28	(M)
26	099	Ceramic and ceramic wares	0.81	(B)
26	100	Glass and glass products	1.26	(M)
26	104	Other non-metallic products	1.20	(M)
27	105	Iron and steel	0.89	(M)
28	106	Secondary steel products	1.20	(M)
28	107	Non-ferrous metals	0.97	(M)
28	108	Cutlery and hand tools	1.41	(M)
28	110	Structural metal products	0.74	(B)
28	111	Other fabricated metal products	0.97	(M)
29	112	Engines and turbines	1.19	(M)
29	113	Agricultural machinery and equipment	1.01	(M)
29	114	Food and metal working machines	1.03	(M)
29	115	Special industrial machinery	1.07	(M)
29	117	Electrical industrial machinery and appliances	1.24	(M)
29	119	Household electrical appliances	0.76	(B)
30	116	Office and household machinery and appliances	0.79	(B)
31	120	Insulated wire and cable	0.77	(B)
31	121	Electric accumulators and batteries	1.40	(M)
31	122	Other electrical apparatus and supplies	0.95	(M)
32	118	Radio, television and communication equipment	1.12	(M)
33	129	Scientific equipment	0.98	(M)
33	130	Photographic and optical goods	0.99	(M)
33	131	Watches and clocks	0.82	(B)

ISIC Rev.3	I-O Code	1-O Description	DRC	
34	123	Shipbuilding repairing	1.25	(M)
35	125	Motor vehicles	5.18	(M)
35	126	Motor cycles and bicycles	1.29	(M)
35	128	Aircraft	0.87	(M)
36	132	Jewellery and related articles	0.82	(B)
36	133	Recreational and athletic equipment	1.01	(M)
36	134	Other manufactured goods	0.76	(B)
36	080	Wooden fumiture and fixture	0.70	(B)

Note: M = Import Competition Industry, B = Export-oriented, N = Non-traded.

Source: Mingsam et al. 1997.

Export groups with the RCA index greater than one and with an upward trend are:

- Food and beverages (15);
- Office, accounting and computing machinery (30);
- Electrical machinery and apparatus (31);
- Radio, television, and communication equipment (32).

Export groups with the RCA index greater than one but with a decreasing trend are:

- Wearing apparel except footwear (18);
- Leather, leather products and footwear (19);
- Furniture and other manufacturing (36).

Export groups with the RCA index less than one and with a downward trend are:

- Textiles (17), wood and wood products (20), paper and paper products (21);
- Petroleum refineries (23), chemical and chemical products (24);
- Non-metallic mineral products (26), basic metal industries (27);
- Fabricated metal products (28) and machinery and equipment (29).

7.8.2   Domestic Resource Costs (DRC)[14]

The calculated DRC for Thai industrial exports in 1997 fell between 0.57 to 0.84. For example,

- Wearing apparel (DRC = 0.57);
- Made-up textile goods (DRC = 0.63);
- Tyres and tubes (DRC = 0.77);
- Canning and preservation of fish and other sea food (DRC = 0.82);
- Rubber sheet and block rubber (DRC = 0.84).

See Table 7.5 for more detail.

When combining the DRC and RCA indices, we find, as shown in Table 7.6:

1   Exports with the high competitiveness (RCA > 1 with an upward trend and DRC < 1) are:

- Canning and preservation of fruits/vegetables (0.45);
- Fish and other seafood (0.46);
- Office and household machinery and appliances (116);
- Insulated wire and cable (120).

Table 7.5
Thai Industries Classified by RCA and DRC Indices, 1997

	DRC/SER < 1	DRC/SER > 1
RCA > 1	15(045, 046, 049, 061), 17(070),18, 19(076, 077), 25(095, 096, 097), 28(110), 29(119), 30, 31(120, 122), 33(130, 131), 36(080, 132)	15(055, 056), 19(075), 32, 35(126), 36(133)
RCA < 1	17(071), 27, 33(129), 20(079)	15(059, 062), 16, 20(078), 21, 23, 24, 25(098), 26(100), 28(106, 108), 29(112, 113, 114, 115), 31(121), 35(125)

Note: Numbers in parentheses are the Input–Output Code.

Source: DRC calculation are from TDRI 1997; RCA from author's calculation.

Table 7.6
Nominal Rate of Protection (%)

ISIC Rev. 3	1995	1999
15	39.97	25.90
16	51.40	60.00
17	28.90	19.10
18	38.70	42.30
19	15.34	11.15
20	14.19	11.24
21	18.06	15.57
22	20.00	17.10
23	9.39	6.37
24	19.48	13.03
25	35.16	24.39
26	24.81	17.76
27	10.18	9.27
28	22.64	18.45
29	9.62	8.15
30	14.40	10.50
31	15.72	11.79
32	13.90	11.20
33	10.98	7.95
34	38.40	38.50
35	10.35	5.58
36	30.13	18.55
Manufacture	17.22	13.03
Aggregate	16.65	12.23

Note: Calculation weighted with import shares.

Source: UNSD, Comtrade database; and data provided by the Thai authorities.
Quoted in Trade Policy Review Thailand, WTO, 17 November 1999.

2   Exports with reduced competitiveness (RCA > 1 with a downward trend and DRC < 1) are:

- Wearing apparel (072), carpets and rugs (073);
- Leather finishing (076) and footwear (077).

3   Industry with limited competitiveness (RCA < 1 and DRC > 1) are mostly import-competing industries.

Table 7.7
Industry Grouping by their Level of Competitiveness
Group A: Products with High Competitiveness
with RCA > 1 and DRC < 1

ISIC (IO Code)	Products	NRP 1997	Import Content 1998	Export/ Output 1998	*
15(049)	Rice milling	Low	Low	High	R
25(095)	Rubber sheet and block	Medium	Low	High	R
18	Wearing apparel	High	Low	Medium	L
15(045)	Canning and preservation of fruit and vegetables	High	Low	High	R
33(130)	Photographic and optical goods	Medium	Low	High	T
25(097)	Other rubber products	Medium	Low	High	R
15(046)	Canning and preservation of fish	High	Low	High	R
17(070)	Made-up textile goods	Low	Medium	Medium	L
25(096)	Tyres and tubes	Medium	Medium	Medium	R
29(119)	Household electrical appliances	Medium	Medium	Medium	T
19(076)	Leather finishing	High	Medium	Medium	L
30	Office and household machinery and appliances	Medium	Medium	High	T
36(080)	Wooden furniture and fixture	Medium	Medium	Medium	R
36(132)	Jewellery and related articles	Low	High	Medium	L
19(077)	Footwear (except rubber)	Medium	High	High	L
33(131)	Watches and clocks	Medium	High	High	T
31(120)	Insulated wire and cable	Low	High	High	T
31(122)	Other electrical apparatus and supplies	Medium	High	Medium	T
28(110)	Structural metal product	Medium	High	Medium	-

Note: * L = Labour-intensive products, T = Technology-intensive products, R = Resource-based products.

Group B: Products with Medium Competitiveness
with RCA > 1 and DRC > 1

ISIC (IO Code)	Products	NRP 1997	Import Content 1998	Export/ Output 1998	*
15(055)	Sugar	Medium	Low	High	R
15(056)	Confectionery	Medium	Low	Medium	R
15(061)	Animal feed	Low	Medium	Low	-
19(075)	Tanneries and leather finishing	Low	High	Medium	-
32	Radio, television and communication equipment	Low	High	High	T
35(126)	Motorcycles and bicycles	High	Medium	Medium	T
36(133)	Recreational and athletic equipment	Low	Low	Medium	L

Note: * L = Labour-intensive products, T = Technology-intensive products, R = Resource-based products.

Group C: Products with limited Competitiveness
with RCA < 1 and DRC < 1

ISIC (IO Code)	Products	NRP 1997	Import Content 1998	Export/ Output 1998	*
17(071)	Knitting	Medium	Low	High	L
27	Iron and steel	Low	Medium	Low	T
33(129)	Scientific equipment	Low	Medium	Medium	T

Note: * L = Labour-intensive products, T = Technology-intensive products, R = Resource-based products

Group D: Products with Poor Competitiveness
with RCA < 1 and DRC > 1

ISIC (IO Code)	Products	NRP 1997	Import Content 1998	Export/ Output 1998	*
15(059)	Coffee and tea (processing)	Medium	Medium	Low	-
15(062)	Distilling and spirits blending	High	Low	Low	-
16(066)	Tobacco products	High	High	Low	-
20(078)	Saw mills	Low	Medium	Medium	-
20(079)	Wood and cork products	Medium	Low	High	-
21(081)	Pulp, paper and paperboard	Low	High	Medium	-

ISIC (IO Code)	Products	NRP 1997	Import Content 1998	Export/ Output 1998	*
21(082)	Paper and paperboard products	Medium	Medium	Low	-
23(093)	Petroleum refineries	Low	High	Low	R
23(094)	Other petroleum products	Low	High		R
24(084)	Basic industrial chemicals	Low	Low	Low	T
24(085)	Fertilizer and pesticides	Low	Medium	Low	T
24(086)	Synthetic resins, plastic and artificial fibre materials	Medium	Low	Medium	T
24(087)	Paints, varnishes and lacquers	Medium	High	Low	T
24(088)	Drugs and medicines	Low	High	Low	T
24(089)	Soap and cleaning preparations	Low	Medium	Low	T
24(090)	Cosmetics	High	High	Low	T
24(091)	Matches	Low	Low	Low	-
24(092)	Other chemical products	Low	High	Medium	T
25(098)	Plastic wares	High	High	Medium	T
26(100)	Glass and glass products	Low	Medium	Medium	-
28(106)	Secondary steel products	Low	High	Low	T
28(108)	Cutlery and hand tools	Medium	High	Medium	-
29(112)	Engines and turbines	Medium	High	Low	-
29(113)	Agricultural machinery and equipment	Low	Medium	Medium	-
29(114)	Wood and metal working machines	Low	Medium	Low	-
29(115)	Special industrial machinery	Low	Medium	Low	-
31(121)	Electric accumulators and batteries	Medium	Medium	Medium	-
35(125)	Motor vehicles	High	High	Medium	T

Note: * L = Labour-intensive products, T = Technology-intensive products, R = Resource-based products

7.8.3   Nominal Rate of Protection and Effective Rate of Protection (NRP and ERP)

The NRP in 1999 was in between 5.58 and 60.00 per cent, with an average of 13.03 per cent:

- Thai industrial sectors with a relatively high protection rate are tobacco (60 per cent), Wearing apparel except footwear (42.3 per cent), Motor vehicle, trailers and semi-trailers (38.5 per cent).
- Industrial sectors with a relatively low protection rate are petroleum refineries and petroleum products (6.37 per cent), machinery and equipment (8.5 per cent), medical, precision and optical instruments, watches and clocks (7.95 per cent) (see Table 7.7 for detail).

The ERP in 1997 was in between –45 per cent and 757 per cent, with a simple average of 32 per cent and a weighted average of 90 per cent.

- Generally, export industries received a negative protection rate (an average ERP of –3 per cent), while import-substitution industries enjoyed a large protection rate (an average of 193 per cent);
- Those highly protected industries were motor vehicles (496.9 per cent), petroleum refinery (237.3 per cent), tanneries and leather finishing (180.9 per cent).

A comparison of the ERP between 1990 and 1997 indicates that:

- Industries received a high protection rate (positive ERP) tended to receive lower protection;
- Industries received a negative protection tended to receive higher protection;
- If considering the industries by their stage of production, the primary industries mostly received a negative protection, while intermediate industries partially received a low protection and final product industries enjoyed a high protection.

Combining RCA, DRC and NRP together, we observe the following results (Table 7.8):

1   Group A: Exports with High Competitiveness with RCA > 1 and DRC < 1:

- Products in this group received a variety of nominal rates of protection, ranging from 0 to 60 per cent;
- Products classified as labour-intensive, resource-based and technology-based industries are also found in this group proportionally.

Table 7.8
Spearman's Rank Correlation Coefficient
Between NRP and DRC Ranking

Rank Correlation	Export Goods	Import Goods
NRP vs DRC	—	0.4237
ERP vs DRC	–0.205	0.3268

Source: NRP, ERP and DRC are reported in Appendix.

- High tariff rates are found on some differentiated product and luxury imports for government revenue reasons.

2   Group B: Exports with Medium Competitiveness with RCA > 1 and DRC > 1:

- No negative protection is found in this group. Products with high-import content had low tariffs.

3   Group D: Exports with Poor Competitiveness with RCA < 1 and DRC > 1:

- Industries fallen into this group are mostly technology-based. Their import-content is medium to high, and their export–output ratios are medium to low;
- Industries with high-import content have low tariffs, except for motor vehicles, plastic wares, and tobacco.

7.9   RELATIONSHIP BETWEEN DRC AND ERP

We have tested the relationship between DRC and ERP by use of Spearman's Rank Correlation. Industrial products are classified as export and import-substitution goods. The results, shown in Table 7.9, indicate that

- For import-substitution goods, industries with comparative disadvantages tended to receive more protection (these results are hardly a surprise);
- For export goods, industries with better trade performance received increasing levels of support, but those whose performance were worsened received lower support.[15]

NOTES

1   The final draft will include a comparative study of Thailand's international competitiveness with some Asian countries and the role of Thai government policy after the crisis. Thai industrial policies will be emphasised.
2   For other definitions, see Leamer and Stern (1990), and IMD.
3   Note integrated analyses of these various indicators are not yet determined.
4   Industrial surveys recently conducted by the Ministry of Industry with the technical assistance of the World Bank provided us with TFP estimates of some manufacturing sectors. For details, see Dollars et al. 1998.
5   For example, see Radelet and Sachs 1998, Siamwalla 2000.

6   World export grew just 4 per cent in 1996, while rose up to 17 per cent in average in 1994–95. Thai exports in dollar terms fell 1 per cent in 1996 after two years of growth in excess of 20 per cent. The volume of exports stagnated in 1996, while there was little change in prices.

7   Another measure of real exchange rate, namely relative prices of traded and non-traded goods, shows a similar result. However, Warr 1998 showed that the common measure of real effective exchange rates by the International Monetary Fund or Morgan Guaranty highly underestimates the magnitude of a real appreciation.

8   Radelet and Sachs 1998, p. 32

9   Overall, the zero growth of Thai exports in 1996 was due to the stagnation of export volume, while there was little change in unit values (Radelet and Sachs 1998, p. 31).

10   Siamwalla 2000, p. 23 showed a slightly difference in the REER appreciation after the crisis due to the different measure of the REER.

11   In the second half of 2000, Thai economy showed signs of slowing down due to the slowing down of the world economy and world trade.

12   *Quarterly Report on Conditions of Manufacturing Industries*, Office of Industrial Economics, Ministry of Industry, Bangkok, Oct.–Dec. 2000.

13   The RCA indexes by SITC code are available upon request.

14   Calculation based on the input–output table in 1997. For mapping from input–output code to ISIC code, please see Appendix.

15   This result differs from the past study by Warr and Nidhiprabha 1996, which showed the contradictory results for export goods during 1974–84.

REFERENCES

Dollars, D., et al. (1998), 'Short-term and Long-term Competitiveness Issues in Thai Industry', background paper for the conference on *Thailand's Dynamic Economic Recovery and Competitiveness,* Bangkok, May.

Krugman, P. (1994), 'Competitiveness: A Dangerous Obsession', *Foreign Affairs*, **73**, 28–44.

Leanmer, E.E. and R.M. Stern (1990), *Quantitative International Economics*. Boston: Allyn and Bacon.

Radelet, S. and J. Sachs (1998), 'The East Asian Financial Crisis: Diagnosis, Remedies, Prospects,' *Brooking Papers on Economic Activity, 1.*

Siamwalla, A. (2000), 'Anatomy of the Thai Economic Crisis', mimeo.

Warr, P.G. (1998), 'Thailand: What Went Wrong?', background paper for Conference on *Thailand's Dynamic Economic Recovery and Competitiveness*, National Economic Studies and Development Board and the World Bank.

Warr, P.G. and B. Nidhiprabha (1996), *Thailand's Macroeconomic Miracle: Stable Adjustment and Sustained Growth*, Washington, DC: World Bank.

APPENDICES

Appendix 7.1
Code Mapping: ISIC, SITC, I-O., HS in the Study

ISIC (Rev.3)	Description	Value added (GDP Table)	SITC (Rev.3)	HS	TSIC	IO-Code
15	Food and beverages	1+2	011, 012, 016, 017, 022, 023, 024, 025, 034, 035, 036, 037, 042, 046, 047, 048, 056, 058, 059, 061, 062, 071, 072, 073, 074, 081, 091, 098, 111, 112, 211, 411, 421, 422, 431	02, 03, 04, 07, 08, 09, 11, 15, 16, 17, 18, 19, 20, 21, 22, 23, 41,	31	042-064
16	Tobacco	3	122	24	31	065-066
17	Textiles	4	261, 263, 264, 265, 268, 651, 652, 653, 654, 655, 656, 657, 658, 659	50, 51, 52, 53, 54, 55, 56, 57, 58, 59, 70, 60, 63	32	067-071
18	Wearing apparel except footwear	5	613, 841, 842, 843, 844, 845, 846, 848	43, 61, 62, 65,	32	072
19	Leather, leather products and footwear	6	611, 612, 831, 851	41, 42, 64	32	073-077
20	Wood and wood products	7	244, 246, 247, 248, 633, 634, 635	44	33	078-079
21	Paper and paper products	9	251, 641, 642	47, 48	34	081-082

ISIC (Rev.3)	Description	Value added (GDP Table)	SITC (Rev.3)	HS	TSIC	IO-Code
22	Printing, publishing	10	892	48, 49, 85	34	083
23	Petroleum refineries and petroleum products	12	325, 334, 342, 344	27, 28	35	093-094
24	Chemicals and chemical products	11	232, 245, 266, 267, 335, 511, 512, 513, 514, 515, 516, 522, 523, 524, 525, 531, 532, 533, 541, 542, 551, 553, 554, 562, 571, 572, 573, 574, 575, 591, 592, 593, 597, 598, 882	27, 28, 29, 30, 31, 32, 33, 34, 35, 36, 37, 38, 39, 40, 54, 55, 71, 85,	35	084-092
25	Rubber and plastic products	13	579, 581, 582, 583, 621, 625, 629, 893	39, 40	35	095-098
26	Non-metallic mineral products	14	661, 662, 663, 664, 665, 666	25, 38, 68, 69, 70,	36	099-104
27	Basic metal industries	15	282, 283, 284, 285, 288, 289, 671, 672, 673, 674, 675, 676, 677, 678, 679, 681, 682, 683, 684, 685, 686, 687, 689, 971	26, 71, 72, 73, 74, 75, 76, 78, 79, 80, 81,	37	105
28	Fabricated metal products	16	691, 692, 693, 694, 695, 696, 697, 699, 711, 811, 812	73, 74, 76, 82, 83, 84	38	106-111

ISIC (Rev.3)	Description	Value added (GDP Table)	SITC (Rev.3)	HS	TSIC	IO-Code
29	Machinery and equipment n.e.c.	17	712, 718, 721, 722, 723, 724, 725, 726, 727, 728, 731, 733, 735, 737, 741, 742, 743, 744, 745, 746, 747, 748, 749, 775, 891	73, 84, 85, 87, 93	38	112-115, 117, 119
30	Office, accounting and computing machinery	17	751, 752, 759	84, 90	38	116
31	Electrical machinery and apparatus	18	716, 771, 772, 773, 778, 813	85, 94	38	120-122
32	Radio, television and communication equipment	18	761, 762, 763, 764, 776	85	38	118
33	Medical, precision and optical instruments, watches and clocks	na	774, 871, 872, 873, 874, 881, 884, 885	85, 90, 91	38	129-131
34	Motor vehicle, trailers and semi-trailers	19	713, 781, 782, 783, 784, 786	84, 87	38	123, 127
35	Other transport equipment	19	714, 785, 791, 792, 793	84, 86, 87, 88, 89,	38	125-126, 128
36	Furniture and other manufacturing	8	269, 667, 821, 894, 895, 897, 898, 899, 961	36, 42, 59, 63, 66, 67, 71, 92, 94, 95, 96,	39	080, 132-134

Appendix 7.2
Thailand–RCA Indices By ISIC, 1995–98

ISIC(REV.3)	RCA			
	1995	1996	1997	1998
01	2.0821	2.1813	1.8024	1.5257
10	0.0000	0.0000	0.0000	0.0000
11	0.0635	0.0741	0.1049	0.1149
12	0.0000	0.0000	0.0000	0.0000
13	0.0642	0.0823	0.1020	0.0638
14	0.8746	1.0437	1.1076	1.5145
15	2.6539	2.7657	2.6433	2.7443
16	0.0091	0.0243	0.0356	0.0652
17	1.0708	1.1121	1.1345	1.1419
18	2.8221	2.1364	1.8752	2.0030
19	4.0204	2.9947	2.6697	2.5895
20	0.5477	0.5359	0.5200	0.6309
21	0.2678	0.1903	0.3309	0.4793
22	0.5874	0.1222	0.1241	0.1423
23	0.2793	0.5627	0.8923	0.7842
24	0.3714	0.3394	0.4243	0.4553
25	1.7103	0.9937	0.9857	0.9494
26	0.8666	0.9337	1.0089	1.0180
27	0.2151	0.2306	0.4173	0.4549
28	0.5984	0.6393	0.6110	0.6664
29	0.4968	0.5392	0.5037	0.5163
30	2.1092	2.5738	2.4157	2.7555
31	1.2327	1.2863	1.3389	1.3564
32	1.4550	1.5864	1.5466	1.5235
33	0.6367	0.7005	0.6391	0.6344
34	0.0720	0.0880	0.1448	0.1823
35	0.5567	0.6545	0.4279	0.1519
36	1.9652	1.9790	1.6612	1.4516
40	0.0000	0.0000	0.0000	0.0000
92	0.3418	0.0375	0.0230	0.0361
other	0.3074	0.4490	0.9562	0.5671
TOTAL	1	1	1	1

Source: Author's calculations.

Appendix 7.3
RCA Index Comparisons for Selected Countries, 1998

ISIC (Rev.3)	Indonesia	Korea	Malaysia	Hong Kong	China	Singapore	Thailand	Japan	Philippines
01	1.4722	0.1300	0.6264	0.0042	0.9375	0.3188	1.5257	0.0196	0.6743
10	6.9650	0.0003	0.0004	0.0000	1.4655	0.0008	0.0000	0.0003	0.0000
11	6.4539	0.0000	2.2470	0.0000	0.4084	0.0000	0.1149	0.0014	0.0012
12	0.0000	0.0000	0.0662	0.0000	0.0000	0.0000	0.0000	0.0000	0.0000
13	0.0099	0.0084	0.0724	0.0000	0.1276	0.0623	0.0638	0.0010	0.7919
14	0.2931	0.2895	0.2297	0.0072	2.2042	0.1168	1.5145	0.1783	0.4078
15	1.5741	0.2966	1.4944	0.2043	0.7574	0.2968	2.7443	0.0788	0.8853
16	0.6518	0.0817	0.6336	1.8766	0.6429	3.3052	0.0652	0.1463	0.0863
17	1.6575	2.9140	0.5327	1.9287	2.4753	0.2717	1.1419	0.5251	0.3523
18	1.6325	1.0690	0.9529	11.9263	4.9709	0.3936	2.0030	0.0320	2.3882
19	2.3290	1.4599	0.2074	0.2012	5.4433	0.1640	2.5895	0.0432	1.0973
20	4.9262	0.0789	3.2464	0.0314	0.6036	0.1974	0.6309	0.0145	0.4003
21	1.9405	0.5662	0.1472	0.6041	0.2363	0.2397	0.4793	0.2295	0.1774
22	0.0395	0.3162	0.1844	4.1173	0.3840	0.8238	0.1423	0.1992	0.0695
23	1.3028	2.2413	0.8216	0.0852	0.5828	4.8176	0.7842	0.1816	0.3490
24	0.4923	0.7973	0.3368	0.2980	0.5743	0.6922	0.4553	0.7847	0.1106
25	0.3173	0.9957	0.5788	0.6157	1.1353	0.3592	0.9494	0.8493	0.2679
26	0.4962	0.3613	0.5356	0.1054	1.4612	0.2029	1.0180	0.7925	0.3509
27	1.1501	2.1958	0.3869	0.4518	0.5683	0.5299	0.4549	0.9154	0.3576
28	0.3131	0.8622	0.4204	0.4935	1.4460	0.3888	0.6664	0.6580	0.2089
29	0.1055	0.6585	0.3044	0.2406	0.4631	0.5618	0.5163	1.3801	0.1461
30	0.3007	0.7520	2.9278	0.8601	1.1832	5.1246	2.7555	1.5859	2.8220
31	0.4443	0.5679	1.2183	0.9377	1.3219	1.2932	1.3564	1.5904	1.2231
32	0.4154	2.6024	4.0873	1.6677	0.9575	3.1879	1.5235	1.7302	6.2291
33	0.1512	0.6687	0.5329	3.2020	0.9549	0.9113	0.6344	1.6414	0.4128
34	0.0375	0.7992	0.0712	0.0102	0.1284	0.0725	0.1823	1.8696	0.1177
35	0.2562	1.5942	0.5212	0.0081	0.4556	0.3772	0.1519	1.0987	0.0621
36	1.3106	0.6024	0.8049	1.3025	2.5367	0.7376	1.4516	0.6537	0.6914
40	0.0000	0.0000	0.0000	1.2656	1.6004	0.0067	0.0000	0.0000	0.0000
92	0.0658	0.5176	0.0313	0.5302	0.2370	0.1366	0.0361	0.0859	0.1546
other	5.3987	0.0000	0.2841	0.4807	0.0000	0.4736	0.5671	1.0539	0.0077
Total	1.0000	1.0000	1.0000	1.0000	1.0000	1.0000	1.0000	1.0000	1.0000

Appendix 7.4
Ranking of the RCA indices for Selected Countries, 1998

ISIC (Rev.3)	Indon-esia	Korea	Malay-sia	Hong Kong	China	Singa-pore	Thai-land	Japan	Phili-ppines
01	2	7	5	9	3	6	1	8	4
10	1	5	4	7	2	3	7	6	7
11	1	7	2	7	3	7	4	5	6
12	2	2	1	2	2	2	2	2	2
13	6	7	3	9	2	5	4	8	1
14	4	5	6	9	1	8	2	7	3
15	2	7	3	8	5	6	1	9	4
16	3	8	5	2	4	1	9	6	7
17	4	1	6	3	2	9	5	7	8
18	5	6	7	1	2	8	4	9	3
19	3	4	6	7	1	8	2	9	5
20	1	7	2	8	4	6	3	9	5
21	1	3	9	2	6	5	4	7	8
22	9	4	6	1	3	2	7	5	8
23	3	2	4	9	6	1	5	8	7
24	5	1	7	8	4	3	6	2	9
25	8	2	6	5	1	7	3	4	9
26	5	6	4	9	1	8	2	3	7
27	2	1	8	7	4	5	6	3	9
28	8	2	6	5	1	7	3	4	9
29	9	2	6	7	5	3	4	1	8
30	9	8	2	7	6	1	4	5	3
31	9	8	6	7	3	4	2	1	5
32	9	4	2	6	8	3	7	5	1
33	9	5	7	1	3	4	6	2	8
34	8	2	7	9	4	6	3	1	5
35	6	1	3	9	4	5	7	2	8
36	3	9	5	4	1	6	2	8	7
40	4	4	4	2	1	3	4	4	4
92	7	2	9	1	3	5	8	6	4
other	1	9	6	4	8	5	3	2	7

Appendix 7.5
Real Wage and Labour Productivity in 1988 Prices:
The Whole Kingdom

	Value added per worker		Real wage	
Year	(Baht per person)	Growth	(Baht per month)	Growth
1980	40 596	—	1812.03	—
1981	39 742	−2.11	1703.60	−5.98
1982	41 085	3.38	1728.08	1.44
1983	42 774	4.11	1856.43	7.43
1984	43 811	2.42	2002.16	7.85
1985	46 107	5.24	1911.68	−4.52
1986	47 130	2.22	1906.38	−0.28
1987	49 845	5.76	1904.52	−0.10
1988	52 968	6.27	1984.69	4.21
1989	57 027	7.66	2034.86	2.53
1990	62 875	10.25	2182.15	7.24
1991	66 540	5.83	2291.71	5.02
1992	69 778	4.87	2568.69	12.09
1993	76 404	9.5	2861.61	11.40
1994	83 442	9.21	2911.76	1.75
1995	90 001	7.86	3136.93	7.73
1996	100 710	11.89	3189.22	1.67
1997	97 535	−3.15	3371.98	5.73
1998	91 128	−6.57	3186.69	−5.49
1999	93 246	2.32	3268.83	2.58
2000	90 367	−3.09	3165.64	−3.16
Periods				
1981–85	42 704	2.61	1840.39	1.24
1986–90	53 969	6.43	2002.52	2.72
1991–95	77 233	7.45	2754.14	7.60
1996–2000	93 069	0.28	3236.47	0.26

Source: From NESDB and NSO refer to Pranee and Chalongphob 1998, p. 44, Table 21 for 1980–95, for 1996–2000 from author's calculation.

Appendix 7.6
Thailand Real Effective Exchange Rate (REER), 1990–2001

Jan-90	100.42	Oct-92	98.77	Jul-95	98.00
Feb-90	100.95	Nov-92	99.55	Aug-95	100.63
Mar-90	102.06	Dec-92	99.25	Sep-95	102.62
Apr-90	102.32	Jan-93	99.72	Oct-95	102.86
May-90	101.76	Feb-93	100.23	Nov-95	103.00
Jun-90	102.26	Mar-93	99.27	Dec-95	103.30
Jul-90	101.38	Apr-93	98.37	Jan-96	103.27
Aug-90	100.23	May-93	98.16	Feb-96	103.45
Sep-90	99.16	Jun-93	98.27	Mar-96	103.72
Oct-90	99.33	Jul-93	99.16	Apr-96	103.93
Nov-90	99.40	Aug-93	98.91	May-96	104.08
Dec-90	99.62	Sep-93	99.25	Jun-96	104.45
Jan-91	99.37	Oct-93	99.05	Jul-96	104.64
Feb-91	98.84	Nov-93	99.28	Aug-96	105.12
Mar-91	100.36	Dec-93	99.50	Sep-96	105.38
Apr-91	102.01	Jan-94	101.60	Oct-96	106.05
May-91	102.36	Feb-94	100.84	Nov-96	106.31
Jun-91	103.05	Mar-94	100.81	Dec-96	106.51
Jul-91	102.15	Apr-94	100.25	Jan-97	107.17
Aug-91	101.94	May-94	100.80	Feb-97	108.89
Sep-91	101.84	Jun-94	100.69	Mar-97	109.73
Oct-91	101.46	Jul-94	99.47	Apr-97	109.69
Nov-91	100.11	Aug-94	99.42	May-97	109.15
Dec-91	99.09	Sep-94	99.58	Jun-97	108.69
Jan-92	98.79	Oct-94	99.29	Jul-97	94.46
Feb-92	99.20	Nov-94	98.49	Aug-97	91.92
Mar-92	99.50	Dec-94	98.70	Sep-97	83.31
Apr-92	99.31	Jan-95	99.25	Oct-97	81.87
May-92	99.90	Feb-95	99.18	Nov-97	80.05
Jun-92	99.40	Mar-95	97.55	Dec-97	72.55
Jul-92	98.85	Apr-95	95.93	Jan-98	63.75
Aug-92	99.29	May-95	96.95	Feb-98	72.49
Sep-92	98.70	Jun-95	97.11	Mar-98	82.00

Apr-98	76.21	Jul-95	98.00	Apr-98	76.21
May-98	88.39	Aug-95	100.63	May-98	88.39
Jun-98	84.04	Sep-95	102.62	Jun-98	84.04
Jul-98	86.67	Oct-95	102.86	Jul-98	86.67
Aug-98	86.86	Nov-95	103.00	Aug-98	86.86
Sep-98	86.11	Dec-95	103.30	Sep-98	86.11
Oct-98	86.87	Jan-96	103.27	Oct-98	86.87
Nov-98	90.46	Feb-96	103.45	Nov-98	90.46
Dec-98	90.10	Mar-96	103.72	Dec-98	90.10
Jan-99	88.93	Apr-96	103.93	Jan-99	88.93
Feb-99	89.31	May-96	104.08	Feb-99	89.31
Mar-99	89.43	Jun-96	104.45	Mar-99	89.43
Apr-99	88.48	Jul-96	104.64	Apr-99	88.48
May-99	89.75	Aug-96	105.12	May-99	89.75
Jun-99	90.04	Sep-96	105.38	Jun-99	90.04
Jul-99	89.53	Oct-96	106.05	Jul-99	89.53
Aug-99	86.12	Nov-96	106.31	Aug-99	86.12
Sep-99	81.18	Dec-96	106.51	Sep-99	81.18
Oct-99	81.20	Jan-97	107.17	Oct-99	81.20
Nov-99	83.16	Feb-97	108.89	Nov-99	83.16
Dec-99	84.49	Mar-97	109.73	Dec-99	84.49
Jan-00	86.64	Apr-97	109.69	Jan-00	86.64
Feb-00	87.61	May-97	109.15	Feb-00	87.61
Mar-00	86.97	Jun-97	108.69	Mar-00	86.97
Apr-00	86.43	Jul-97	94.46	Apr-00	86.43
May-00	85.79	Aug-97	91.92	May-00	85.79
Jun-00	84.66	Sep-97	83.31	Jun-00	84.66
Jul-00	82.90	Oct-97	81.87	Jul-00	82.90
Aug-00	82.25	Nov-97	80.05	Aug-00	82.25
Sep-00	80.79	Dec-97	72.55	Sep-00	80.79
Oct-00	79.10	Jan-98	63.75	Oct-00	79.10
Nov-00	76.98	Feb-98	72.49	Nov-00	76.98
Dec-00	78.26	Mar-98	82.00	Dec-00	78.26

Note: 1994 = 100.

Source: Bank of Thailand.

Appendix 7.7
Manufacturing Exports Classified by Technological Activities

Labour-intensive products	Technology-intensive products	Resource-based products
Garment	Computers and parts	Sugar
Textile and yarn	Integrated circuits	Molasses
Footwear	Telecom equipment	Canned foods
Toy and games	Other electrical circuit apparatus	Cement
Precious stones, jewellery	Electrical appliances	Rubber products
Travel goods	Transformers, generators, motors	Furniture and parts
Artificial flowers	Chemicals	Ceramic products
Sports goods	Plastic products	Petroleum products
Leather products	Motor vehicle and parts	
	Base metal products	
	Ball bearings	
	Electrical wire, cables	
	Clocks, watches	
	Medical and surgical instruments	
	Photo, cinema apparatus	
	Optical appliances	
	Containers	

Source: Bank of Thailand.

8. Anti-trust Law and Competition Policy in Vietnam: Macroeconomic Perspective

Le Viet Thai, Vu Xuan Nguyet Hong and Tran Van Hoa

8.1 ISSUES AND ASPECTS OF ANTI-TRUST LAW AND COMPETITION POLICY IN VIETNAM

8.1.1 Changes in Perception on Competition and Monopoly during Vietnam's Economic Transitional Process

Competition

The traditional viewpoint on competition during the transitional period of a centrally planned economy such as Vietnam is that competition was an element of the market economy and capitalism. It was thought to be ugly and immoral, like 'big fish eats small fish', because it caused economic crisis and turmoil, bankruptcy, unemployment, and so on. It was even blamed by some mass media organisations for causing social evils such as fraud and corruption, which in fact were not created by competition but by human greed and the desire to do better than other competitors or to serve blindly the shareholders (the cases of Emron and WorldCom in the US during 2002 were typical examples of these). Capitalism and its competitive (or animal) spirit sometimes also communicated incorrect news to reduce competitiveness on some products. In addition, economic or financial policy decisions made by some state bodies and officials often discriminated one firm against the others, especially in business registration and quota allocation. All this has had the impact of impeding competition and distorting competitive relations in the market.

Since the international economic integration began in earnest worldwide recently, this kind of traditional perception on competition has changed and for the better. Both the Government and entrepreneurs have recognised the important

139

role of competition in the economy, especially in the global integration context. Many aspects of a positive impact of competition on the economy such as accelerating the reform, re-allocating resources and selecting viable businesses have been recognised. Firms in particular, and the economy in general, are gradually considering competition as a basic principle of the market economy even one with a socialist orientation.

This change in perception has also had a positive impact on the firms' performance and the content of the governmental policy in laying the foundation for a healthy competitive business environment in Vietnam. Many enterprises have invested in new technology and products to improve their competitiveness. Many policies and legal documents have been issued to create a legal framework conducive to the setting up of a competitive environment. One of these documents is the newly promulgated Enterprise Law, which permits on a large scale the entry of new businesses into the market.

Monopoly/Oligopoly

In Vietnam, monopoly goes closely with the issue of the definition of the role of State in the economy and this definition clearly affects the state intervention in it. There are a number of reasons for this. First, it is a strong belief that the monopoly of the state-owned enterprises (SOEs) is the only one that presently exists in Vietnam. Second, this monopoly has been created and maintained by government regulations. In other words, *all current monopolistic firms in the economy were established through administrative decisions, and no firm has become monopolistic through competition.* Third, bearing in mind the perception that monopoly or oligopoly of SOEs could help the Government to better manage the economy, many governmental agencies have been set up with the sole purpose of supporting, directly or indirectly, monopoly in a number of industries. The arguments for the maintenance of this monopoly are: national security, the leading role of the state sector and domestic production protection. In addition to the regulations issued by the central government, the local governments have also issued their own, which, to many, have irrationally segmented the market and created a monopolistic power for the enterprises located in the territories under their control.

Monopoly exists in diverse areas such as corporations and labour supply whereas the monopoly of patterns and innovations (this kind of monopoly is good for promoting innovations) is not being seriously supported. This neglect discourages research and development (R&D) in Vietnam, and therefore limiting the enhancement of the country's competitiveness.

Over the past years, however, at least the perception on competition has changed specially at the executive and administrative level of governance. This was expressed clearly in the speech by Prime Minister of Vietnam, Phan Van Khai, at the conference on Assessment of Organiseal and Operational Models of 90 and 91 – General Corporation (GC) in Hanoi on 1–2 March 1999: 'If monopoly exists business talents cannot be mobilised. Monopoly should be crossed out/regulated to improve the business performance, increase the competitiveness of goods and services'.[1]

8.1.2 Progress in Improving the Competitive Business Environment in Vietnam

Major changes in policies have been made to establish and develop a competitive business environment in Vietnam

Economic reform in Vietnam began with policies on expanding the rights of the people in doing business, including production, trade, and price setting, and, subsequently, of diversifying the form of ownerships in the economy. By issuing the Foreign Investment Law (1987) and the Company and Private Enterprise Law (1990), the form of multiownerships was officially recognised and legally protected. More specifically, the 1992 Constitution (Article No. 28) confirms that the rights and benefits of producers and consumers are protected.

The legal framework for economic transactions in the market-oriented economy has been gradually established through many codes, laws, and legal documents such as the civil code, criminal code, labour code, taxation laws, commercial law, legal documents on economic contracts, and so on. The rights to make decisions of both producers and consumers have also been expanded. The dual-price systems have been gradually scaled down to the level that the Government only sets prices for some strategic goods and services. The prices of almost all goods and services are currently set by the conditions of supply and demand in the market. The so-called situation 'forbid to cross the river, and open up the market' was changed into the one whereby goods are freely traded all over the country. During the process of preparing to join the regional and international trade organises (such as the ASEAN and APEC and currently the WTO), many trade liberalisation measures have been applied in order to gradually open up the economy to the outside world.

As a result, many important aspects of development, including ownership diversification, gradual production, trade, price liberalisation, and gradual international integration, have created the basic conditions for the establishment and operation of a competitive business environment. Competition has taken place not only in the goods and services sectors of Vietnam but also between Vietnam's locally made products and imported products; not only among the domestic firms but also between domestic and foreign-invested companies.

Many achievements have been gained by improving the competitive business environment

Lifting the barriers to entry to the market has improved the quantity, quality and variety of the supply of goods and services in many industries in the country.

Consumer choices have been expanded. Trading activities have become more 'exciting'. Many firms have produced highly competitive products, which not only have taken more significant shares in the domestic market but also gained a share in the international market.

At the same time, many firms have made losses due to their weak competitiveness. Their products cannot be sold sufficiently even to break even, and therefore, their workers have lost their jobs. Theoretically, this is a process of so-called 'selection and elimination' of the competitive mechanism. While this process creates partial losses (losses for firms, which are inevitable, but the workers could move to other employment), it improves quality and performance of the overall industry, accelerates the economic restructuring in the right direction, and therefore generates benefits for the society as a whole. The process can be regarded as 'a creative destruction' in the sense that it puts pressure on firms to improve or renovate technology, products, sale methods, distribution channels, and organise. As a result, this pressure increases the firms' competitiveness and successful entry into the international market.

Competition policies such as foreign trade liberalisation, including lifting quota on export-import licenses, reducing the number of prohibited and restricted import-export goods and services, increasing the number of export–import firms and so on, are beneficial to the export–import environment in Vietnam. These policies have the effect of reducing the transaction costs of exporting and importing and increasing export–import value, and therefore increasing the degree of openness of Vietnam's economy.

8.1.3   Problems of Discrimination

Discrimination is often observed and it occurs in many fields in all human endeavours. In economics, it is present not only in the policy-making process and in the contents of the legal documents, but also in the attitude and behaviour of the officials formulating the process or implementing the legal documents.

During the full-cycle administrative process of doing business, from registration to resources access (such as land, credits and labour supply) and production, the discrimination of one firm against the others, especially a SOE against non-SOEs or domestic against foreign-invested firms, is always there. Discrimination also exists in the legal documents and policies made by both the central and local governments. It exists particularly in the regulations of business registration and establishment, in the amount of taxes and the level of prices imposed on domestic and foreign invested firms, in the regulations of credit access, and in the allocation of the land of the state, and in dealing with private firms.

In Vietnam, regulations in the law on encouraging domestic investment for example, which aim at officially mobilising the resources of business of all kinds of ownership, also discriminate between state and private firms. Although many private firms have been certified to be provided with preferential treatment according to this law, they have not actually received as much as the state enterprises.[2]

Many governmental agencies regard private firms as dishonest businesses. This attitude possibly explains why government inspection agencies visit private firms more frequently than the state ones. In addition, bank staff also hesitate in lending to private firms because they think the probability of being tracked down and held responsible for lending to the private sector would be higher than the one of lending to state enterprises when loans cannot be collected or repaid.

While there have been many changes, the attitude of the public towards private firms is still unfavourable. As a result, these firms can attract a smaller number of competent workers than the state firms or governmental agencies. The 'trader' in the country is still not as respectable as the entrepreneurs in other developed countries. The mass media has reported the cases of bad business deals of private firms more often than those of the state sector. This kind of behaviour by the public distorts seriously the image of the private sector. To some extent, in the eye of the public, the private sector means tax invasion, fraud, and so on.

The discrimination of state against private firms may lead to the development that some individuals can take advantage of the preferential treatment given to the state firms to seek profits for themselves and to 'squeeze' money from the state budget. The discrimination also affects negatively the competitive business environment, and more importantly, it affects the people's confidence in the policies of reform and the strategy of the Government and the Vietnamese Communist Party.

8.1.4 Problems of the Market Structure

Administrative obstacles to market entry and exit

Administrative obstacles in business establishment and registration Although the Government and the Vietnam Communist Party encouraged the development of a multisectoral economy by issuing the Company and Enterprise Law in 1990, changes arising from the regulations have taken place only slowly. The old perception that 'people can only do business in the fields that the Government allows' has prevented people from entering the market. This has led to a stagnation of the economy. As a result, the number of firms in many fields has remained quite small, and these firms did not have the pressure exerted upon them to renovate or to restructure.

The Enterprise Law, promulgated in 1999, came into effect on 1 January, 2000, and was a breakthrough for lifting almost all administrative barriers to market entry, and has created a new atmosphere for the business community. For the first time, the rights of the people in doing business, which were regulated

---

Box 1:
Private Enterprises: Public Perceptions

In 1999, the Mekong Project of Development Facility (MPDF) conducted a survey on the attitude of the public towards private firms in Vietnam. Results of the survey showed a picture of the private sector through the perceptions of the public as follows:[3]

1   According to public opinion, the private sector is not good. They are opportunists and pure profit-seekers.
2   Private firms are not good employers. Students and their parents do not want to work for private firms.
3   Credit agencies do not want to lend money to private firms since they are dishonest, risky and not backed by the state.
4   Officials said that the fixation about the private sector is driven by ideology.

Consequently, there is discrimination of the commercial banks in lending to the private firms:[4]

•   Only 18 per cent of the total number of interviewees supported lending to the private sector while 80 per cent preferred lending to the state although both private and state firms can meet the conditions required by the banks.
•   Three out of four most important conditions in the lending of banks are in favour of state firms (95 per cent of state firms can meet the conditions while only 10 per cent of private firms can).

The above opinions was expressed even 93 per cent of interviewees said the private sector was important to economic development, and 23 per cent said the private sector was efficient (the number of state firms being efficient was 15 per cent).

---

in the Constitution, were institutionalised. People can do business in all fields that are not legally prohibited. As a result of this law, in 2000, 14 400 new enterprises were established, an increase of 350 per cent from 1999. It should be noted that, during its implementation period, the law faced many objective as well as subjective difficulties. At the moment, some remaining barriers to entering the market still exist:[5]

1   Some Governmental agencies have not issued constructive legal documents to guide the implementation of the Enterprise Law. Many investors could not register in some industries because many regulations on the conditions of those industries have not yet been issued.

2   Many public authorities have delayed the implementation of the Law, or contravened the Law. For example, a number of districts or communes did not follow correctly the new procedures for business registration in the household economies, or refused to let investors register in some industries which were legally permitted. Other districts or communes even still maintain the old licences, which had already been made redundant according to the new Law. Some of these licences include, for example, licences on slaughter and electronic installation businesses.

The above obstacles have reduced the potential positive impact of the Enterprise Law, and maintained a number of barriers to the market entry. This state of affairs not only has a negative impact on improving the competitive business environment but also discourages the people from doing business. It reduces the confidence of investors, and therefore affects badly the country's economic development. The maintenance of an inappropriate licence system will have the effect of nurturing the old mechanism of the so-called 'ask-give', creating opportunities for corruption, slowing down the pace of economic restructuring, and will be a reason for numerous firms for not actively renovating to increase their corporate performance. The experiences of the implementation of the Enterprise Law show that, in order to implement successfully this Law, a comprehensive administrative reform is also needed. Therefore, the determination of the leadership in carrying out this reform is seen as a vital factor for the success of the implementation of the Law.

Obstacles in bankruptcy   Theoretically, bankruptcy is a normal activity during the selection–elimination process of the free market. The consequences of bankruptcy are only short term. Bankruptcy is in fact a factor to speed up economic restructuring, to re-allocate efficiently resources, and to increase the competitiveness of the economy as a whole.

In Vietnam, the Bankruptcy Law was issued in 1993. However, due to many reasons, the Law has not yet been effectively implemented. Specifically, the parties that have the rights to claim bankruptcy (such as enterprises, labour union, creditors) all do not want the firms to go bankrupt, due to complicated and unclear administrative procedures. In the US, there were 1.5 million firms that applied for bankruptcy in 1998, 1.3 million in 1999, and 1.25 million in 2000. In Vietnam, seven years after the promulgation of the Bankruptcy Law, only 100 firms have applied for bankruptcy. In Ho Chi Minh City, only three firms have gone bankrupt, four were in the process, and the remaining nine were not eligible to go bankrupt.[6]

The weak effectiveness of the Bankruptcy Law has had a negative impact on the competitive business environment and the economy. It has been claimed that the Law maintains viable firms, therefore slows down the process of resource re-allocation and economic restructuring. At the moment, many 'dead' firms are still 'fed' by the banks with the hope that these banks can collect their loan repayments. This not only supports the inefficient firms but also wastes the scarce capital of the banks.

High capital accumulation of SOEs in some industries   One of the important factors hindering competition in Vietnam is the market structure. Although the country has prepared to move to a market-oriented economy, it still heavily depends on the state sector that has a high accumulation of capital. During the 1980s, almost all industries had enterprise associations which associated all enterprises horizontally, and associations of enterprises which associated all enterprises vertically. When more autonomy was given to the enterprises, almost all above associations revealed their weaknesses and therefore went into divestitures. At about the same time, competition began. However, the establishment of a group of so-called 90 and 91 – General Corporation (GCs) distorted the market structure until 1994–95.

Figure 8.1 shows the accumulation of capital of GCs, especially 90-GCs. The revenue and contribution of GCs to the state budget seem to demonstrate

---

Box 2:
Capital Accumulation Through Administrative Measures
by Establishing the General Corporation[7] (GCs)

At the moment, the number of members in the GCs, independent accounting enterprises, was 1140. This accounts for 20 per cent of the total number of current state enterprises, 54 per cent of total state capital value, 68 per cent of total revenue of all state enterprises, and 82 per cent of total contribution of state enterprises to the state budget. More specifically, 18 GCs had 342 independent accounting-company members, making up 6 per cent of total number of state enterprises, 36 per cent of total state capital, 57 per cent of total revenue and about 60 per cent of total contribution of state enterprises to the state budget.

---

that GCs operate efficiently. However, this performance is probably attributed to the monopolistic position of GCs in the economy. Assuming that these GCs are really in the competitive environment (perhaps by removing all import barriers), then it is certain that the trend in the above figure would change. The establishment of GCs can be a positive development but it may hamper the setting in train of a competitive business environment, and create unnecessary monopoly in some industries.

In some provinces in Vietnam, the local authorities have set up barriers to protect local enterprises by preventing goods produced outside from entering the local market. For instance, a number of authorities have issued regulations that local restaurants could only sell beers produced locally, or local construction

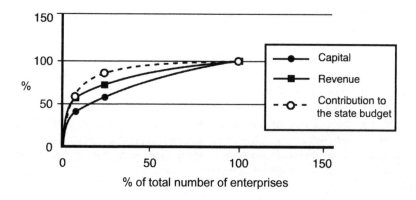

Figure 8.1   Capital Accumulation of GCs in the State Economic Sector

companies could only use local cements, or school students could only buy insurance from local insurance companies, and so on. This kind of administrative measures has a negative impact on the consumers' benefits.

8.1.5   Collusion Among Companies Impedes Competition

Collusion of firms may have either a negative or positive impact on the economy. Those firms that aim at nationalising, standardising, specialising production, and especially at empowering their negotiating positions in the international market, clearly bring benefits to the economy. On the contrary, those firms that aim at setting high prices and dividing the market will have a negative impact on the competitive business environment in particular, and affect the society in general.

In many countries, the regulations prohibiting negative collusions are the major contents of the anti-trust law. Depending on the local situations, some of these countries forbid horizontal collusion, while some others forbid vertical one.[8] At the primary stage of economic transition, the state sector accounts for a large part in the economy's activities. In this case, the collusion driven mainly by the ideology of the centrally-planned regime is usually harmful to the economy because it sets high prices and divides the market. However, this behaviour sometimes is artificially justified by very 'attractive' objectives such as price management or consumer protection from the private traders. It is a popular belief in Vietnam that local enterprises often collude with each other to become an association to set high prices. The association of taxi companies or transportation firms can be regarded as a typical example.

The collusion against competition is usually difficult to be prove. Therefore, it is more difficult to solve this issue than other problems. However, if a country has no appropriate measure to eliminate this kind of collusion, the consequences may be very serious.

8.1.6   Monopoly and Regulating Monopolies

Monopolistic companies in Vietnam

The monopolistic companies or oligopolistic companies in Vietnam were established through administrative decisions rather than through competition. Therefore, there were only state monopolies and no private or foreign invested monopolies. Many forms of monopoly existed in Vietnam: monopoly, monopsony, oligopoly, oligopsony, national monopoly or local monopoly.[9] The concept of natural monopoly has not yet been studied in line with current technological development.[10] Many industries artificially have a status of monopoly because they are regarded as natural monopolies. For example, electricity and water production and distribution are currently essentially state monopolies although they can be contracted out to the private sector.

Apart from the above subjective reasons, there are technically objective reasons for being a monopoly in Vietnam. Specifically, the capital requirement of a number of industries is fairly high when compared to domestic aggregate demand such as steel and cement. This means that so long as these products cannot be exported, the oligopoly of the state companies in this industry remains.

Box 3:
Price Collusion Broken Up, Consumers Benefited

Decision No. 19 of the Prime Minister abolished the association of 14 taxi companies in Ho Chi Minh City. At the same time, the entry of the Sao Viet Transportation Collective with 300 vehicles which offered much lower fares than the above association (VND8000 against VND12 000 per km) created a fierce competition against the association. Sao Viet in fact broke up the price collusion of the association that previously was supported by government regulation. This regulation stopped licensing taxi business and the one-price fees for taxi services under the control of the Department of Road Transport, Ministry of Transportation and Communication. In fact, this department did not legally have the authority in taxi-fare management.

It is notable that the above association was maintained for quite a long time with the support of the central government's agencies and local authorities whose objective was to regulate the over-supplied taxi market in Ho Chi Minh City. However, the trend of increasing prices of taxi services until 2000 proved that supply was still lower than demand, and therefore competition in this market could bring benefits to the consumers.

In view of the above reasons, while a market-oriented economy has been officially introduced into Vietnam over the past decades, the monopoly and oligopoly of SOEs still exist in such industries as coal mining, metal production, electricity and water production and distribution, telecommunications, financing, banking and insurance services. In these industries, there is a GC (either 90- or 91- GC) such as Coal GC, Tobacco GC, Electricity GC, Telecommunications GC, Insurance GC and so on. These GCs consist of many state enterprises. In this case, it is a state monopoly as a result of a collusion of state enterprises.

Regulating monopolies
Due to a lack of competition, the price of goods and services in monopolistic industries is usually high. These industries also do not provide good services to the customers. As a result, the Government must supervise and regulate monopolistic companies to prevent them from abusing their monopoly power and doing harm to the benefits of the customers. The remedy includes the supervision of prices and quality of goods and services.

Table 8.1
Prices of Goods and Services in Vietnam in Comparison
with Other Countries (USD)

Goods and services	Prices in Vietnam	Prices in other countries
Telecommun- ications • Instalment (/time)	In Hanoi and Ho Chi Minh cities: USD 90	Singapore: USD 57.64 Malaysia: USD 52.35
• Telephone to Japan (3 minutes)	USD 7.75	Singapore: 2.17; Malaysia: 3.15; Philippines: 3.75; Thailand: 3.24; Indonesia: 2.31; China: 4.3
• Telephone	From Ho Chi Minh city to America: 3.8/ minute	America to Ho Chi Minh: 1.5/minute
Electricity 6-22 KV	0.06/kwh	Singapore: 0.05; Malaysia: 0.052; Philippines: 0.09; Thailand: 0.03; Indonesia:0.014; China: 0.044
Fresh water	0.21-0.47/m^3	Malaysia: 0.3; Philippines: 0.26; Thailand: 0.25; Indonesia: 0.2; China: 0.13
Sugar	0.48/kg	0.2/kg
Cement	57/ton	43/ton

In Vietnam, the capability to supervise prices is weak due to poor or underdeveloped receipt and accounting systems. Therefore, price supervision cannot yet be done effectively.

In addition to high prices, the quality of goods and services in monopolistic industries is very poor. Customers are always the losers in this case. For example, they have to bear all the costs when the supply of water, electricity and telecommunications to their residences is cut off or their aviation flights are delayed. Meanwhile, the suppliers or producers can always terminate the supply contracts when the customers do not pay on time. While the association of consumers' protection has been established in some cases, the role of these organises is very negligible.

Other negative impact on the economy of monopoly
Negative impact on the business environment High prices not only create losses for the consumers but also distort the business environment. They particularly affect foreign investment. Many foreigners have to give up their plans to invest in Vietnam not only because of the complicated administrative procedures but also of high prices of the essential services when compared to other countries in the region.

Creating income inequality and distorting resource allocation Monopolistic profits also are not taxed properly. They go partly into the individual's pockets, therefore causing disparity in the income of the workers in the monopolistic industries. On the other hand, these profits do not indicate correctly the performance of monopolistic industries. This leads to a misallocation of resources in the sense that the investment flows into these industries are, in fact, inefficient. The examples for this situation can be found in the mechanical, cement and sugar industries in Vietnam.

In addition, the profits of monopolistic or oligopolistic industries do not reflect the efficiency of these industries. Being protected, the prices of goods and services in these industries are higher than the world prices in similar industries. As a result, the enterprises in the monopolistic industries can earn profits although their technologies are outdated. A bizarre outcome of this situation is that, since profits can still be made, the local authorities may establish more state firms in these industries to reap profits for the local budget. Now if the number of these industries increases, the prices in them may fall. This may lead many state firms to go bankrupt. As a result, the state has to rescue these firms. Thus, the society as a whole has to bear the resulting high costs. In Vietnam, the cement and sugar industries are two typical examples of this situation.

Vietnam is different from the developed or even developing market economies. The monopolistic status in the country is affected by identifying the role of the state sector in it. Many experts have regarded SOEs as the leading example of state monopoly. While state monopoly may be maintained by the

Table 8.2
Income in State Sector[11] (1999, VND/person/month)

	Amount	%
Average income	698 300	100.0
Five highest income industries		
1. Transport, storehouse, communications	1 322 200	189.3
2. Electricity, gas, and water production and distribution	1 244 900	178.3
3. Mining industry	1 234 300	176.8
4. Real estate and consultant service	1 076 000	154.1
5. Financing and banking industries	896 000	128.3
Five lowest income industries		
1. Educational and training services	487 600	69.8
2. Agricultural and forest industries	493 400	70.1
3. Cultural and sport industries	495 400	70.1
4. Health service	515 500	73.8
5. Technological and science industries	543 000	77.8

state, it should also allow other SOEs to enter the industries. This policy will bring benefits to the whole society. For example, recently, the Government allowed a military telecommunications company, Vietel, to do business in the area from Hanoi to Ho Chi Minh City. The price of telecommunication services of Vietel is half of that of another post and telecommunications company that had the monopoly in this industry.

8.1.7 Unhealthy Competition

Competition is a very important factor in the market economy. As we all are aware, competition may have both negative and positive impact on the economy. Therefore, it needs to have a framework or policy that minimises the negative impact and maximises the positive impact. Due to a lack of an appropriate legal framework and the usually poor compliance of the law by the people, many unhealthy competitive activities[12] have taken place in Vietnam during its transition period.

While there has not yet been a unified definition of unhealthy competition, unhealthy competition is, generally speaking, an action which competes by using illegal tools or immoral measures. Recently, these unhealthy competitive actions appear more frequently with increasingly sophisticated tricks used by the companies concerned. Some of these tricks are described below.

Fake goods

Fake goods appear frequently in Vietnam and in several forms such as fake quality, fake trademark, fake of both quality and trademark.[13] The phenomenon that a good's quality is only good at the time of the good's offering stage is popular even in business dealings with foreigners. The trick of using the trademark of 'real' goods has decreased but still exists. In fact, there is a recently reported case to imitate the trademark which has the name and logo similar to the real goods.

Dishonest advertisement

Over the past decade, the advertisement industry in Vietnam has developed quickly ranging from a simple introduction of goods and services to impressive and sophisticated advertisement programmes. However, the advertisement sometimes exaggerates the real characteristics of the products or hide their bad features. This happens especially for new medicine and chemical goods. Even a new medicine like Malatonin, which is forbidden abroad, was still advertised for sale in Vietnam.[14]

Fake promotion

Besides advertisement, Vietnam's firms often use promotional programmes to attract customers. Apart from the real promotional programmes, there are signs that these companies do not carry out promotional programmes honestly. For example, recently, a milk company, Foremost, held a promotional programme from 15 January 2001. As announced, a customer would win the highest prize worth VND100 million if there were three stars on the milk bottle they bought. However, two customers, one in Kontum and one in Ho Chi Minh City, got the bottles with three stars, but the company did not give them the VND100 million prizes as advertised. Instead, the company gave only two photographic equipments worth VND1.05 million apiece with the argument that the three stars on their milk bottles were not on one continuous line. This condition was, in fact, not informed to the consumers before.[15] In addition, almost all results of the promotional programmes were not publicly informed, therefore, the customers have a feeling of being cheated in these promotional programmes.

Slandering to damage images of rivals

Slandering rivals to damage their images has been used by many companies in Vietnam. This appears in various forms such as verbal communications or using modern technical tools.[16] More dangerously, some Government agencies either intentionally or unintentionally have assisted in these behaviours by passing wrong judgment on some victims who were slandered.

Dumping
A typical example for this anti-competitive behaviour is the competition in the soft drink market. After entering Vietnam's market, two companies, Coca Cola and Pepsi, reduced prices many times.[17] These kinds of dumping were hidden under the campaign of 'aggressive' promotion programs. Consequently, many Vietnamese soft-drink companies went out of business unjustly. Since that 'victory', Coca Cola has increased the prices of its products by 25 per cent, and currently competing with only Pepsi, its permanent rival.[18]

In addition to the above 'formal' unhealthy competitive actions, there are other 'informal' ones that it is hard to find clear evidence of. These include such actions as collusion in bidding and corrupting officials to inspect unreasonably rivals. The last case needs amplification: if there is an inspection by the Government agency in front of the company's customers, immediately customers will think badly of the company although inspectors do not find anything wrong with the company. As a result, it is hard for the company to restore the image in the eyes of its customers.

8.1.8   Overall Assessment of Factors Creating Achievements and Remaining Problems

Overall assessment
1   More than 10 years after the introduction of the open policy of Doi Moi (renovation), a competitive mechanism was established and has been operated in Vietnam in the sense that the number of firms in the market has increased, the prices of goods and services are set through the demand and supply conditions in the market, the rights of doing business have been expanded, and so on. Competition has positively impacted the economic reform in accelerating economic restructuring, pressuring firms to innovate to increase their competitiveness, increasing economic efficiency, integrating into the international economy, and improving the living standard of the country's population.
2   Although the Anti-trust Law has not been promulgated yet, a number of regulations have been issued to regulate activities relating to competition. These include the Foreign Investment Law, the Enterprise Law, the Civil Code, the Commercial Law, and so on.
3   In order to improve the competitive environment, the number of firms in the industries should be increased further. In this regard, the Enterprise Law has made significant contributions. However, if the obstacles hindering the implementation of the Enterprise Law are not solved quickly, the economy still remains not a level-playing field for businesses.
4   Economic reform goes into a new phase that requires high determination and radical changes of perception. In the previous phases, changes in the

perception to recognise the existence of the multisector economy were a factor for the resulting success. From now on, in order to achieve more successes, the state must eliminate all forms of discrimination among the enterprises.

5   Unhealthy competition occurs everywhere. This can only be eliminated if the legal framework and the law compliance of the firms and people are improved, and law violation is judged and settled seriously.

6   The establishment of GCs, especially monopolistic GCs, has negative impact on the market structure and the competitive business environment.

7   Monopolies or oligopolies in the market must be regulated properly, including the supervision of prices and quality of goods and services. Additionally, there should be a Government agency to be officially responsible for this issue with the assistance of the consumers association.

8   An asymmetric information system, especially in legal and policy information, is also a reason for inequality in the market.

Factors create achievements

The achievements of the above objectives in improving the competitive business environment can be attributed to the following factors:

1   Strong determination of the Government and the Communist Party in transforming the economy to a socialist-market-oriented economy by using less centrally planned management tools, and increasingly using the instruments of the market.

2   Ideological reform in making policies, mobilising domestic resources and, at the same time, attracting foreign investment.

3   Formulation of appropriate legal framework for competition.

4   State sector reform in the direction of creating for it a competitive environment.

5   Decrease in state subsidies to state firms in order to establish a level playing field for all businesses.

6   International integration to create pressure on local firms to improve their competitiveness and on policy-makers to establish a competitive business environment.

Remaining problems

Problems of viewpoints and perception on competition

1   The different viewpoints on the role of competition and monopoly in the economy have not yet been clarified. Discrimination occurs both in reality, in policies and regulations especially in business registration, bankruptcy, capital, labour and land access, as well as exports and imports.

2   The leading role of the state sector is identified with a monopolistic role, this therefore does not motivate the state firms to reform to improve their performance. This situation would create losses for the society as a whole. There are many unreasonable arguments that were being used for maintaining a state monopoly. As a result, the number of monopolistic industries is quite large. That clearly limits competition.

Institutional problems

1   The legal framework on competition has not yet been completed. Law compliance is poor, there are therefore many unhealthy competitive actions in Vietnam.
2   There have not yet been regulations and an official institution to regulate monopolies.
3   The administrative procedures for doing business are not yet clear. They are in fact complicated, unspecified, inappropriate, and not transparent. This discourages investors and creates room for corruption.

Other problems

1   The administrative procedure is complicated. Therefore, the transaction costs in doing business in Vietnam are high for some firms, but low for others. This does not create a level playing field in doing business.
2   SOE reform has been implemented slowly. Many SOEs are still assisted by the state providing capital. This not only eats up the state budget but also creates inequality in the business environment.

8.2   RECOMMENDATIONS

8.2.1   Experience of the Countries in the Region and Other Transitional Economies

Establishing the legal framework or policy for competition is very important in building a healthy competitive business environment, in increasing competitiveness and in speeding up the international integration process. Many countries have tried to establish this legal framework.[19] Based on the experience of these countries, some lessons can be drawn:

1   In order for competitive policies to be most effective, the benefits of the society as a whole must be the first priority. More specifically, economic efficiency and consumers' benefits are preferential objectives in formulating

these policies. It may be the case that a group of people may be worse off as a result, but that is the short-term transitional costs.

2   Establishing a giant corporation such as a chaebol in Korea does not only have a negative impact on the business environment but also distorts the performance of the corporations, and creates room for collusion between officials and firms to create losses for the society. In addition to this factor, a weak financial management and supervision can lead to the financial crisis of Thailand, Korea and other regional economies.

3   Equitisation, privatisation and competition have an interactive relationship. Privatisation took place at the beginning of the economic transition period in Russia. Anti-trust law was promulgated to assist in this process. Nevertheless, due to a weak law compliance and serious corruption, the privatisation process in Russia changed its situation from a controllable monopoly of state firms to an uncontrollable monopoly of private firms. This was a main factor that had destabilised and heavily depressed the Russian economy.

4   The reform process in Russia was carried out in line with the country's administrative reform. Since the perception and working habits of Russian officials were unchanged, the Government had to intervene heavily in the economy. Administrative offices also were regulated by the Anti-trust Law of Russia. This Law regulated that authorities and Governmental bodies were not allowed to issue legal documents that discriminated one firm against the other. It did not allow the establishment of a ministry or commission that monopolised an industry, and it did not allow public agencies to negotiate to impede competition.

5   Due to the existence of a huge state sector, the Anti-trust Law in China aims mainly at fighting unhealthy competition. It rarely regulates the market structure. China is different from Russia and the administrative reform in China has not yet been implemented radically and its Anti-trust Law does not regulate the behaviour of the administrative offices. As a result, the Anti-trust Law has not had profound and clear impact on the economy so far.

8.2.2   Major Viewpoints on Formulating Competition Policy in Vietnam

(a)   Acknowledging that regulated competition is a motivation of development
Competition is an important element of the market economy. However, unregulated competition would lead to monopoly sooner or later. This, in return, obstructs competition and will be a great obstacle to economic development. Due to a lack of responsibility on the part of the producers

in the market, competition may have negative impact on economic development. Thus, the Government needs to establish a legal system aiming at ensuring a healthy competitive business environment and bringing benefits to the society as a whole.

(b) **Improving legal system and its effectiveness in doing business to ensure equality in giving business opportunities to all individuals and organisations**

The Constitution and many other legal documents regulate the rights of doing business and equality among all economic units in the country, the practice is different. Discriminating one economic unit against another exists in many areas. Once there is no equality in the business process, competition cannot either take place or bring satisfactory results. Thus, the positive characteristics of the market economy cannot be made fully viable. That is a reason why the pre-condition to improve the competitive business environment should ensure equality in giving business opportunities to all people.

(c) **Ensuring freedom of consumers to make choices**

Being free to make choices is very important for the consumers. In the market economy, the producers supply whatever the consumers need. Thus, the choice of the consumers is a factor to formulate proper business strategies of firms. The price, quality and after-sale service of goods and services are the main criteria for the consumers to choose. These criteria help to measure the competitiveness of firms. We can therefore say that only when the customers are free to choose, the positive features of competition can be attained and promoted.

(d) **Players in the market must be responsible for their activities and enjoy the benefits according to the quality of their products**

The players or producers in the market make their own decisions and are responsible for them. It is up to the quality of those decisions to either reward or punish these players. If firms renovate and strengthen their competitiveness, they will make more profits and enhance their market share and prestige. On the contrary, if firms do not renovate and continue to rely on the assistance of the Government, they will suffer losses, a market share reduction and even bankruptcy. If this rule to innovate is institutionalised, firms will be careful in making decisions, and therefore the competitiveness of the economy as a whole increases.

(e) **State only should monopolise a very necessary industry, and this must be supervised closely**

During the economic transitional process in Vietnam, the state sector continues to account for a major portion of industries. Most of these SOEs are granted many privileges, and are, therefore, more predominant than other firms. Reserved privileges in the market economy will hinder and distort competition. Thus, they should be reduced. In the case that the privileges cannot be cut off immediately, the state supervision of these SOEs must be strictly undertaken to prevent them from abusing their monopolistic power.

8.2.3   Short-term Measures

Based on the observed practices of competition in Vietnam, the international experience, and the viewpoints presented above, a number of short-term measures need to be taken by the state or the implementing agencies as follows:

1   Gradually reducing until ending discrimination in business.
2   Minimising unhealthy competition activities in the market.
3   Reducing the number of sectors that are monopolised by SOEs or abolishing barriers to other firms to enter the market to reduce a dominant role of the state sector.
4   In the case that the state monopoly must be maintained, the Government should not let one SOE monopolise that sector.
5   In the case that a monopoly still exists, there should be appropriate measures to regulate and supervise it, particularly in the price and quality of the products, to avoid the abuse of monopolistic position.

Sets of measures

Measures for discrimination
1   Repeal the legal documents that contain discrimination provisions.
2   Preferential treatments should be framed on the basis of 'post-preferential' and clear conditions to minimise the subjective factors impacting the approval process.

Measures for anti-competition
3   Establishing rules to prevent the collusion of firms in areas such as: price collusion, collusion to fragment the market and collusion to boycott outsiders.

Measures to reduce and regulate monopolies
4   Identifying and rationalising clearly the role of the state in the economy as well as of the leading role of the SOEs. Based on this, the number of monopolistic SOEs should be reduced.
5   Minimising administrative barriers to entering the market according to the Enterprise Law.

6   Studying in-depth the necessity for the existence of each GC. If GCs are indeed not essential, they should be divided into smaller ones to facilitate competition in that sector; identifying correctly the natural monopoly sectors (for example, in generating and supplying electricity, only power generation is a natural monopoly, while electricity transmission is not). This identification is a basis for dividing GCs into smaller groups.

7   Public services can be provided by the private sector through bidding, but not necessarily provided by SOEs. Government should keep only enterprises that play a strategic role in the economy.

8   Formulating appropriate regulations and mechanism to supervise enterprises which control markets in terms of its prices and quality of goods and services.

Measures for unhealthy competition

9   Clearly defining the concept of 'unhealthy competition' and formulating sanction measures, particularly for the cases which are not yet stipulated by the Civil Code, the Criminal Code, and the Commercial Law.

Measures to improve the information system

10   Encouraging the establishing of consumer associations with the main activities in providing information to the consumers and to identifying anti-competition activities.

11   Improving the legal and economic information system toward transparency; and simultaneously, quickly reforming the administrative system to further facilitate enterprises' operation.

Implementing organisation

1   Based on the documents of the IX Communist Party Congress, the Government has been issuing resolutions about controlling monopolies and encouraging a healthy competition in business. Consistent understanding about competition is a decisive factor to improve the business competitive environment regulated by laws in Vietnam.

2   Propagating the correct concept of competition through the mass media to aim at promoting a healthy competitive spirit in the market.

3   Ministries, agencies and local authorities should revise regulations in their authority that contain discriminative treatment.

4   Ministries, agencies and local authorities should consistently implement issued policies in respect of competitive environment improvement. Some of these are the Enterprise Law and other related Governmental Degrees, Degrees on assigning, selling and contracting small SOEs, import and export liberalisation (reducing the number of limited import and export commodities, lifting the quota, and so on).

5   Comprehensive studies about GCs should be carried out to select GCs that

are necessary to be kept by the state. The rest will be re-arranged to split into smaller companies to be able to compete with each other.

6   Drafting an anti-trust law to submit to the next National Assembly and based on the above key viewpoints; Amending the Bankruptcy Law.

7   Capacity-building and training officers about competition policy and preparing to establish a specialist organisation in this area.

8.2.4   Long-term Solutions

Basically, long-term solutions will focus on three directions: adjusting the market structure (diminishing accumulation of capital), regulating business behaviour and supervising monopolistic firms in the market.

Regulating business behaviour

The process of Vietnam's economic transition had been implemented over 15 years. A number of markets have been set up, but the competition mechanism has not yet been well operated. Many business behaviours which may be regarded as hindering the positive aspects of competition still are in existence. These behaviours can be categorised into three groups: unhealthy competitive behaviours, the behaviours of limiting competition and the content of discriminative treatment in the legal documents or in the behaviours of officers in the state agencies.

The discriminative provision in legal documents and in officials' attitude should be stamped out

Notably, the origin of this type of discrimination can be found in the state documents or in the attitude of the officials implementing the legal documents. As a result, the regulated objective of the Anti-trust Law and related legal documents should not only include the relevant enterprises but also the state bodies and Governmental officials.

Preventing unhealthy competition

Preventing unhealthy competition aims at facilitating efficiency of a mechanism of reward and punishment for competition. In addition, it protects the consumers' and producers' benefits. In order to do so, it is necessary to clearly and specifically define unhealthy competition. This definition needs to be legalised and a simultaneous sanction for violation should be established. A supervising organise should also be set up. All cases of violation should be solved by an appropriate legal organise.

Preventing collusion that hinders competition

Preventing collusion that impedes competition is a major content of the anti-trust law in almost all countries. Discovering and solving this collusion is not easy, because the evidence is hard to find. While this phenomenon is not popular in Vietnam, the regulations should be quickly established to prevent its occurrence in the future.

Adjusting the market structure
A high level of capital accumulation in economic structure in Vietnam is due to many subjective and objectives reasons (discussed earlier). As a market structural adjustment needs time to be carried out, this adjustment may depend on the following factors:

- Progress of the SOE reform;
- Deregulating the business in terms of entering and exiting the market; and establishing a fair business competitive environment;
- Capability to widen the markets for Vietnam's products.

In the years to come, the measures that can be taken to gradually adjust the market structure may be as follows:

Splitting the GCs which are not necessary to be kept by the government The relationship between the members in GCs presently is only in the administrative level. This relationship does not strengthen their competitiveness. By contrast, it gives to GCs an opportunity to control the market. Therefore, splitting GCs will facilitate further a competitive environment and promote SOE equitise.

Easing the conditions for market entry and exist A strict implementation of the Enterprise Law on the basis of ensuring the freedom of doing business according to the laws will strongly encourage domestic and foreign investors to invest in Vietnam. This does not only accelerate economic growth but also lessen the capital accumulation requirement of many state firms in the economy.

Stimulating SOE reform, initially, shifting from regulating state-owned enterprises by the SOE law to the Enterprise Law, and selling, contracting, and leasing small- and medium-sized SOEs. The Government should restructure SOEs by the above measures. By doing this, the collusion of SOEs and the government intervention in the business of SOEs will be reduced and the autonomy of the SOEs will increase. This can be considered an element of the necessary market structure adjustments.

Supervising monopoly

Reviewing and reducing the number of monopolistic sectors When the Government grants monopolistic or market-controlled position to one (or many) company/ies, the following principles should be carefully considered: the Government only invests and intervenes in the sectors that will have strong social impact on the whole society. In principle, the Government should allow the private sector to freely join the market. The Government should also split unnecessary monopolistic GCs into small groups. The maintaining of monopolistic GCs should be considered carefully. For example, the electricity industry should be only a monopoly for the distribution electricity network, but for electricity generation, it can be done by the private sector.

Strictly supervising prices of monopolistic products   The Government should not set a profit target for monopolistic SOEs rather than the targets of quality and prices. In this case, prices should be fixed in such a way as to maximise the benefits of the whole society. The Government should supervise the market-controlled companies to prevent them from increasing prices to harm consumers and from reducing prices to put pressure on their competitors.

Regulating minimum quality for monopolistic products   A popular phenomenon in the country is 'monopoly and authoritarian behaviours are always side by side'. Once there are no minimum criteria for monopolistic products, the consumers will certainly have to consume poor-quality goods. These criteria should be publicly informed to the consumers to be on the lookout. A compensative regulation should be established for the detection of poor quality products.

Encouraging and supporting establishment of consumer associations   The consumers associations will counteract the actions of market-controlled companies. They will be the most active player to help the state to supervise the quality and prices of the products. The Government should therefore encourage and support the establishment of such consumers associations.

Tendering for providing public services   In the past, the public services were provided by SOEs and they were considered as a sector that should be monopolised by the state. Recently, this kind of services has been tendered instead, and some positive results have been obtained in some areas. Thus, tendering and bidding are completely suitable in these fields.

8.3   COMPETITION POLICY AND ITS PROSPECTS IN VIETNAM

8.3.1   Necessary Conditions to Introduce Competition Policy in Vietnam

In order to carry out successfully the recommendations proposed in the previous sections, a number of basic conditions are required:

1   First, there must be a unified point of view from the central government to local authorities about the equally important existence of the non-state sector in the economy. Based on this view, subsidies to SOEs should be reduced step-by-step and gradually stamped out.

2   The Government must have a stable and sound policy to support the process of formulating and implementing its competition policy. The instability of the economy may lead to conducts of speculation, thereby nullifying the positive impact of the competitive mechanism in the market.

3   The Government should especially pay attention to the highly fair environment of the input factor markets, such as the credit market, the real estate market and the labour market.

4   The process of equitisating SOEs must interact with the improvement of the competitive environment. Without a level playing field, the driving forces of equitise will be nullified. On the other hand, the market structure will be affected by the equitisation of SOEs, so that a competitive policy can be easily implemented. As a result, the process of equitise of SOEs in particular and the reform of SOEs in general should be accelerated.

5   One of the main targets in the next stage of development is to integrate Vietnam into the world economy successfully. This integration would bring about both opportunities and challenges to the Vietnam economy. For a successful integration, the Vietnamese economy must raise its local and international competitiveness. In order to do this, the competitive environment must be established and maintained. In this context, an integration agenda must take into account the requirement of competition policy. Vice versa, competition policy must consider the conditions of international integration.

6   In the short term, when the capital accumulative level of corporations (SOEs and GCs alike) in the economy cannot be reduced immediately, the Government must supervise closely the monopolistic and oligopolistic enterprises. In order to do this, the accounting and auditing system must be improved to help the financial supervision of enterprises in general and large firms in particular.

7   There must be consumers associations to provide a counterbalance to monopolistic companies. Through these associations, unhealthy competition and abusive activities of companies will be fully investigated and brought to the attention of the public and, when appropriate, suitable punishment imposed.

8.3.2   Implementing Competition Policy in Vietnam: The Costs

The formulation and implementation of competition policy and law in Vietnam will certainly bring benefits to all in the society. However, this process can affect benefits of a number of groups in it.

Changing the thinking about the role of the state in the economy

Although the economic reform process has been carried out for more than 15 years, the way of thinking as well as the activities of the State officials have not changed very much. These officials still keep thinking that they have the rights to give favour and to manage the corresponding relationships with the people. This is an important factor that obstructs the mobilise of the potential of the people in doing business, and hinders the development of the non-state sector. *The renewed thinking of a State, which establishes the legal framework, supports and supervises businesses instead of the State, and which permits and decides the efficiency in economic operation and integration* will make a significant contribution to the development of the country. In this sense, everybody has *the rights to do business in the fields which are not forbidden by the State*. Bearing this idea in mind, the State should strengthen the legal framework, minimise the administrative interference in business and increasingly use indirect measures to manage the economy.

Changing roles of the state economic sector

Until now, the leading role of the state economic sector continues to be affirmed in the strategies and plans of economic development, which were approved by the IX Communist Party Congress. Nevertheless, it is necessary to have a clear and concrete understanding on the 'leading role' of the state economic sector to avoid the misunderstanding that the state economic sector must dominate all fields and must be large in terms of quantity but ignoring quality. In this sense, the cost is the expenses for the state sector reform. There must be some reduction in the number of sectors monopolised by the State. In some areas that the State maintains its monopolistic position, the Government should allow other SOEs to participate in these areas in order to avoid the 'monopoly of one SOE'. This one-SOE monopoly will influence the benefits of some current monopolistic SOEs but the process is for the better of all.

Changing the authorities of some state organises

The process of deregulation and license abolishment will also affect the benefits of some officials who are working in state organises. The ask-give mechanism will be limited. This does not mean that the authority of these organises will decrease. The process will only change the way of carrying out the authority from 'giving' to 'supervising'. In order to do this effectively, the state officials need to be retrained and re-educated and the facilities for working in the new environment need to be upgraded. This costs time and money but the benefits will more than compensate for them.

Solving social problems

Implementing competition policy will create some social problems. For instance, when some business firms go to bankrupt or close down, their workers will lose their jobs. Despite the fact that this is a short-term and structural unemployment, the Government should have timely and appropriate solutions to solve this unemployment situation.

8.3.3 Some Viewpoints on the Draft Anti-trust Law of Vietnam

From different perspectives, the Draft Competition Law of Vietnam[20] can be considered and evaluated differently. Based on our analysis in the preceding sections, some viewpoints on the Anti-trust Law can be given as follows:

The scope and objectives of the Anti-trust Law

- The competitive environment nowadays is not only influenced by the conduct of enterprises but also by administrative decisions of state agencies. Thus, for the effectiveness of this Law, *the Law should regulate also the behavioural decision-making of state agencies.* Specifically, amending and supplementing Clauses No. 1 and No. 2 that: all administrative decisions relating to competition and *state agencies should be subjected to this law.*
- Clause No. 3 is unclear. It is likely to be understood that almost all SOEs fall into a category of 'exceptional cases'. However, if SOEs are not subjected to this law, the unification of the economy will be broken, the market will be unreasonably fragmented, so that the Law cannot be effective and its objectives cannot be attained. Therefore, SOEs must be subjected to this Law.

The regulations on the corporate behaviour in respect of competition in the market

- As explained above, one of the behaviours impeding competition in the market is that of state bodies, such as the behaviour of creating illegal and irrational barriers. To include these behaviours, the Law's scope and objectives must be broadened.
- A criterion to define collusion which hinders competition (in Clause No. 10) is only in regard to the benefits of the consumers. Some other criteria should be added to be in line with the content of Clause No. 9, such as the collusion to boycott the 3rd party or competitor.
- Procedures of explanation are not relevant for all cases. In the case of oral negotiations without written documents, firms may not be able to explain adequately why. Another suitable solution should be found for this situation.
- The draft should provide supplements defining unhealthy competition conducts in Chapter 5 of the Law. These include fake promotion programmes or 'inappropriate' behaviour of state organisations.

Supervising monopoly

- There should be a more specific definition of a market-controlled position, which can be quantitatively measured (Clause No. 18, Article 1). For example, a market-controlled position may be the case when one firm controls more than 40 per cent of the market or the market share of the two biggest firms is over 60 per cent, or of the three biggest firms is over 70 per cent, and so on. While these firms do not collude with each other, they must be supervised because of their market-controlled position (this is a different situation from Clause No. 15).
- The definition of abusive behaviour is not precise, especially section c and d of Article 2 of Clause No. 18 'Capability...' is a status, and it is not a behaviour. All firms, which control the market, have this status.
- Explanation process (Clauses Nos. 20 and 21) is absolutely irrational and makes it difficult for enterprises to comply. This process is unrealistic and unsuitable to the market mechanism when the firms must ask for a permit from the state agencies once they want to change prices. This limits the dynamics of firms and creates room for state agencies to harass the enterprises. Another solution that does not trouble firms but ensure the appropriate supervision of state agencies should be developed.

The adjustment of economic structure

- Adjusting an economic structure is to split big enterprises and supervise the mergers of firms. Chapter 4 of the Law only mentions the supervision of the mergers of firms and it does not take into account the high level of capital accumulation of SOEs in Vietnam currently. Thus, this chapter should have some clauses about the splitting of large SOEs.

State management and Anti-trust Law implementation

- The state management organise on competition must have enough authority to carry out its tasks. When the state agencies are subjected to the Anti-trust Law, the agency which manages competitive issues should be independent in making its decisions. This agency must have authority to punish firms in the cases violating the law and to make decisions (not only being involved in the cases as pointed out in Clause No. 40 and appraised as in Clause No. 41).
- A competitive behaviour is a civilian behaviour, so that it should not be judged in a criminal court. When the behaviour relates to criminal law, this should be made clearly to offending firms in order to avoid penalising an economic relationship.

Other issues

- Important concepts related to competition should be added to the Law; the clauses about information collection and dispute solutions should also supplemented.

NOTES

1 Quy Hao, *Vietnam Economic News*.
2 Based on the reports of local authorities over all the country, the number of private firms, which were certified to be provided investment preferential treatment in 2000 was 1113 projects (accounting for 79.4 per cent of all projects) with a capital of VND10 371 billion (accounting for 67.9 per cent) employing 116 045 workers (accounting for 74 per cent). However, only 412 projects out of 1113 actually received preferential credit from the Development Assistance Fund, accounting for 37 per cent of all certified projects (whereas, the respective number of the state enterprises was 86.2 per cent). Moreover, total preferential credit lending to private firms accounted for only 22.5 per cent of all preferential credit, of which 32.9 per cent was assisted through low interests.
3 These are four out of seven points mentioned in the study No. 9 of the MPDF on the Private Sector.
4 This result was based on the questionnaires for staff of credit agencies.
5 According to the report after the one-year enforcement of the Enterprise Law.
6 *Saigon Economic Times*, No. 16, 12 April 2001.
7 Pham Hoai Thanh, Consolidating and Improving the Performance of GCs, *Enterprise Magazine*, No. 4, 1998.
8 Horizontal collusion is a collusion between firms that provide the same goods or services; vertical collusion is a collusion between firms that use products of each other.
9 Some local authorities use administrative measures to force the local people to buy local products or products of certain companies such as beer, cement, construction materials, insurance. This is a local monopoly.
10 For example, before, network industries such as the telecommunications industry may be considered as a natural monopoly. However, thanks to the development of new technology, nowadays, many telecommunications companies can use the same network, therefore, telecommunications is no longer a natural monopoly industry in several countries.
11 General Statistics Office (*Saigon Economic Times*, 31 August 2000).
12 Currently, there is not yet unified and clear definition of an unhealthy

competition action in the world. However, in general, unhealthy competition action may be defined as an action to compete by illegal tools or immoral measures, which harm consumers and competitors.

13   Le Tat Chien, 'Three kinds of fake goods', *Labor Newspapers*, No. 32/99, 24 February 1999.

14   Dr Nguyen Nhu Phat and Nguyen Thi Thu Hien, A report on practices of unhealthy competition in Vietnam's market in a Conference in September 2000 held by the Institute of State and Law, Hanoi.

15   'One more lesson in giving gifts', *Youth Newspapers*, No. 85, 9 April 2001.

16   In 1996, in some places of Southern Delta, a rumour was spread that eating arca caused leprosy, and a sugar cane laminating-machine killed a worker (according to an article 'Competing by Rumour' of Ho Chi Minh People's police newspaper on 17 July, 1996). In 1999, there was a rumour (even broadcast on VTV1) that Luc Ngan litchi caused encephalitis. Rumours were also communicated through the Internet on some kind of shampoo that caused cancer, injection needles injected HIV, sanitary napkin was made by an organic substance namely amiang, which harmed health.

17   In 1995, Coca Cola reduced its prices by increasing its can capacity from 207 ml to 300 ml without changing the price of VND1500; Pepsi also increased its can capacity to 500 ml with the same price of VND1600. Meanwhile, the prices of two Vietnamese soft drinks, Tribico and Festi, were VND1100/bottle of 207 ml, and VND2200/bottle of 200 ml respectively. In 1996, Coca Cola had a promotion campaign that buying three bottles would get one free, meaning 25 per cent cheaper in price. With the tax rate of corporate income of 8 per cent, and the tariff rate of input of 30 per cent, this price was much lower than costs.

18   Report by Tran Van Truong, and a report by Dr Nguyen Nhu Phat, and Nguyen Thi Thu Hien, *op. cit.*

19   For example: Pakistan (1970), Thailand (1979), Korea (1980), Sri Lanka (1987), Taiwan (1991); Hungary and Poland (1990), Bulgaria, Czech Republic, Kazakhstan, Latvia and Romania (1991), Belarus, Georgia, Moldovia, Ukraine and Uzbekistan (1992), Estonia and China (1993).

20   Draft 1st (Dated 8 May 2001).

REFERENCES

BMWi (1995), 'Wettbewerbspolitik in der sozialen Marktwirtschaft', Working Paper, Germany: Ministry of Economy.

CIEM (1998, 1999, and 2000), various papers presented at workshops on *Competition Policy,* Hanoi.

CIEM (1993), *Monopoly and Anti-Monopoly*, CIEM Research Program Paper, Hanoi.

CIEM (1995), *Measures and Policies to Encourage Competition and Regulate the Monopoly in the Market Economy*, CIEM Research Program Paper, Hanoi, 1995.

Dang Vu Huan (1996), 'Competition, Anti-illegal Competition and Monopoly Supervision', Working Paper, Ministry of Justice, Hanoi.

Government Committee on the Prices of Goods and Services (1996), *Solutions Control Monopoly and Unhealthy Competition in the Process of Vietnam Economic Transition,* Hanoi: Vietnam–Netherlands Research Program.

Laws of Some Countries: United Republic of Germany, United States, Russia, China, and Bulgaria, *passim*.

Le Viet Thai (2000), *Theoretical Basis and Practices for Building Competition Policy in Vietnam,* Hanoi: Labour Publishing House.

Oesterdiekoff (1992), 'Wettbewerbspolitik', paper by Friedrich Ebert Stiftung, Germany, Hanoi: CIEM.

Pittman, R. (1999), 'Why Competition Policy – Especially for Developing Economies', Discussion Paper, Hanoi: CIEM.

Schmidt, I. (1999), *Wettbewerbspolitik Kartellrecht*, Stuttgart: Lucius & Lucius,.

Various articles from *The Labour, The Young Newspapers, Saigon Economics Time, People Police Newspaper, and Business Forum,* passim.

Yasuda, N. (2000), 'The Evolution of ASEAN Competition Law within the APEC Framework', Working Paper, Hanoi: CIEM.

9.   Competition and SMEs in Vietnam

Charles Harvie

9.1   INTRODUCTION

Vietnam stands at an important crossroad in its transition from a planned to market oriented economy. Since the implementation of economic reform started with Doi Moi in 1986, supplemented with further reform from 1989, the economy experienced rapid economic growth during the period of the 1990s until 1997. Since this time GDP growth has noticeably slowed, partly due to the onset of the financial and economic crisis to afflict the region in 1997–98, and partly due to a disconcerting, and related, decline in foreign direct investment flows. Despite this adverse development there has been a remarkable transformation of the economy that has seen it become more globally oriented, as exemplified by a rapid growth of both exports and imports and with a significant contribution to the economy from the foreign-invested sector.

For Vietnam to once again re-establish high and sustainable rates of economic growth further restructuring and reform efforts are required. In particular, achieving further progress in establishing the institutional framework for a market economy is necessary, including: the enforcement of contracts; financial discipline and a hard budget constraint on state-owned enterprises; establishing the rule of law; and restructuring of the banking sector so that it operates along commercial lines. The country will also be required to make further progress in ownership reform, focusing upon: ensuring free and unrestricted entry to markets for all ownership forms, and the development of a start-up private sector; encouraging foreign direct investment; allowing the private sector a larger role in the management and ownership of currently state-owned enterprises; allowing unviable state-owned assets to be liquidated and their assets put to more productive use; and encouraging fair competition between different ownership forms, with the state, as a buyer, not discriminating against any form of ownership. These should form the core of the country's competition policy.

This chapter focuses upon the need for competition policy to encourage the nurturing, growth and development, specifically, of private sector small and medium enterprises (SMEs). Private entrepreneurship and enterprise reform can play a crucial role in the reform of the Vietnamese economy. There is a recognition that a dynamic non-state manufacturing sector, in particular, is a precondition for attaining the twin objectives of: (1) restructuring and slimming state enterprises; and (2) expanding non-farm employment and income opportunities. In particular, the ability to nurture and encourage the development of SMEs is of crucial importance not only in terms of creating employment, but also as a means of achieving sustainable economic development, a more efficient allocation of resources along the lines of the country's comparative advantage – that is, labour-intensive manufactured goods, expanded exports, a more equal distribution of incomes – and is essential for rural and regional development.

It has been increasingly recognised by regional economies in the wake of the financial and economic crisis that there needs to be a change in emphasis for industry policy. Industry restructuring, with a greater focus upon the development of SMEs, has occurred. Unless Vietnam is similarly able to restructure its economy, with an emphasis on the development of SMEs, it will find itself in a relatively weaker competitive position, vis-à-vis its regional neighbours, to capitalise on the recovery in the region as it gathers pace.

The chapter proceeds as follows. Section 9.2 conducts a review of Vietnam's recent economic performance and the contribution of the private sector to this. Section 9.3 provides a profile of Vietnam's SMEs. Section 9.4 identifies strategies for the promotion of the SME sector and for the development of the private sector in general. Section 9.5 discusses the important role of the Government and the key areas for the support and promotion of SMEs. Section 9.6 briefly identifies the core ingredients of an effective competition policy. Finally, Section 9.7 provides a summary of the major conclusions from this paper.

9.2 VIETNAM'S RECENT ECONOMIC PERFORMANCE AND THE CONTRIBUTION OF THE PRIVATE SECTOR

9.2.1 Vietnam's Recent Economic Performance

During the period of the 1990s Vietnam was one of the fastest growing economies in the world, achieving an annual average GDP growth rate of 7.4 per cent. This contributed to a rapid improvement in GDP per capita (see Figure 9.1). During this period of rapid economic growth there was a noticeable change in the structure of the economy, with the contribution of the agriculture sector to GDP declining from 40.6 per cent in 1990 to 23.8 per cent in 1999, the GDP share of the industry sector increasing from 22.4 per cent in 1990 to 34.3 per cent by 1999, and the share of the services sector increasing from 36.9 per cent of GDP

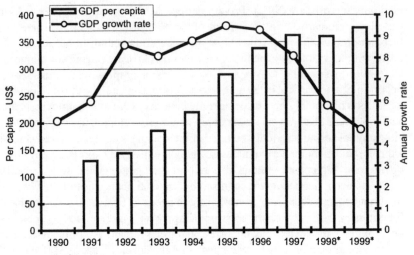

Note: * Preliminary.

Source: GSO Statistical Yearbooks, and UNDP computation.

Figure 9.1   Vietnam GDP, 1990–99

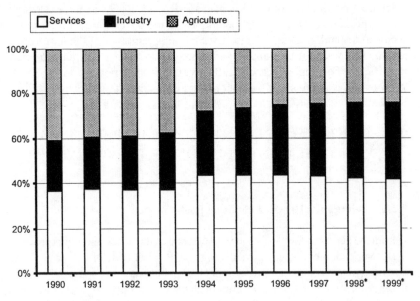

Note: * Preliminary.

Source: GSO Statistical Yearbooks.

Figure 9.2   Sectoral Shares of GDP, Vietnam, 1990–99

in 1990 to 41.9 per cent in 1999 (see Figure 9.2). Such a structural transformation is a typical and nearly universal feature accompanying economic development (see, for example, Chenery and Syrquin 1975).

On further analysis it can be found that this rapid rate of economic growth was led by the industrial sector. Table 9.1, taken from Belser (2000), shows that the average annual growth of GDP over the high growth rate period 1993–97 was an impressive 8.9 per cent. The major sector contributing to this growth was the industrial sector, where value added increased at an average annual rate of 13.4 per cent. The services sector also grew impressively at 9.4 per cent a year during this period, while the agriculture sector lagged behind with an average annual increase of 4.3 per cent. This accounts for the share of industry and services in GDP increasing relative to that of agriculture. The period of the 1990s has seen a rise in the importance of both the non-state sector and the foreign-invested sector in industrial production (see Figure 9.3). In 1990 the state sector contributed almost 68 per cent of industrial production, falling to just over 50 per cent by 1995. However in 1999 there was a further decline in its contribution to industrial production, down to just under 44 per cent. Therefore over half of industrial production in 1999 was from the private domestic and foreign sectors, with the contribution of the latter, in particular, worthy of note.

The rapid growth of the industrial sector has contributed to an expansion in industrial employment. Cross-country evidence provided by Gillis et al. (1987) indicates that over the period 1965 to 1983 developing countries experienced on average a growth elasticity of employment in industry of around 0.6. That is, industrial employment expanded at around 60 per cent of the rate of industrial output growth. In the case of Vietnam, however, industrial output growth has had only a moderate impact on employment. As indicated by Tables 9.2 and 9.3 the growth rate of industrial employment in Vietnam between 1992–93 to 1997–98 was 4 per cent per year. While respectable, this represents less than 30 per

Table 9.1
Industrialisation of Vietnam

	Average annual real GDP growth during 1993–97 (%)	Estimated share in total output in 1992 (%)	Share in output 1997 (%)
Total	8.9	100	100
Agriculture	4.3	31.6	25.2
Industry	13.4	27.3	33.1
Industry less construction	13.1	20.7	24.7
Services	9.4	41.1	41.7

Source: Belser 2000, p. 2.

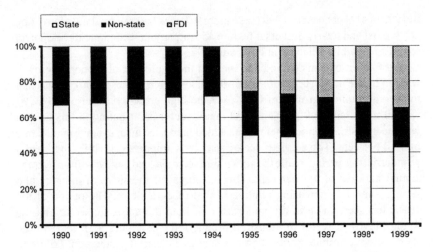

Note: * Preliminary.

Source: GSO Statistical Yearbooks.

Figure 9.3   Industrial Production by Ownership, Vietnam, 1990–99

Table 9.2
Industrial Employment Growth

	1992–93 (million)	1997–98 (million)	Absolute increase 1992/93 to 1997/98 (million)	% increase per year 1992/93 to 1997/98	Incremental employment distribution 1992/93 to 1997/98
Total employment	36.8	40.3	3.5	1.8	100.0
Agriculture	26.2	26.8	0.6	0.4	16.7
Industry	4.3	5.3	1.0	4.0	27.0
Industry less construction	3.8	4.3	0.5	2.6	14.8
Services	6.3	8.2	1.9	5.6	56.3

Note: Employment data is for people between 15 and 65.

Source: Vietnam Living Standard Surveys, 1 and 2.

Table 9.3
Employment by Sector

	Share in total labour force 1992–93 (%)	Share in total labour force 1997–98 (%)	% Change from 1992/93 to 1997/98
Agriculture	71.2	66.4	-4.7
Industry	11.8	13.1	+1.3
Industry and construction	10.3	10.7	+0.4
Services	17.0	20.5	+3.4

Source: Vietnam Living Standard Surveys, 1 and 2.

cent of the rate of industrial output growth. Consequently, despite the rapid growth of the industrial sector the share of industrial employment in total employment has only increased from 11.8 per cent to 13.1 per cent. Interestingly, when construction is excluded from the industry sector the record is even worse. Hence a key issue for policy makers in Vietnam is how best to benefit in terms of employment growth in the context of rapid growth in the industrial sector. In this regard the contribution of the private sector and SMEs will be of particular importance.

Table 9.4
Contribution to Industrial Production and Employment by Sector

	Industrial production growth (%) 1995–98	Share in industrial production growth (%) 1995–98	Share in industrial GDP (%) 1998	Share in industrial employment 1997–98 (%)
State sector	10.2	37.2	46.2	24.2
Foreign investment	22.7	46.5	31.8	11.5
Domestic non-state sector	9.2	16.2	22.0	64.3
Of which:				
• private and mixed	21.6	11.1	7.9	25.2
• collective	8.7	0.3	0.6	1.3
• households	4.0	4.7	13.5	37.8

Sources: General Statistical Office and Vietnam Living Standard Survey, 2.

There are a number of reasons to explain this sluggish growth of employment, and this can be identified with the aid of Table 9.4. This shows that in industry the state and the domestic non-state sectors grew rapidly over the period 1995–98. However, it is clear that the state sector dominates the domestic non-state sector, more specifically the private sector. In 1998 the state sector's contribution to industrial value added was more than twice that of the domestic private sector. State enterprises therefore contributed substantially to the expansion of industrial production, amounting to 37.2 per cent of Vietnam's total industrial growth between 1995 and 1998. This compared to only 16.2 per cent for domestic private companies. Foreign investment, however, was the most important single contributor to expanded industrial production.

By comparison to its contribution to industrial production the state sector's contribution to industrial employment is considerably less. State sector industrial employment was less than 25 per cent of total employment in this sector. The domestic non-state sector, by contrast, although contributing only 22 per cent of industrial output employed more than 64 per cent of industrial workers. A large proportion of these workers were in household enterprises. Of particular interest is the employment contribution of the registered private and mixed companies. Although contributing only 7.9 per cent of industrial GDP in 1998 they employed more workers than that of the SOEs.

Vietnam's slow employment growth in the industrial sector, therefore, arises from the state sector's strong growth but low labour intensity, and the private sector is still relatively small size. This poor employment performance can therefore be partially explained as a by-product of the transition period to a market economy, in which the growth of private enterprises is rapid but their overall contribution is small as a result of starting from a much lower base. Also, state enterprises, which tend to be concentrated in import substituting activities and are sheltered from both foreign and domestic competition, typically draw capital and other resources away from the private sector. This could have prevented higher rates of private sector growth and employment, and could be of concern for the attainment of longer-term growth and employment creation.

Another important feature of Vietnam's development process has been the increasing significance of international trade. Table 9.5 indicates that between 1992 and 1999, for example, the dollar value of imports and exports more than quadrupled, increasing the share of trade in GDP from 52 per cent to 58 per cent. In 1997 the share of trade in GDP reached a remarkable 86 per cent, a high level by international standards. Table 9.6 indicates that Vietnam's export growth was led by impressive growth in light manufactured exports, which in real terms grew by no less than 45 per cent a year and whose share in total exports rose from 13.5 per cent in 1992 to 36.7 per cent in 1997. Also remarkable is the strong rise in the value of agriculture exports, mainly reflecting the spectacular take-off in rice and coffee production. In only a few years Vietnam turned from

Table 9.5
Exports, Imports and the Share of Trade in GDP

Year	1992	1997	1999
Value of exports (million US$)	2581	9185	11 500
Value of imports (million US$)	2540	11 592	11 600
(Exports + Imports)/GDP (%)	51.6	85.7	58.0

Sources: General Statistical Office and UNDP.

Table 9.6
Export Growth by Sector

	Estimated average annual real growth 1992–97 (%)	Share in total exports in 1992 (%)	Share in total exports in 1997 (%)
Total exports	18.8	100.0	100.0
Agriculture	11.1	49.5	35.3
Heavy industry and minerals	12.3	37.0	28.0
Light industry	45.1	13.5	36.7
of which:			
• textiles and garments			16.4
• footwear			10.6

Source: Belser 2000, p. 5.

being a net rice importer into the world's second largest exporter with over 3.5 million tons in 1998.

The performance in manufacturing exports was supported by foreign investment. Vietnam's trade and taxation regimes now contain special provisions that allow export-oriented foreign enterprises to import duty free intermediate goods from abroad and to enjoy preferential tax rates. In addition, many joint ventures are also exempted from import duties on equipment goods, machine components, spare parts and transport equipment and materials. Table 9.7 shows that the dollar value of exports by foreign-invested companies, about 40 per cent of which stem from light manufacturing, grew by 80 per cent per year between 1994 and 1997. This raised the share of exports by foreign-invested companies from less than 4 per cent in 1994 to almost 20 per cent of total exports in 1997.

Table 9.7
FDI and its Contribution to Exports

	1994	1997
Total exports by foreign companies (US$ million)	161.1	1 790
Total light industrial exports by foreign companies (US$ million)	na	728
Share of FDI in total exports (%)	3.9	19.5
Share of FDI in light industry exports (%)	na	21.6

Source: Belser (2000).

9.2.2   Contribution of the Private Sector to the Economy

The Prime Minister in his opening speech to the National Assembly in November 1999, emphasised the importance of creating a climate conducive to private sector development. Farmers, household microenterprises, private SMEs and relatively large foreign-invested enterprises comprise the private sector in Vietnam. The decollectivisation of agriculture, together with the approval of the Domestic and Foreign Investment Laws in the late 1980s, as well as the Commercial Law in the early 1990s, were extremely effective in promoting growth of the private sector from a negligible base. The economic reforms of the 1980s were remarkably effective in galvanising the energy of millions of Vietnamese individuals who diversified and expanded their agricultural production rapidly, and set up many microhousehold-enterprises as well as domestic private registered SMEs. Foreign firms invested in majority foreign-owned joint ventures or in wholly foreign-owned enterprises. Tapping the potential of individual farmer's drive and dynamism through 'Doi Moi' was key to the rapid growth and employment generation of the 1990s (see World Bank 1999). In the early part of the twenty first century, unleashing the potential of the private non-farm sector, to produce and to export, is likely to be the key to restoring higher growth of income and employment during the next decade.

While systematic data on the performance of the domestic private sector is limited, what does exist suggests a significant expansion and diversification of private sector activities in the last ten years. Five important facts about the performance of the private sector can be usefully highlighted.

Table 9.8
Private Sector's Share in 1998 GDP (%)

	Total GDP	Manufacturing GDP
State sector	49	54
State-owned enterprises	na	na
Private sector	51	46
Foreign-invested sector	10	18
Domestic private sector	41	28
Of which:		
• Household enterprises/farmers	34	18
• Private SMEs	7	10

Source: General Statistical Office, *Statistical Yearbook*.

First, the share of the private sector in total GDP in 1998 was about 50 per cent (see Table 9.8), approximately the same share as in 1993. Hence the domestic private sector's share of GDP remained stagnant during this period. During the period 1995–98 the domestic private sector, despite its many constraints, grew at 9 per cent a year, only a percentage point lower than the growth of the state-owned sector.

Second, less than half of manufacturing GDP in 1998 was produced by private firms, but the share is increasing, with the domestic private sector dominating that share (see Table 9.8). The domestic private sector, especially household enterprises, has had an important role in manufacturing. Household microenterprises and private SMEs account for 28 per cent of manufacturing GDP. As of 1999 there were around 600 000 microhousehold enterprises in manufacturing, contributing 18 per cent of manufacturing value added, and 5600 private SMEs in manufacturing accounting for 10 per cent of manufacturing GDP. However, with the introduction of the Enterprise Law in 2000 the situation was changing rapidly, especially for private registered SMEs, with more than 10,000 new firms registered during the first nine months of 2000.

The period of the 1990s has seen a steady decline in the contribution of the state sector towards industrial output, from around 62 per cent in 1990 to 44 per cent by 1999 and to just over 42 per cent in 2000 (see Table 9.9). While the domestic private (non-state) share has actually declined during this period the foreign-invested enterprises' share has increased considerably. Most of this was due to very rapid growth of foreign-invested enterprises in the oil and gas sector as well as in manufacturing. Household enterprise growth stagnated after the first half of the 1990s as the environment for domestic private enterprises was

Table 9.9
Industrial Output: Growth and Share by Sector, 1990–2000

	1990	1995	1999ᵖ	2000ᵉ
Total industrial growth (%)	3.2	13.8	10.4	15.5
Percentage of industrial output				
State-owned enterprises	61.7	50.3	43.5	42.2
Domestic private (non-state)				
sector	29.5	24.6	21.8	22.7
Foreign-invested sector	8.8	25.1	34.7	35.2

Notes: p = preliminary figure; e = estimate.

Source: General Statistical Office, *Yearbook*.

not sufficiently favourable to promote their rapid growth. Thus foreign-invested enterprises now have a much bigger share of total private industrial output than was the case in 1990.

Third, the domestic private sector is considerably more labour intensive in comparison to the state sector and the foreign-invested sector. Referring to Table 9.4 again, it can be seen that in 1998 the state sector contributed 46 per cent to industrial production but employed only 24 per cent of the industrial workforce. The foreign-invested sector contributed 32 per cent of industrial production but employed only 11.5 per cent of the industrial workforce. By contrast the domestic non-state-sector, household enterprises and private SMEs, contributed only 22 per cent of industrial production but employed 64 per cent of the industrial workforce. The relatively large share of the private sector in employment and in labour intensive exports indicates that it has been outperforming other enterprises in exploiting Vietnam's comparative advantage in labour-intensive production. Indeed, private sector development in Vietnam, through its effect on growth and employment, can have a significant impact on poverty reduction.

Fourthly, private SMEs in manufacturing, especially the larger ones, are highly export oriented. In Vietnam there are around 457 private manufacturers with more than 100 full time workers (see MPDF 1999) that operate mainly in labour intensive sectors like garments, footwear, plastic products, seafood and so on (see Table 9.10). On average these SMEs export around three-quarters of their production, and consequently have a greater export orientation than SOEs. By comparison foreign-invested enterprises export only around a half of their output.

Finally, private foreign-invested enterprises are playing an increasingly important role in the economy, accounting for about a fifth of manufacturing

Table 9.10
Private Registered Manufacturers – Export Orientation

	Number of firms	Exports/Output (%) (unweighted average)
Garments and textiles	159	80.5
Leather products	34	85.0
Rubber and plastic products	22	75.0
Food and beverages (incl. seafood)	71	63.2
Wood products	65	75.1
Other non-metallic products	39	73.2
Basic metals	9	na
Chemical products	9	20.0
Others	49	74.4
Total	457	75.3

Source: Mekong Project Development Facility 1999.

output and employing 300,000 workers in 1998. There has been a slight trend away from joint ventures with state enterprises and an increase in wholly foreign-owned investments. A large share of foreign investment in industry is in the production of import competing goods in capital-intensive sectors. This is a reflection of the incentives offered to foreign investors in the form of protection to these sectors. In particular, import-licensing restrictions with unlimited protection have encouraged over investment for the domestic market, at the cost of export markets. This structure of foreign investment partially reflects Vietnam's high barriers to heavy industrial imports that not only protect state enterprises but also attracts foreign investors into import substituting and capital-intensive activities, often with SOEs. This form of foreign investment is generally inefficient. It creates local monopolies and raises the price of products relative to those that would have prevailed under free imports. Thus, although foreign investment has boosted local production it has done little to create employment. Improving the climate for export-oriented foreign investors would certainly assist Vietnam towards more labour-intensive export-led growth in line with its comparative advantage.

The adoption of the 1987 Law on Foreign Investment and subsequent amendment established an 'open door' policy for investors and increasingly simplified investment procedures. This gradual improvement in the investment climate led to a large increase in foreign capital inflows, mainly from Asian countries. During the period 1993–97 the inflow of disbursed foreign investment increased by almost 46 per cent per annum (in terms of current US dollars), reaching nearly US$2.1 billion during 1997. Most of this foreign investment was capital intensive. Although the share of FDI going to light industry has increased in recent years, most investment entered oil-related production, heavy industry or real estate. By the end of 1998 less than 13 per cent of the total stock of FDI was in the labour-intensive light industrial sector, where about 80 per cent of production is exported (according to information from the Ministry of Planning and Investment). This indicates that the amount of export oriented and labour intensive foreign investment attracted by Vietnam's high human capital and low labour costs has been relatively small. It is therefore not surprising that foreign investment, while accounting for 31.8 per cent of industrial production in 1998, and half of industrial growth over the period 1995–98, employed only 11.5 per cent of all industry workers in 1997–98.

Despite a number of favourable developments the private sector remains more constrained in Vietnam than in other countries in the region, including China[1]. The private sector continues to face various unnecessary restrictions on entry arising from the remaining business license requirements, whose modification and rationalisation are still needed. Access to, and transactions in, land use rights remain difficult despite recent changes in land law and security regulations. New institutional arrangements like registries, and procedures for selling foreclosed land use rights are not in place. Access to capital and credit is also more difficult for private SMEs in part because banks are in dire financial straits, and in part because lending to SOEs is viewed more favourably than lending to the private sector. But improving the climate for day to day operations of private investors – making interactions with the bureaucracy easier – will necessitate deep seated behavioural changes in the way private activity is perceived by the civil service, the dominant state-owned commercial banks, and, most importantly, by the political leadership.

9.3   VIETNAM'S SMES – A PROFILE

The Vietnamese economy is characterised by a large number of small- and medium-sized enterprises with little capital. Total SME capital accounts for just 20 per cent of the total business capital value of all enterprises, with a small number of state-owned enterprises holding most of the capital of the whole country.[2] More than half of all SMEs are not owned by the state and are therefore, officially at least, private. In practice many companies that appear to be private are really not. Before 1988 Vietnam had no private enterprises, 'apart from family firms, which were politically above suspicion if only because, at least officially, they did not employ any wage labour' (Wolff 1999, p. 72). There were, however, some enterprises that were run virtually along market-economy lines, particularly in the south of the country. Currently, the most important organisational form of private enterprise is still the household firm, employing an average of three employees each (Wolff 1999, p. 73).[3] The next largest element of what Wolff calls *the semi-formal private sector*, are the industrial cooperatives and quasi-cooperative 'production groups' (Wolff 1999). The number of non-state enterprises has increased dramatically recently[4] and the number of enterprises in the collective and state sectors has tended to decrease. The number of private enterprises, excluding business households or groups working below the limit of legal capital, has been increasing most quickly. Only 5.7 per cent of non-state enterprises were established before 1990.[5]

9.3.1   The Number and Structure of Small- and Medium-Sized Enterprises

In Vietnam, SMEs are officially defined by the Government as enterprises with chartered capital of under VND[6] 5 billion (or US$36 000) and fewer than 200 staff[7]. In 1998 there were more than 30 000 registered enterprises in Vietnam, including more than 23 000 non-state enterprises. Of these registered firms, approximately 22 000 were SMEs. SMEs in Vietnam account for 87.7 per cent of the number of State firms, 30 per cent of joint ventures, and 96 per cent of total private firms in Vietnam. (Central Institute for Economic Management (CIEM) 1998).

If we classify SMEs by their amount of investment capital (those enterprises with investment capital below VND 5 billion) and by their number of employees (less than 200), then around 90 per cent of the total number of enterprises in Vietnam are classified as small- or medium-sized. Despite making up the preponderance of Vietnamese enterprises the capital value of these SMEs accounts for only 20 per cent of the total business capital value of all enterprises.[8] The considerable capital value of the SOEs, particularly the large ones, accounts for this, in addition to the fact that the capital value of the non-state SMEs account for only just over half (52 per cent) of the total capital value of non-state enterprises.

Figure 9.4 indicates the growth in number of private registered SMEs over the period 1994–97. In 1994 there were 10 859 privately registered SMEs of which most were in the industry sector (4392) and trade sector (3894). While overall industrial growth has outstripped service sector growth, growth in the number of private SMEs has been far higher in services than industry. This reflects the bias in industrial growth in favour of capital intensive and large sized enterprises. Trading SMEs more than tripled in number between 1994 and 1997 (Figure 9.4), while those in construction and other services more than doubled. The faster growth of service SMEs is largely because this sector is less dominated by state enterprises and thus experiences fewer restrictions on private participation. In 1997, 56.5 per cent of all SMEs were in trade and

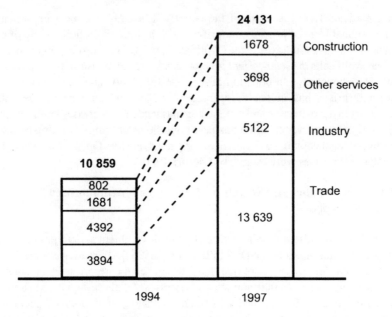

Source: General Office of Statistics.

Figure 9.4   Private Registered Small- and Medium-Sized Firms

repairing services; 21.2 per cent were in the industry sector; 6.9 per cent were in the construction sector; and the remaining 15.3 per cent in other services. Most (90 per cent) of the more than 5122 SME firms in industry in 1997 were in four sub-sectors: food and beverages (56 per cent); garments and shoes (9 per cent); metals and metal products (17 per cent) and wood and paper products (11 per cent). SMEs are typically well represented in sectors in which size and scale are not significant cost advantages. Such activities offer the greatest potential for future expansion of private SMEs (World Bank 1998, p. 30).

The contribution of non-state SMEs under a number of categories for various economic sectors in 1997 is contained in Table 9.11 and that for the economy as a whole in Table 9.12.

9.3.2   Contribution to GDP and Production

In Vietnam there are almost no figures available for the contribution of SMEs to the economy. The following is an attempt to draw a general picture of the sector based on data available for economic inputs. In 1995 the share of 'value added' produced by the non-state sector to GDP was 65 per cent. The contribution of non-state enterprises, including SMEs, to GDP was approximately 36.6 per

Table 9.11
Contribution of Non-State SMEs in the Main Economic
Sectors, 1997 (%)

Sector	Capital	Labour	Turnover	Tax payments
Fisheries	55	80	57	87
Processing industry	15	49	22	24
Construction	22	56	33	19
Trade	21	60	42	18
Service and hospitality	19	56	43	63

Source: General Statistical Office 1998

Table 9.12
Contribution of Non-State SMEs in the Economy, 1998 (%)

Capital	Labour	Turnover	Tax payments
10.2	47	35	16

Source: Ministry of Planning and Investment 1999

cent. The share of capital value of SMEs in the total business capital value of all non-state enterprises was approximately 52 per cent.[9] It is therefore possible to assume that the proportion that SMEs provided of the total value added produced by non-state enterprises was also 52 per cent, that is 19 per cent of GDP. The share of value added produced by SOEs as a whole is equal to 25 per cent of GDP.[10] Assuming that the value added by state SMEs is equal to one fifth of this then the contribution of state SMEs to value added is equal to approximately 5 per cent of GDP. Thus, the share of value added produced by all SMEs in the country, in all economic sectors, is estimated to be approximately equal to 24 per cent of GDP (see Table 9.13). This corresponds with the figure of 25 per cent of GDP quoted by the World Bank (2001, p.49), suggesting that the proportion of GDP contributed by all SMEs has not changed by much during the latter half of the 1990s.

Tables 9.4 and 9.9 indicate that the state sector dominated the industrial sector during the period of the 1990s. However by 2000 its contribution had fallen to 42 per cent of industrial production, and foreign-invested enterprises, including joint ventures with SOEs, contributed a further 35 per cent of industrial production. The domestic non-state sector contributed the remaining 23 per

Table 9.13
Contribution of Vietnamese SMEs to GDP, 1995

No.	Vietnamese SMEs by Ownership	% of GDP
1	Non-state SMEs	19
2	State-owned SMEs	5
Total		24

Source: Ministry of Planning and Investment 1998.

Table 9.14
Distribution of Industrial Output by Ownership (%), 1997 Figures

	Total Industry	Garments	Textiles
State-owned enterprises	51.4	36.0	60.0
Foreign-invested enterprises[1]	24.4	15.0	16.0
Non-state	24.2	49.0	24.0
Of which: private companies[2]	2.4	18.0	14.0

Notes: 1   Includes 100 per cent foreign-owned companies and joint ventures with SOEs.
            2   Private registered enterprises and others not in partnership with SOEs.

Source: World Bank 1998, Table 2.4, p. 30.

cent of industrial production, with the bulk of this being produced by household microenterprises. While private registered companies (SMEs), overall, contributed a very small proportion of industrial output, only about 2.4 per cent of industrial production in 1997 (Table 9.14), they were very important in the production of key export items including that of garments and textiles. However, the share contributed by all SMEs (including state SMEs, private local SMEs and those with foreign investment) to the total industrial gross output has been estimated by one source to be equal to 31 per cent.[11] However, compared with other countries in the region, where SMEs contribute on average 50–60 per cent of GDP,[12] the performance of Vietnamese SMEs remains modest.

9.3.5   Contribution to Industrial Employment

The non-state sector contributes significantly to employment. As indicated in Table 9.4 the non-state sector contributed 76 per cent of industrial employment in 1997–98, with the domestic private sector contributing 64 per cent of total industrial employment. Private SMEs contributed 27 per cent and household enterprises contributed 37 per cent of total industrial employment in 1997–98 (see Table 9.15). The World Bank (2001, p. 49) has asserted that total SMEs for all sectors contribute 50 per cent of total labour force employment.

9.3.6   Contribution to International Trade

As identified previously, Vietnam has made considerable advances in increasing the openness of its economy. Between 1991 and 1995 private firms were allowed to engage in foreign trade by obtaining a license, tariff exemptions were introduced for imported inputs used in the production of exports, licensing procedures were simplified, an interbank foreign exchange market was introduced, and quotas on exports were removed except for rice. Vietnam signalled its intention to integrate with the region by joining ASEAN in 1995, and is now also seeking membership of the WTO. Since 1998 the trade regime

Table 9.15
Industrial Employment by Sector (%), 1997–98

Ownership	% of workforce
State sector	24
Foreign-invested	12
Private SMEs	27
Household enterprises	37

Source: GSO: *Vietnam Living Standard Survey* 2, 1999.

Table 9.16
Shares in Non-Oil Exports and Total Imports

	Non-oil exports		Total Imports	
	1997	Mid-2000	1997	Mid-2000
State-owned enterprises	65	46	68	57
Foreign-invested enterprises	23	32	28	27
Domestic private SMEs	12	22	4	16
Total	100	100	100	100

Source: Ministry of Trade.

has been opened up further. The most significant measure was the freeing up of trading rights for firms registered in Vietnam. These firms were allowed, for the first time, to export and import goods directly without a license.[13] This newly provided right for domestic firms encouraged significant participation of private firms in foreign trade. Domestic private SMEs' share of non-oil exports rose from 12 per cent in 1997 to 22 per cent in mid 2000. Their share of imports increased from 4 per cent to 16 per cent over the same period (see Table 9.16). There is therefore considerable potential for an expansion of exports by SMEs, particularly given that they primarily produce labour-intensive products that are in line with the country's comparative advantage.

9.3.7   Distribution of SMEs by Location

According to Ministry of Planning and Investment calculations, see Table 9.17, more than 55 per cent of the total number of SMEs are located in the Southeast and the Mekong River Delta. The figures for the Red River Delta and the North Central Coast are 18.1 per cent and 10.1 per cent, respectively. This suggests that there is considerable scope for an expansion of SMEs in the north of the country, where in the past SOEs have traditionally dominated.

9.4   SME PROMOTION AND PRIVATE SECTOR DEVELOPMENT

9.4.1   Overview

The Central Committee of the Communist Party of Vietnam has drafted a Socio-

Table 9.17
Distribution of SMEs by Region

Region		Percentage
1	Southeast Coast & Mekong River Delta	55.0
2	Red River Delta	18.1
3	North Central Coast	10.1
4	Other Regions	16.8
Total		100.0

Source: Ministry of Planning and Investment 1998.

Economic Development Strategy (SEDS) 2001–10 that is 'aimed at accelerating industrialisation and modernisation in the socialist orientation and creating a foundation for Vietnam to become an industrialised country by 2020'.[14] This envisages that GDP will double from 2000 to 2010.[15] Vietnam in 2000 faced serious challenges in employment generation with unemployment figures at more than 7 per cent, underemployment around 30 per cent and an expected growth of the workforce of 11 million people over the next 10 years. Since unemployment and underemployment are the major factors contributing to poverty, the creation of new jobs, and particularly in the rural sector, will be crucial for the reduction of poverty.

To accomplish these aims the SEDS gives particular emphasis to SMEs and private enterprises, especially given their ability to generate employment and opportunities for the poor. In 2000 overall SMEs, both state and private, generated approximately a quarter of GDP, employed around 50 per cent of the Vietnamese labour force and were the fastest growing type of enterprise in terms of numbers (see World Bank 2001, p. 49). A flourishing private sector and a growing number of SMEs have the potential to: generate new jobs as well as absorb labour made redundant by the ongoing reform of the SOEs; provide the engine for economic growth; contribute to export growth; and play a vital role in the modernisation and industrialisation of Vietnam. Therefore the government realises that it will be essential, to achieve the targets set under the SEDS, to support the further development of the private sector and SMEs.

Meeting the draft strategy's investment targets will require total domestic private investment having to rise to 11–13 per cent of GDP. This is unlikely to occur without a significant improvement in the climate for the private sector, and for SMEs in particular. The climate for the private sector, however, still remains grudging rather than supportive. This contrasts markedly with China where the private sector has been recognised openly as a key partner in the country's development.[16] Despite this there are indications that the climate is improving. In mid 1998 the Law on Promotion of Domestic Investment was revised providing new incentives for the domestic private sector. This was followed by the approval and implementation of the Enterprise Law in 1999 and 2000. Together with the elimination of more than 100 different business licenses that restricted entry in different sectors, ongoing implementation of the Law is improving the policy environment for domestic private SMEs significantly. The Enterprise Law 2000 substantially simplified business start up and led to the registration of more than 10 000 additional domestic firms in the first nine months of 2000. However, domestic private registered firms (private SMEs) still numbered only around 30 000[17] and produced less than 10 per cent of GDP. Creating a level playing field for the private sector will require a shift in the social and administrative culture from one of reluctance and control towards one of active support and encouragement. The private sector will also benefit from the introduction of a transparent and predictable regulatory framework, where discretionary actions on the part of officials are minimised.

In addition three recent government policies have gone some way to reducing the restrictions on private SMEs. First, firms are allowed to export directly. This will help small firms most of all as they were least able to bear the additional transactions costs of previous restrictions. Second, requirements to import through state enterprises, to satisfy stipulated conditions of capital and qualified personnel needed for being registered as an importer, have been removed. Third, foreign investors are now allowed to own 30 per cent of shares in existing domestic enterprises, permitting private firms to seek foreign partners.

More needs to be done in the area of finance and access to credit for SMEs, particularly for efficient enterprises in rural industry. So far, farmers, SOEs and private foreign firms have driven growth. Private small- and medium-sized enterprises have played a negligible role, especially in industry. But private SMEs have been the most efficient users of resources in other countries of the region and key to employment creation. They need to be encouraged in Vietnam. A vigorous private SME sector will need more freedom to operate and better services from a vigorous and modern banking sector, neither of which Vietnam has at present. A precondition for promoting such entrepreneurship will be to introduce reforms to reorient the country's banks towards the needs of private SMEs and to restructure, equitise and liquidate SOEs, to improve their efficiency. A more open trade regime and less import protection for heavy industry will mean more investment in labour-intensive sectors and exports (garments, footwear, travel goods, processed agricultural products, tourism), stimulating rural industry and agriculture. While registered private firms can export or import more easily, registration of private businesses, a prerequisite for trading, still remains difficult.

The most cost effective prospect for generating off farm employment is through promoting SMEs (that is, registered private companies with 50–300 employees) Each job generated in an SME is estimated to require a capital investment of about US$800 (VND 11 million, in book value). In contrast, one job created in an SOE requires approximately US$18 000 (VND 240 million). Empirical evidence from other countries also indicates that SMEs are more efficient users of capital under most conditions.[18]

During the early period of reform in the late 1980s agricultural growth, made possible by allowing farmers greater decision making freedom, was the main engine for Vietnam's initial surge of growth. Eliminating the existing restrictions on SMEs has the potential to result in a second round of growth by boosting labour intensive manufactures and processed agricultural exports, thereby protecting rural areas from the current slowdown. So far private SMEs (that is, registered corporate firms) have played a minor role in industrial production and have grown very slowly. Household enterprises play a much larger role. This contrasts sharply with the experiences of its rapidly developing regional neighbours.

9.4.2   Promoting Vietnam's SMEs

As discussed previously, despite an improvement in the private sector business environment its growth and development still remains more constrained in Vietnam than in other countries of the region. According to survey conducted by the Vietnam Chamber of Commerce and Industry in 1999, the main difficulties encountered by SMEs in Vietnam are:

*   the majority (80 per cent) lack capital for production and trade;
*   most have obsolete equipment and machinery;
*   they lack adequate physical and human resources;
*   they lack current information on technical, market and legal issues;
*   they lack support from the state, especially in technology transfer, credit guarantees and loans.

In this section four of these issues are given particular focus: access to finance; access to technology and use of information technology; access to market information; and human capital deficiencies. Each of these is now briefly discussed in turn.

Access to finance
Government policies on mobilising financial resources have been implemented through taxation, interest-rate management, and investment promotion strategies. Domestic production did develop rapidly in the first half of the 1990s as did domestic savings and gross investments. From 1991–95 domestic private investment (mainly by SMEs) accounted for 30 per cent of total gross investment (approximately equal to US$6 billion). The remainder of the capital for enterprises was mobilised from formal domestic and international institutions.

Despite the increase in investment nearly all (80 per cent) of Vietnamese SMEs lack capital for production or business, according to official statistics (Ministry of Planning and Investment 1999). The VCCI study in 1999 found that: 55 per cent of enterprises had difficulty in obtaining capital; 67.5 per cent of enterprises had to borrow from relatives and friends; 25 per cent of enterprises had to deliver materials in advance; only 42.5 per cent of enterprises borrowed from the banks; and 20 per cent of enterprises borrowed from other financial organisations.

Other surveys of SMEs by government management agencies and other organisations give similar results. These surveys also pointed out that the share of bank loans allocated to the non-state enterprises has tended to increase, but not in accord with their number and their contribution to GDP. For instance, bank loans to these enterprises, as a proportion of total loans, were: 10.3 per cent in 1990; 18.2 per cent in 1992; 33.1 per cent in 1993; 37.1 per cent in 1994; and 50 per cent in 1995.[19] However, this has not satisfied the demand for credit by non-state enterprises. The financial system can satisfy only 25.6 per cent of the credit demand by the non-state enterprises. According to CIEM, in 1995, among 407 SMEs surveyed, 316 had to borrow from informal financial sources.

Difficulty in accessing financial resources by SMEs has partly resulted from the obstacles created by some of the policies and regulations on capital mobilisation. The effect of these policies has been as follows. First, the majority of external resources, such as Foreign Direct Investment and Official Development Assistance, have been allocated to the state sector. Second, there are still irrational regulations that seriously hamper the capital mobilisation of SMEs. For example, the regulations on short-term credit issued by the State Bank give preferential treatment to the state-owned enterprises, which enjoy cheaper financing in comparison to their counterparts in the private sector. Compulsory insurance is also unreasonably required for those assets financed by bank loans, even when such loans had not yet been given by the banks and when the ownership documents related to the assets are not available. Collateral for bank loans is required for non-state enterprises while it is not for SOEs. There is still no guidance document available on collateral procedures. According to Decision 198/NH on 16 September 1994 by the State Bank and Decision 217 on 17 August 1996, the maximum bank loan is defined to be equal to 70 per cent of the value of the collateral written in the loan contract. However, in practice, enterprises are given loans equal to less than 50 per cent of collateral, regardless of the fact that the asset values determined by the banks are usually different from the actual values. Third, there are no special financial institutions for SMEs, except for a number of foreign funds such as the SME Development Fund, which operates through the existing commercial banks, and the Mekong Project Development Facility (MPDF) that mainly provides technical assistance for private sector SMEs.

Access to technology and use of information technology

Technology and equipment in SMEs   A draft development strategy for SMEs prepared by the Ministry of Planning and Investment (MPI 1999) indicated that their technology level, as well as the nature of their equipment and machinery, was in poor shape. Moreover, the rate of renovation is too low, approximately at the level of 10 per cent of annual investment. The strategy document proposed, in order to improve conditions for the development of technology, that:

- competition should be created to encourage enterprises to adopt new technology and renovate existing technology;
- the economy should be open to access and exchange information;
- enterprises should be encouraged to improve their capacity to apply new technology.

Presently, the majority of Vietnamese enterprises, especially SMEs, are using obsolete technology that is perhaps three or four generations behind the world's average level. Their technological and technical capacity is limited, and the capital level per employee is low (only 3 per cent of the level in the large industrial enterprises).[20]

In a recent survey by the Central Institute for Economic Management, specialists in government organisations and other SME support institutions recognised that the technology level in SMEs is obsolete, that technology management skills are poor, and that product quality is low. At the same time the government has not provided supporting policies for technological advance. Among 40 enterprises surveyed only two had been able to get any technological support.[21] Policies that support the enhancement of technology for SMEs have many weaknesses. These are:

- there are no policies specific to SMEs (that is specific policies on training and improving the skills in management, technology, etc.);
- no research and development organisation has been created specifically for SMEs;
- the specialised organisations in science, technology, and training that exist are not strong enough to provide the supporting and consulting services required for SMEs;
- the existing promotion centres were established mainly to meet the requirements of international assistance projects rather than to satisfy the need to support SMEs;
- there is still no master plan or national strategy for the development of SMEs in the country.

Access to information technology – electronic commerce Electronic commerce has yet to be systematically developed in Vietnam. In the country as a whole there are only four Internet Service Providers (ISPs), and fewer than 100 companies with their own registered websites. The Internet is still a luxury to most people, with high service charges (two US cents for each minute online) and extremely limited banking infrastructure support for e-commerce.

As in many other countries e-commerce could play a vital role in Vietnam in the future. Currently however, especially in rural areas, lack of proper telecommunications, hardware and software, training, human skills and access to appropriate technology constitute major obstacles to the development of e-commerce especially for SMEs. Today only 72 000 Internet connections are registered in Vietnam. Major effort is required by the government to improve the current situation.

Availability of information

One of the first steps in entering the export business is to get adequate and reliable information on market opportunities. This is a major difficulty for many SMEs. Most obtain information through the media or by personal contacts and not through formal channels. These personal contacts could be relatives or friends living overseas, or acquaintances made at trade fairs, conferences or on private trips. Only the more dynamic SMEs tend to contact formal organisations like the SME Club, the Chamber of Commerce and Industry and the various Trade Associations for such information. However, the average SME can neither digest nor effectively use the large quantity of statistical data and general information from the above sources, even if they manage to obtain it. The lack of reliable and useful market information often leads to a situation where local firms export their products with lower prices than the competition or miss out on good business opportunities.

The availability of specific information regarding new technology has been improved with the opening of technology centres such as the Technology Presentation House (TPH) in Ho Chi Minh City. These centres have been established with the aim of introducing new technologies and advanced products – both local and international – that can be implemented in Vietnam.

Human capital – skills and qualifications

The skills of employees in SMEs do not meet desirable standards according to the Vietnamese government, because the majority of them, especially in small businesses, have not received any training while their educational level is low. Only about 5 per cent[22] of employees in the non-state sector have a university degree. The majority of the owners of non-state enterprises established in recent years have also not received any training, but they have a higher level of general education. Nevertheless, only 31.2 per cent of the owners of non-state enterprises have a university or higher degree,[23] and 51.8 per cent of proprietors have a management qualification. The percentage in proprietorships that have no management qualifications is 70.5 per cent and in limited liability companies 26.4 per cent.

9.5 GOVERNMENT'S ROLE AND SUPPORT FOR SMES

9.5.1 Background

Until the beginning of the 1980s in Vietnam there were only two significant institutional forms in the economy: state-owned enterprises (SOEs) and co-operatives. Private production and business units were allowed to operate but their scale and scope were negligible. Economic management during this period was based on the mechanisms of central planning. Enterprises did not have any autonomy in their production and business process since the government controlled and distributed resources and applied a monopoly policy on trade.

Economic reform started in 1986, but by 1988 inflation was increasing at an annual rate of 40 per cent with a large current account deficit. The events of 1989 convinced the Vietnamese Government that it would get no further help from its previous benefactor, the Soviet Union. Starting in that year it therefore adopted a package of measures introducing strict structural reforms and macroeconomic stabilisation, in line with IMF orthodoxy (Reidel and Comer 1997, pp. 195–7). The 'shock therapy' included the adoption of a policy of trade liberalisation and switching the economy to a market price mechanism that accelerated reform. The abolition of the majority of subsidies helped, and indeed forced, enterprises to operate within the market mechanism. The shift to a market focus was a key element in the policy of economic reform and contributed substantially to the development of the private sector in Vietnam. The policy of creating a market economy through the liberalisation of business activities relied on two factors: that market forces determine production and business decisions, and that the valid rights of enterprises are protected by the state (Woo 1997). One of the essential components of economic reform is defined in the policy for multisectoral development that recognises the permanent existence of a variety of forms of enterprise and provides for their equal treatment under the law.

9.5.2 Government's Long-term Vision

The draft Socio-Economic Development Strategy (SEDS) 2001–10 of the Central Committee of the Communist Party of Vietnam (SEDS), emphasises accelerating industrialisation and modernisation of the country and creating a foundation for Vietnam to become an industrialised country by 2020. In order to accomplish these aims the SEDS emphasises the importance of SMEs and private enterprises. A flourishing private sector and a growing number of SMEs would: absorb new workers as well as labour made redundant by the ongoing reform of the SOEs; be a key engine of economic growth; contribute to export growth; and play a vital role in the modernisation and industrialisation of Vietnam. The role of the government in supporting the further development of the private sector and SMEs will be essential, and involve levelling the playing field between SOEs and private companies and enhancing the business environment by: simplifying the tax system; streamlining administrative procedures; reducing red tape and corruption; restructuring the banking system; and strengthening existing or, when necessary, creating additional support institutions. Particular focus is required for the development of SMEs in the rural sector where non-agricultural jobs are scarce, underemployment is high, and poverty widespread.

9.5.3   Achieving the Long-term Vision

Since the change to the Constitution in 1992, recognising the right of freedom of business and equality before the law for all sectors of economy, the government has taken steps to develop the private sector and SMEs. Most recently the SEDS, the PSPAP[24] and a *draft* Governmental Decree on SME Promotion Policies Structure provide details of Government plans for further action in this area. These plans focus upon the following areas: enhancing the legal environment for SMEs; strengthening existing and/or establishing new institutions; easier access to capital; trade promotion and export development of SME/private enterprises; and improving the image of the private sector. These are now discussed in turn.

Enhancing the legal environment for SMEs
Since 1986 important achievements have been made in adopting and elaborating legal measures and in creating the legal framework within which all types of enterprises can operate. Up to the end of 1996, 55 laws (codes, laws and acts), 64 decrees and 251 resolutions had been promulgated.[25] However, the soundness and validity of the fundamental reform legislation is in doubt. Significant problems are being caused by the proliferation of legal instruments, many contradictory, which are issued at every hierarchical level. This is due partly to a lack of experience in constructing the legal framework and partly because of the nature of the culture and social structure and the tensions within it. This results in an inability of the state to make any one entity accountable. The effect of which is a proliferation of state agencies with overlapping responsibilities and opposing functions (Kornai 1990).

Although the legal system is still not complete and has many imperfections, it has provided a level of protection higher than before that has helped the economy to operate on a legal basis. However, overall reforms have been slow and moderate and have often been accompanied by arbitrary new rules. A government agency (CIEM 1998) identified the following main shortcomings:

- Legal regulations are too complex, ambiguous and contradictory;
- The legal environment for different types of enterprises is different and creates unequal grounds for enterprises to be established and operated. Many policies give priority to enterprises based on their ownership without supporting measures being linked to the scale of enterprise (so small enterprises which are officially or semi-officially owned receive more protection than larger ones which are not);
- Frequent changes in the regulations provide an unstable legal environment;
- Legal instruments are usually issued hastily, without corresponding support from supporting legislation;

- Some legal documents still lack a rational basis that causes difficulties and restrictions for enterprises, and creates gaps which they can abuse;
- Communication of the nature and implications of legal changes is still limited, and generally enterprises, especially SMEs, have limited knowledge of the regulations.

To advance the development of SMEs Vietnam requires a rule-of-law-based regulatory framework. The current system of vague and frequently changing regulations and excessive bureaucracy has resulted in: increased risk and cost of doing business; a drain on the resources and time of private entrepreneurs that would otherwise be available for investment or for management of the business; and has created an inhospitable business environment. Evidence from other countries shows that bureaucratic stranglehold, exercised through bureaucratic discretion, has been a major drag on private sector dynamism. To establish the rule of law as the basis for government–business relationships there will also be a need for institution-building.

A transparent legal and regulatory framework for the private sector, therefore, needs to be established, to ensure a level playing field for both SOEs and the private sector. Three actions over the medium term will be required to achieve this. First, Government should continue to monitor carefully and implement effectively the Enterprise Law (for example, eliminating, modifying and rationalising the remaining business licenses in other sectors) and the Domestic Investment law, since they are the key instruments for facilitating Vietnamese private entry further. In January 2000 the new Enterprise Law came into effect, permitting for the first time non-discretionary registration of private firms, instead of by Government approval, thereby eliminating bureaucratic steps. It also regulates the approval of establishment of a new business, which has to be decided within 15 days of the submission of the application. While this is a very important development, its implementation and enforcement is not yet consistent. Even though the Government has abolished many licensing requirements, a large number of licenses still need to be obtained, depending on the field of business. The momentum for the elimination of unnecessary licenses needs to be maintained.

The Government has announced its intention to promulgate a Decree on SME Promotion Policies Structure in order to demonstrate a commitment to SME promotion and its strategy for achieving this. This will provide guidelines on support measures for private enterprises and SMEs covering areas such as encouragement policies and the set-up of support institutions. The Decree, originally planned to be promulgated in 2000, requires promulgation as soon as possible. The government also recognises the need to encourage the establishment of new SMEs, and to this end make administrative procedures simpler and more transparent. The problem concerning bureaucracy and complicated procedures in holding back the development of SMEs is acknowledged in the SEDS.[26]

Second, the revised Foreign Investment Law and Decision 24 need to be implemented in the spirit in which they were developed. Foreign investors should be encouraged, not discouraged, from engaging in joint ventures with private Vietnamese firms, to facilitate transfer of technology, and enhance marketing contacts and management expertise. Third, there is a need to make the regulatory framework for private participation in infrastructure more transparent and predictable over the medium term and conclude some of the build-operate-transfer (BOT) transactions in the power sector in the short term. More generally, as recommended in the SEDS, implementation of equal terms for all enterprises regardless of ownership should be carried out as soon as possible in all relevant fields, for example, related to bidding for Government procurement, access to land and credit etc.

In addition, it will be important to improve the situation concerning land use rights. Unclear and cumbersome procedures make it very difficult for private SMEs to acquire land. This presents a major obstacle since access to land use rights is essential, especially to private enterprises, as collateral for accessing credit. In order to improve access to land the following steps are necessary: (i) clarify and speed up procedures for land title allocation; (ii) unify and modernise registers for land and buildings; (iii) reduce heavy fees and taxes on registration; and (iv) provide clear, simple and fair procedures for resolving disputes.

Strengthening of existing and/or establishment of new relevant institutions and changing social and administrative attitudes

Ministries and agencies involved in industry, planning, education and training, such as the Ministry of Industry, Ministry of Planning and Investment and universities, are still geared towards support of the SOEs. These organisations will be required to shift their focus towards the private sector and SMEs in order to enhance the general economic environment. This will require a fundamental change in social and administrative attitudes and a focusing upon an improvement in the image of the private sector in the country. The vital role of private companies for employment generation and modernisation of Vietnam should be acknowledged and disseminated through the media and the educational system at all levels. Given the many years of discrimination against private enterprises and private entrepreneurs, stronger and more frequent endorsement of private business by the Vietnamese leadership is required as was the case in China. Regular public exhortations by top leaders of the Party and Government to the bureaucracy to provide support to private enterprises under the law, would be extremely helpful. Stories in the media of domestic private business successes and visits by top leaders to successful private exporters would help to reinforce the value of private business in Vietnam's development.

Apart from access to capital, most SME entrepreneurs consider lack of access to technical and market information, lack of skilled labour and know-how as their main business obstacles. The government needs to implement measures that will strengthen the business environment for SMEs through enhancing the performance of existing organisations and/or establishing relevant new organisations where appropriate. Measures agreed upon but still not implemented include the establishment of a national SME Agency that will coordinate consistent SME development. At the national level a Council for Private Sector Promotion has been proposed to provide a forum for a regular dialogue between relevant parties such as government agencies, local authorities, business organisations/associations and representatives of the private sector and SMEs. It will also provide advice on private sector and SME encouragement policies and programmes.

Given the importance of mechanical engineering for the industrialisation and modernisation of Vietnam, as well as the enhancement of technical know-how of entrepreneurs, the Government decided to establish three Technical Assistance Centres (TACs) (in North, Central and South Vietnam). The TACs not only concentrate on the enhancement of technical know-how but also support industrial subsectors such as textiles, ceramics, rubber/plastics, food processing and craft products, by providing engineering experts with experience in specific areas required by SMEs.

Providing an information system containing data on the latest developments for private enterprises through an Information Centre for Private Enterprises would benefit private enterprises. At the provincial and local level the authorities should be encouraged to incorporate the private sector and SME promotion into their local development plans. In addition appropriate institutions on the provincial and local level should be established or strengthened in order to support private business activities.

Measures that include a strengthened provision of Business Development Services (BDS), to assist the private sector and SMEs improve their access to resources, markets, new technologies and qualified labour, would be beneficial. International experience shows that a growing number of private companies are the most flexible and effective providers of BDS to the diverse and fast changing demands of the private sector. A number of public organisations, including business associations, already exist in Vietnam providing these services and they should be part of the future support to the BDS market as well. Since many SMEs are not aware of the existence of, and benefits from, BDS and/or are unable to pay market rates, the development of a well-functioning BDS market needs to be supported by the Government and/or local authorities.

In many countries business associations are playing a crucial role in identifying and advocating the needs and demands of the business community and in establishing a policy dialogue between the business community and relevant authorities. This has been acknowledged by the New Enterprise Law, which regulates, and the draft Decree on SME Promotion Policies Structure, which supports, the establishment and operation of private business associations.

Easier access to capital

A major constraint facing private SMEs in Vietnam is a shortage of funds. Private SMEs lack access to long-term loans, an equity financing system and access to collateral. The strict collateral requirement by banks and the low incentives for State-owned Commercial Banks (SOCBs) to lend to SMEs, and on the other hand the unwillingness of private SMEs to deal with SOCBs, are serious constraints. This generates a vicious circle that prevents many SMEs from entering the formal credit sector, and forces them to rely on informal credit. Financial policies have an important impact on capital mobilisation and development of enterprises. Vietnam's banking reforms aim to address the shortages and problems of availability of credit and capital for the economy. However, the impact of these reforms on the domestic private sector will continue to remain limited if the private sector continues to experience difficulties in securing access to land use rights, their potentially most valuable source of collateral.

The Private Sector Promotion Action Plan (PSPAP), the so called Miyazawa Plan, agreed between Japan and Vietnam in 1999, includes more than 40 measures to diminish the constraints faced upon the growth of the private sector. It is based on three common principles: defining Government policy to promote the private sector; securing equal treatment for private enterprises vis-à-vis SOEs; and granting private enterprises freedom to conduct business within the laws of Vietnam. A number of these include measures to improve the financial environment of SMEs. Some of these have already been implemented such as: the promulgation of the Decree on the Lending Guarantee; the Circular related to the Auction System; the Decree Liberalising Transactions involving Land Use Rights in 1999; and the establishment of the Stock Exchange Centre in 2000.

Others key steps to achieve further improvement in the financial environment for SMEs are the creation of a Two-step Loan Fund and a Credit Guarantee Fund. An agreement for a Two-step Loan Fund was signed between the Japan Bank for International Cooperation (JBIC) and the Government of Vietnam in 1999. It intends to provide long-term credit to SMEs through selected participating financial institutions (PFI), including joint stock commercial banks. It is expected that 70 per cent of the beneficiaries from this fund will be private SMEs. The Credit Guarantee Fund for SMEs aims to further encourage financial institutions to lend to SMEs by absorbing a part of the credit risk, thereby alleviating current borrowing constraints as a result of their insufficient collateral capacity.

Other measures proposed include further improvement of the regulatory framework on lending, mortgaging and leasing, and the pending banking sector reform will also provide SMEs with better access to credit.

Trade promotion and export development of SMEs/private enterprises

The government has applied a relaxed policy on restricting imports and exports and, as a result, the growth in the value of exports and imports from 1992 has increased rapidly. During the period 1992–99 the value of exports and imports increased more than four times. However, the number of trade licenses given to enterprises in the private sector only accounts for 15–20 per cent of the total number of trade licenses (figures from Ministry of Trade, 1998). A number of general trade restrictions remain. Non-state enterprises are allowed to export commodities produced by them and can import the input factors necessary to their production. However, they have to get permission from the Prime Minister if they want to participate in other export and import activities. At the beginning of 1997 regulations limiting licences on exported commodities were abandoned. In addition, access to domestic and international markets for some valuable trade items is severely restricted. Licences to trade in rice, petroleum, fertiliser, black cement, cars and motorcycles are only given to a few favoured enterprises. Only 19 enterprises are allowed to export rice and 25 enterprises are allowed to import fertiliser. Abandoning these regulations would greatly increase trading opportunities.

In addition to requiring export or import licenses, the Ministry of Trade still has the right to require specific additional licenses related to certain groups of exported or imported commodities. Furthermore, for some commodities additional export or import licenses must be obtained from the line ministries. The tariff system also remains extremely complicated with many tariff lines, and nominal rates are high and the range of tariff rates is excessively wide. The system of tariff codes is not compatible with the system of product codes.

While trade procedures have gradually improved, a number of problems remain. Institutional support for trade is still not available. Effective measures to prevent a large inflow of smuggled goods are not available. Some policy measures, such as the 90/CP or 91/CP decrees, which established the state-owned general corporations, and the special preferential treatment to SOEs though the credit and trade policies, are disadvantaging SMEs in the private sector.

More recently, the promulgation of three new implementing decrees related to the New Enterprise Law in 2000, and the removal of some quantitative restrictions in import management, represent a significant step forward in improving the trade and business environment for private sector development and SME support in Vietnam. Export licensing and trade management by quota is becoming less important than in the past. However some of the quotas now accessible to private enterprises need to be further opened up, and the bidding system should be more transparent. Also, special attention should be directed at the proper implementation of the new decrees, regulations and instructions of the Government.

At present, the major obstacle preventing SMEs from seizing trade opportunities is their limited experience of global trade. Fragmentary knowledge and understanding of foreign markets are some of the basic trade barriers. This applies not only for information about management accounting, technical requirements, marketing skills, import regulations and consumer preferences, but also for assessing the suitability of imported goods. Limited language skills of the entrepreneurs is also a problem. Lack of these fundamental skills could be a severe problem when Vietnam further integrates into the global economy in the coming years.

Overcoming these difficulties requires not only an extended exposure of Vietnamese entrepreneurs to the world market, but also an intensive teaching and training of SMEs. Tapping into the expertise existing in neighbouring and other foreign countries would be particularly beneficial.

Beyond the information gap, the low level of competitiveness and the restricted ability to produce larger numbers of identical items of similar quality and on time, are other severe trade barriers for local SMEs. Therefore, tailor-made quality management systems have to be propagated and implemented in order to enhance the export opportunities of SMEs.

Image of the private sector

The image of the private sector has to be improved in the country. The vital role of private companies for employment generation and modernisation of Vietnam should be acknowledged and disseminated through the media and the educational system at all levels. Negative social and administrative attitudes towards private enterprises impact adversely upon behaviour towards those engaged in private activities. They influence individual's decisions to enter the private sector and, once entered, constrain their ability to unleash their full potential. Growing one's business and increasing its visibility through success is seen as a risky proposition by many entrepreneurs in Vietnam, because private business has tended to be viewed negatively.

With greater freedom for the private sector also comes the need for improved corporate governance. There are at least three problems of corporate governance that will need to be addressed if the private sector is to grow in a transparent, accountable and effective manner. First, a key characteristic of the private SMEs is that their organisations are quite opaque. Not only is the ownership structure of most of these SMEs not known but also the way decisions are made is unclear. This is not much of a problem when firms are small, but, as they become bigger and owner-managers' span of control is less adequate, absence of appropriate decision-making processes will constrain their growth. Second, most SMEs now do not maintain sufficient accounts or make any public disclosure of their accounts. Various types of restrictions and insufficient social acceptance of business success leads SMEs to misreport financial and other flows, when reporting is required. In the coming decade it will be necessary to put in place a framework that will ensure that such enterprises act in a transparent and accountable manner.

9.6   IMPLEMENTING AN EFFECTIVE COMPETITION POLICY

From the earlier sections of this chapter it is apparent that if Vietnam is to move forward to become a more market-oriented economy, the implementation of an effective competition policy is essential. There are a number of key ingredients. First, there is a need for ongoing ownership reform and the generation of growth of *new* private enterprises. This requires a removal of barriers to new business so that entry into markets for all forms of ownership is free. The growth of SMEs in industry, agriculture and transport, and especially in services where the greatest deficiency previously existed, should be encouraged. This adds to economic activity, greater competition and efficiency in existing markets, and the development of new products and markets. Ownership reform can be seen as an evolutionary process in which the state and private sectors exist permanently side by side, with the relative size of the private sector steadily increasing through time due to: the entry of new private firms; the sale of state property rights to the private sector: and through the liquidation of inefficient state-owned enterprises that prove to be unviable. All these three processes should be encouraged but not forced, allowing scope for experimentation and trials of various forms of ownership reform.

Second, encouragement should be given to foreign investment in the country. This not only alleviates the acute shortage of capital but also paves the way for attaining new technologies, adopting modern management methods, enhancing the skills of domestic workers and gaining access to foreign markets. Foreign capital should not be encouraged to go into certain markets and not into others. Traditionally, in Vietnam, foreign capital was encouraged to go into import substituting sectors that were more capital intensive and whose production was aimed at satisfying domestic demand. As a result such investment did not focus upon those sectors of the economy where the country's comparative advantage lies. That is in the production of export-oriented labour-intensive manufactured goods. Restrictions on foreign sector investment, therefore, should be eliminated.

Third, unviable state-owned enterprises should be allowed to exit the market, and their resources put to more efficient and productive uses elsewhere in the economy. This will require exit mechanisms such as the introduction of bankruptcy and liquidation procedures. This is also an important component in the process of ownership reform, requiring greater involvement by the private sector in their ownership and management including in the form of privatisation (equitisation). Remaining state-owned enterprises should be subject to hard budget constraints.

Finally, a level playing field in terms of access to markets and fair competition between the various forms of ownership needs to be created. Public ownership should not be forced out where it is capable of standing up to market competition, while there should be no discrimination against private ownership. The state as a buyer should not make public procurement decisions based on the form of ownership of the seller, instead purchases should be made on the basis of which seller offers the best price and conditions.

9.7   SUMMARY AND CONCLUSIONS

Ongoing reform in Vietnam will require the revitalisation and equitisation (privatisation) of the country's many unprofitable SOEs, the development of a robust and dynamic private sector, as well as a further opening of the economy to foreign investment, competition and trade. This reform, in the short term, runs the danger of increased unemployment and rising poverty, and potential social unrest that the authorities would wish to avoid. Such instability could be avoided if reform proceeds slowly, but would likely contribute to a stagnating economy that would fall further behind its already reforming regional neighbours. Hence the authorities face difficult choices. This chapter has argued that the role of SMEs, particularly in the private sector, have the potential to play a crucial role in the future development of the economy by: stimulating competition; harnessing latent entrepreneurial zeal; creating new jobs for those made unemployed by a restructuring of state enterprises and for those living in the countryside; bringing about a more efficient allocation of resources in line with the country's comparative advantage; expanding exports; bringing about a more equitable distribution of income; alleviating poverty in the rural sector; and promoting regional development. To date their contribution to the economy remains below what it could be, as demonstrated by the experiences of its regional neighbours. Hence greater emphasis needs to be placed upon their development.

A World Bank report observed that allowing farmers greater freedom of decision-making after the introduction of Doi Moi in 1986, made possible the agricultural growth that was 'the main engine for Vietnam's first great wave of growth' (World Bank 1998, p. 30). It recommended that 'unshackling SMEs from existing restrictions could unleash a second round of growth by boosting labour-intensive manufactures and processed agricultural exports, thereby protecting rural areas from the current slowdown' (World Bank, 1998, p. 30). To date, however, private SMEs (that is registered private firms, have, according to the Bank, 'played a minor role in industrial production, contributing only

2 per cent of industrial output and have grown very slowly. Household enterprises play a much larger role' (World Bank 1998, p. 30).

The most cost-effective way of generating non-agricultural employment in Vietnam, according to a World Bank Consultative Group, is through promoting SMEs, that is registered private companies with between 50 and 300 employees (World Bank 1998, p. 29). Each job generated in an SME is estimated to require a capital investment of about US$800, compared with an investment of US$18 000 in a State-owned Enterprise (SOE) (World Bank 1998, pp. 29–30). This conforms, says the Bank, to empirical evidence from other countries indicating that SMEs are more efficient users of capital under most conditions.

In line with this evidence the Government has stated that it will support the development of SMEs through favourable policies and assistance in finance, market information and staff training (specified in a draft strategy to develop SMEs in Vietnam to 2010 prepared by the MPI). To support SMEs, the Vietnam Chamber of Commerce and Industry is working with relevant agencies, including the MPI, on the establishment of a credit guarantee system. It is clear that further government support is needed to help SMEs develop. It will be necessary to offer additional tax incentives, and support in funds and floor space to develop production, as well as to devise reasonable financial policies to attract money from the public and encourage effective investment by the private sector. Priority for enterprises will need to be given to trade categories focused upon traditional trades, handicraft, consumer goods, exports and hi-tech products. In addition, the State needs to reform the way it manages SMEs, so that procedures can be simplified and made easier to implement. SME development in the rural sector to expand employment and reduce poverty should also be given priority.

If the changes in policy identified in this chapter address the four key areas of: enhancing the legal environment for SMEs; strengthening existing and developing new institutions; enable easier access to finance; trade promotion and export development; and improving the image of, and attitudes to, the private sector as well as its corporate governance, then the optimistic growth of the private sector outlined in the SEDS can be achieved. In addition, the implementation of a competition policy that focuses upon ownership reform and the elimination of market barriers to entry, encourages foreign investment, enables the closure of unviable enterprises, and puts all forms of ownership on an equal basis, will be an essential pre-requisite for the growth of the private sector and a return to high and sustainable growth. As China, another transition economy, has demonstrated, private firms, if given the right environment, can grow rapidly, from 100 000 to 1 million in number in just 6 years and make a major contribution to the economy. In the case of China, however, there is clear commitment from the government to bring about this structural transformation, while for Vietnam there is still the perception that the authorities are dragging their feet.

Despite the capital-intensive nature of much of Vietnam's growth, there have been encouraging signs in the last few years of the emergence of a labour-intensive export sector. Changes in trade policies have been an essential component of the doi moi policy adopted since 1986. Licensed private companies are now allowed to engage directly in international trade, breaking the trade monopoly of a small number of state-owned enterprises operating under central or provincial authorities. However, until very recently, private enterprises had to satisfy a number of fairly restrictive conditions to obtain the necessary licenses. The recent removal of trade licensing, allowing companies to freely engage in trade within the registered scope of their business activities, should further improve the environment for export-oriented industries. In addition, over the years, most export quotas have been lifted and export taxes have been reduced to generally very low levels. These reforms, together with sound macroeconomic management, have allowed Vietnam to exploit its comparative advantage in labour intensive manufactures, putting the country on track for export led growth. This is a major lesson to be learned from the rapid growth of its regional neighbours.

NOTES

1   See Chapter 5 of this volume.
2   Vietnam had approximately 5300 SOEs in 2000.
3   Ironically, the Government of Vietnam does not consider family-owned businesses to be private companies (Vietnam News Agency, 2000).
4   The size of registered capital of these newly established enterprises has been decreasing.
5   General Statistical Office, 1996.
6   Vietnamese Dong.
7   Ministry of Planning and Investment, 1998.
8   General Statistical Office, 1996.
9   Ministry of Planning and Investment, 1998.
10   General Statistical Office, 1998.
11   Central Institute for Economic Management, 1998.
12   Ministry of Planning and Investment, 1999.
13   For imports: registered domestic firms could only import products that were specified in their registration license, and foreign-invested firms could not do so until the recent revision to the Foreign Investment Law had eased those restrictions somewhat.
14   Central Committee of the Communist Party 'Socio-Economic Development Strategy 2001–2010' (draft) p. 1.
15   Central Committee of the Communist Party 'Socio-Economic

Development Strategy 2001–2010' (draft) p. 6.

16 See for example Harvie (2001) and Chapter 5 of this volume.
17 By the end of 2000.
18 See World Bank 1998, pp. 29–30.
19 Sources: State Bank of Vietnam, Ministry of Finance, Central Institute of Economic Management.
20 Ministry of Planning and Investment 1999.
21 Central Institute for Economic Management 1998.
22 General Statistical Office 1996, p. 97.
23 General Statistical Office 1996.
24 Private Sector Promotion Action Plan (PSPAP) agreed between Vietnam and Japan in 1999. Also called the Miyazawa Plan.
25 Malesky et al. 1998, pp. 10–15, 73–4) provide an excellent summary of the nature and significance of these legal provisions.
26 Central Committee of the Communist Party 'Socio-Economic Development Strategy 2001–2010' (draft) p. 30.

REFERENCES

Appold et al. (1996), 'Entrepreneurship in a Restructuring Economy: Small Private Manufacturers in Hanoi', *Journal of Asian Business*, **12** (4), pp. 1–29.

Belser, P. (2000), 'Vietnam: on the Road to Labour Intensive Growth?', background paper for the Vietnam Development Report 2000 'Vietnam Attacking Poverty', Joint Report of the Government of Vietnam–Donor–NGO Poverty Working Group.

Business Vietnam (1996), 'Direct Foreign Investment 1995', **7** (12), [December 1995–January 1996], 31, Hanoi, Vietnam.

Central Institute for Economic Management (1997), *Economic Report*, Hanoi, Vietnam: Government of the Socialist Republic of Vietnam.

Central Institute for Economic Management (1998), *Report on Industrial Small and Medium Enterprises*, Hanoi, Vietnam: Government of the Socialist Republic of Vietnam.

Chenery, H. and M. Syrquin (1975), *Patterns of Development 1950–70*, New York: Oxford University Press.

Economist, The (1997), 'Nothing is really private in Vietnam', **343** (8017), 17 May, 45–7, London.

Economist, The (2000), 'Goodnight Vietnam', **354** (8152), 65–7, 8 January, London.

Edwards, A. (1997), 'Vietnam Economist Calls For New Wave of Reforms', Hanoi, Reuter, 15 August, *Vietnam Insight* (vinsight@netcom.com), <www.vinsight.org/>.

Fforde, A. (1991), *Country Report – Vietnam*, Hanoi and Stockholm: Swedish International Development Authority.

Fforde, A. and A. Goldstone (1995), *Vietnam to 2005: Advancing on All Fronts*, London: Economist Intelligence Unit.

Freeman, D. (1996), 'Doi Moi Policy and the Small Enterprise Boom in Ho Chi Minh City, Hanoi', *The Geographical Review*, **86** (2), 178–97.

General Statistical Office (1996), 'The Non-state Sector in the Open Period 1991–1995', Hanoi, Vietnam: The Statistical Publishing House, Government of the Socialist Republic of Vietnam.

General Statistical Office (1997), *Statistical Yearbook 1996 (NGTK)*, Hanoi, Vietnam: Statistical Publishing House, Government of the Socialist Republic of Vietnam.

General Statistical Office (1998), *Statistical Yearbook 1997 (NGTK)*, Hanoi, Vietnam: Statistical Publishing House, Government of the Socialist Republic of Vietnam.

Gillis, M., D. Perkins, M. Roemer and D. Snodgrass (1987), *Development Economics*, New York: Norton and Company.

Gittings, J. (2000), 'No Easy Victory in Hanoi's War on Poverty', *The Guardian*, [27 April], **20**. London and Manchester.

Government of the Socialist Republic of Vietnam (1995), *Report to the Sectoral Aid Co-ordination Meeting on Education*, Hanoi: Government of the Socialist Republic of Vietnam.

Harvie, C. (2001), 'China's SMEs – Their Evolution and Prospects in an Evolving Market Economy', in Charles Harvie and Boon-Chye Lee (eds), *The Role of Small and Medium Enterprises in National Economies in East Asia*, Chapter 2, Cheltenham, UK: Edward Elgar.

Jamieson, N.L. (1993), *Understanding Vietnam*, Berkeley and Los Angeles: University of California Press.

Kornai, J. (1990), *The Road to a Free Economy,* New York: W.W. Norton & Company.

Kornai, J. (2001), 'Lessons of the Transformation in Eastern Europe', presentation given at the UNDP, Hanoi, Vietnam, March.

Kurths, K. (1995), *Private Small Scale Industries in Vietnam: Development Environment and and Empirical Results,* Working Paper Series in Economics and Finance, No. 57, Stockholm: Stockholm School of Economics.

Li, B. and A. Wood (1989), *Economic Management Capabilities in Vietnam: an Evaluation and Assessment of Needs with a Suggested Priority Project for UNDP's Management Development Programme,* New York: UNDP.

McMillan, J. and C. Woodruff (1999), 'Inter-firm Relationships and Informal Credit in Vietnam', *Quarterly Journal of Economics*, **114** (4), 1243–85.

Malesky, E., V.T. Hung, V.T. Dieu Anh and N. Napier (1998), *The Model and the Reality: Assessment of Vietnamese SOE Reform–Implementation at the*

Firm Level, Working Paper No. 154, July, Ann Arbor, MI, William Davidson Institute, University of Michigan.

Mekong Project Development Facility (MPDF) (1999), *Vietnam's Under Sized Engine: a Survey of 95 Larger Private Manufacturers*, International Finance Corporation.

Ministry of Labour, War Invalids and Social Affairs (1998), *Labour Forces and Jobs in Vietnam*, Hanoi, Vietnam: Government of the Socialist Republic of Vietnam.

Ministry of Planning and Investment (1998), *Report to Government*, Hanoi, Vietnam: Government of the Socialist Republic of Vietnam.

Ministry of Planning and Investment (1999), *Draft Strategy for SME Development in Vietnam*, Hanoi, Vietnam: Government of the Socialist Republic of Vietnam.

Ministry of Trade (1998), *Annual Report*, Hanoi, Vietnam: Government of the Socialist Republic of Vietnam.

Pham Ghia Hai et al. (eds) (1996), *184 Surveyed Small and Medium Sized Enterprises of Vietnam: Evaluation and Analysis Report*, Hanoi: GTZ and VICOOPSME.

Pistor, K. (1998), 'The Implementation of Enterprise Reform in Vietnam', paper presented at an OECD Conference on *Enterprise Reform and Foreign Investment in Vietnam*, 19–20 January, Hanoi, Vietnam.

Reidel, J. and B. Comer (1997), 'Transition to a Market Economy in Vietnam', in W.T. Woo, S. Parker and J.D. Sachs (eds), *Economies in Transition: Comparing Asia and Europe*, Cambridge, MA: MIT Press, pp. 189–215.

Richards, D., C. Harvie, H. Nguyen and V.L. Nguyen (2002), 'The Limping Tiger: Problems in Transition for SMEs in Vietnam', in Charles Harvie and Boon-Chye Lee (eds), *The Role of Small and Medium Enterprises in National Economies in East Asia*, Chapter 3, Cheltenham, UK: Edward Elgar.

Ronnas, P. (2000), 'Transformation and Employment in the Private Small-Scale Manufacturing Sector in Vietnam', paper presented to the Ninth Annual Meeting of PECC-HRD Pacific Economic Cooperation Council Human Resource Development Task Force, Hualien, Taiwan, 21–2 October.

Taylor, K. (1983), *The Birth of Vietnam*, Berkeley: University of California Press.

Verbiest, J-P. (1998), 'State Enterprise Reforms in Vietnam: Current Situation and Reform Agenda', paper presented at an OECD Conference on *Enterprise Reform and Foreign Investment in Vietnam*, 19–20 January, Hanoi, Vietnam.

UNDP (1994), *Human Development Report*, New York/Oxford: Oxford University Press for UNDP.

UNDP (1999), *Human Development Report*, New York/Oxford: Oxford University Press for UNDP.

Van Arkadie, B. (1993), 'Managing the Renewal Process: The Case of Vietnam'. *Public Administration and Development*, 13, 435–51.

Vietnam Economic Times (1996), 'What it Takes', 14–20 January, Hanoi, Vietnam.

Vietnam Economic Times (1999), 'Little by Little', August, Hanoi, Vietnam.

Vietnam Investment Review (2000), 'Vietnam Income, GDP targets outlined', 1 March, Hanoi, Vietnam.

Vietnam News Agency (2000), 'Simplified Rules Boost Business Registrations in Vietnam', 29 March.

Wallroth, C., C. Rosvall and N. Austriaco (1990), *A Strategy for the Development of Management in Vietnamese Enterprises*, Stockholm: Swedish International Development Authority.

Webster, L. and T. Taussig (1999), 'Vietnam's Undersized Engine: A Survey of 95 Larger Private Manufacturers', Private Sector Discussions No.8, Mekong Project Development Facility, Hanoi.

Wolff, P. (1999), *Vietnam – The Incomplete Transformation,* London and Portland: Frank Cass.

Woo, W.T. (1997), 'Improving the Performance of Enterprises in Transition Economies', in W.T. Woo, S. Parker and J.D. Sachs (eds), *Economies in Transition: Comparing Asia and Europe*, Cambridge, MA: MIT Press, pp. 299–324.

World Bank (1996), *World Development Report-From Plan to Market*, New York: Oxford University Press for The World Bank.

World Bank (1998), *Vietnam: Rising to the Challenge*, Economic Report of the World Bank Consultative Group Meeting for Vietnam, Hanoi, 7 December, New York: World Bank.

World Bank (1999), *Vietnam: Preparing for Take-off?*, Informal Economic Report of the World Bank Consultative Group Meeting for Vietnam, Hanoi, 14–15 December, New York: World Bank.

World Bank (2001), *Vietnam Development Report 2001: Vietnam 2010: Entering the 21st Century,* Washington, DC: World Bank.

10. Australian Competition Law: Experience and Lessons for Drafting Competition Law

Hank Spier

This chapter discusses the issue of competition law for developing economies. It gives an overview of, and lessons from, the Australian regime.

10.1 AUSTRALIA'S COMPREHENSIVE NATIONAL COMPETITION POLICY

Australia has sought to have a comprehensive National Competition Policy since 1991. It has had comprehensive competition law since 1974 (Trade Practices Act) after two earlier less successful attempts in 1906 and 1965.

In 1991, the Council of Australian Governments, consisting of all the Federal, State and Territory Governments of the Australian federation, agreed to examine a national approach to competition policy. The first step in this process was the establishment in the following year of the National Competition Policy Review.

The six key elements of Australian National Competition Policy were identified as:

1   Limiting anti-competitive conduct of all businesses, mainly via the Trade Practices Act;
2   Reforming laws and regulations which unjustifiably restrict competition;
3   Reforming the structure of public monopolies to facilitate competition;
4   Providing third-party access to certain facilities that are essential to competition;
5   Restraining monopoly-pricing behaviour; and

6   Fostering competitive neutrality between government and private businesses when they compete.

On completion of the report in August 1993, Commonwealth, State and Territory Governments began extensive negotiations on implementation of its recommendations.

The main reform elements, to be implemented progressively, were as follows:

- the Trade Practices Act was amended so that, with enabling State and Territory legislation, the prohibitions of anti-competitive conduct contained in Part IV apply to all businesses in Australia. Constitutional limitations had previously prevented application of the competitive conduct rules to unincorporated businesses operating solely in intra-State trade;
- immunity for State and Territory Government businesses was removed, with Government Business Enterprises (known as 'GBE's') being subject to the Act from 21 July 1996;
- the scope for exemptions from the Act was sharply cut back;
- a new Part IIIA was added to the Trade Practices Act, and came into effect on 6 November 1995, establishing a legislative regime to facilitate access to the services of certain infrastructure facilities of national significance.

The reform legislation was complemented by two intergovernmental agreements:

10.1.1   The Conduct Code Agreement

This sets out processes for amendments to the competition laws of the Commonwealth, States and Territories and for appointments to the Australian Competition and Consumer Commission.

It also sets up a process in relation to any exemptions from national competition law.

10.1.2   The Competition Principles Agreement

This covers:

- public, independent and transparent review of all anti-competitive legislation and regulations over a five-year period;
- structural reform of public monopolies;
- access to services provided by significant infrastructure facilities;

- the principles that governments will follow in relation to prices oversight of GBE's; and
- the elimination of any competitive advantage or disadvantage experienced by government businesses when they compete with the private sector (competitive neutrality).

10.1.3   Exemptions

A competition regime needs to operate in conjunction with other government policies. Inevitably, conflict between policies will arise and it will therefore be necessary to determine priorities based on an assessment of national interests. For this reason, a mechanism is needed to provide for exceptions from the general application of a competition regime.

However, for any competition regime to be effective, sectoral exemptions or exclusions from the law must be kept to an absolute minimum. Even where these are considered necessary, mechanisms and timetables must be implemented from the outset for the phasing out of such exemptions by defined dates.

Exemptions from the competition law may be made by:

- *Legislative exemptions.* Such exemptions will only be permitted where it can be demonstrated that 'the benefits of the restriction to the community as a whole outweigh the costs; and the objectives of the legislation can only be achieved by restricting competition'[1].
- *Administrative exemptions.* The TPA allows the ACCC to 'authorise' proscribed conduct (other than misuse of market power) on a case-by-case basis, where the public benefits of such conduct outweigh the associated anticompetitive detriment. Parties gaining authorisation are granted immunity from legal proceedings under the TPA in relation to the authorised conduct.

10.1.5   Australian Competition Law

The Trade Practices Act 1974 contains parts which deal with anti-competitive practices, unfair trading practices and consumer protection, access to the facilities of natural monopolies and some regulatory provisions concerning such industries as telecommunications, unconscionable conduct, industry codes of conduct and authorisation, as well as parts about the institutions and remedies.

This chapter will largely focus on the traditional anti-trust and consumer protection parts of the Act.

10.1.6   Anti-Competitive Practices

There are two broad principles, which underlie the anti-competitive conduct provisions of the TPA. These principles are:

- that any behaviour which has the purpose, or effect, of substantially lessening competition in a market should be prohibited; and
- such behaviour should be able to be authorised on the basis that the public benefits of particular conduct outweighs the detriment caused to the public by any likely lessening of competition.

These broad principles are expressed in the legislation by way of specific prohibitions of anti-competitive agreements, misuse of market power, exclusive dealing, and resale price maintenance and anti-competitive mergers.

Various penalties and remedies are available for breaches of these provisions of the TPA, including:

- penalties (civil) of A$10 million for companies and A$500 000 for individuals;
- injunctions;
- damages;
- divestiture in relation to mergers; and
- various ancillary orders such as rescission and variation of contracts, orders for specific performance of contracts, and so on.

Australia does not have criminal sanctions for hard-core contraventions such as cartels. Whilst civil penalties have some advantages, in terms of the evidentiary tests and a far more economic underpinning, criminal sanctions and imprisonment should be an option that is available to the ACCC and the Court.

Private individuals and companies may also take action under the TPA to obtain remedies against anti-competitive conduct. However, only the ACCC can obtain penalties for breaches of the law. Private litigants can only seek injunctions and damages. However in relation to mergers private litigants cannot seek an injunction but can seek divestiture and damages once the merger has proceeded.

Private litigation is quite frequent, and this self-enforcing element of the legislation has worked well. It has meant that the regulator can concentrate on issues of broad public impact and not be drawn into inter-company conflicts.

Actions under the Trade Practices Act can largely only be taken in the Federal Court of Australia which has developed specific competition law expertise and being a federal body is more attuned to national issues than would be the State or Territory Courts.

10.1.6 Authorisation

Conduct that may substantially lessen competition may be authorised under the TPA. This is a mechanism that provides immunity from legal proceedings for certain arrangements or conduct that may otherwise contravene the TPA. Anyone who wishes to take part in prohibited conduct may apply to the ACCC for authorisation on the basis that the public benefit of the particular conduct outweighs the detriment to the public caused by any likely lessening of competition.

This leads to a clear separation of the consideration of competition issues and efficiency and other public interest issues.[2]

Authorisation is granted on the grounds of prevailing public benefit. Depending on the arrangement or conduct in question, the ACCC must be satisfied that the arrangement results in a benefit to the public that outweighs any anti-competitive effect; or that the conduct results in such a net benefit to the public that it should be allowed.

Public benefit has been given a broad interpretation over the years and is not restricted to issues of economic efficiency although that is usually the most important factor.

However authorisation is not granted lightly or very often. If it were the aims of the legislation could be undermined. In the past ten years very few mergers have been authorised. More common is the authorisation of anti-competitive agreements and exclusive dealing, particularly involving small business and the rural sector.

Importantly authorisation exempts the conduct from challenge by private parties as well as the regulator and therefore it is all the more important that the process is stringent and transparent.

Authorisation can be granted for all the prohibited conduct except misuse of market power.

The process is very public, with public registers and public decisions. Any interested party has the opportunity to have input.

There is the opportunity of an appeal (*de novo* review) to the Australian Competition Tribunal. A Federal Court judge and lay members including economist's head the Tribunal. Each panel must consist of a judge, an economist and one other.

10.1.7 Unfair Trading Practices

Part V of the TPA contains a range of provisions aimed at protecting consumers and businesses that qualify as consumers by:

- a general prohibition of misleading or deceptive conduct;
- specific prohibitions of false statements or representations;
- product safety and recall provisions;
- prohibiting unfair practices, including the unconscionable conduct provisions that prevent businesses from behaving unconscionably

when they supply goods and services to individual consumers and
when corporations are engaged in commercial transactions; and
* conditions and warranties in consumer transactions and actions against
manufacturers and importers.

Various penalties and remedies are available for breaches of these provisions
of the TPA, including:

* penalties (criminal) of A$200 000 for companies and A$40 000 for
individuals;
* injunctions;
* damages;
* corrective advertising; and
* various ancillary orders such as rescission and variation of contracts,
orders for specific performance of contracts.

Other Features of the Australian Model

The Australian competition agency is an integrated agency which performs both
enforcement and adjudication functions. The integration of these functions is
not an especially controversial issue, partly because the ACCC cannot affect the
legal rights of any person or business without their consent, unless it successfully
prosecutes cases in court. Also where it makes authorisation decisions they can
be appealed.

It is also arguably important in a small economy to have the economic and
legal resources in the one body:

* Australia has a single conglomerate regulator with a proconsumer and
procompetition culture;
* There is a system of cross membership between the national
regulator, the ACCC, and other Federal, State and Territory industry
regulators;
* The Australian regime has high transparency, both through its
legislation and by convention. It also has very high visibility;
* Special attention is given to small business issues and the imbalance
of power between big and small. Australia is a highly concentrated
economy and there is an understood belief that small business suffers
as a result;
* There is significant international focus, including a cooperation Treaty
with the US and informal cooperation agreements with Canada, New
Zealand, Chinese Taipei, and Papua New Guinea. Others are at
negotiation stage;
* In 1988, laws were passed in both Australia and New Zealand whereby
Trans-Tasmanian anti-dumping laws were repealed and the misuse

of market power laws of both jurisdictions applied in each other's jurisdiction;

- Competition laws in Australia and New Zealand are largely harmonised;
- There is no mandatory merger pre-notification. An informal system has worked for many years;
- In 1993, the Act was amended to allow the ACCC to accept enforceable undertakings in its administration of the law. An undertaking is a commitment to the ACCC by a business to take a particular action, for example, to sell assets as part of a merger. These undertakings are enforceable in Court if breached but the Commission only has to prove a breach of the undertaking and not any breach of the substantive prohibitions contained in the Act. This provision has been, and is much used by the Commission and has proved a very valuable tool in the day-to-day administration of the law.

10.1.9 The Role and Functions of the ACCC

The ACCC was established in November 1995 by the merger of the former Trade Practices Commission and the Prices Surveillance Authority.

The ACCC is an independent statutory authority responsible for ensuring compliance with the whole Act especially with Part IV (anti-competitive practices), IVA (unconscionable conduct), IVB (industry codes), V (consumer protection), VA (product liability), and VB (the New Tax System related pricing) of the TPA.

The ACCC also has responsibilities and powers under other parts of the TPA, notably Parts IIIA (access to nationally significant essential facilities), VII (authorisation and notification) and XIB and XIC (telecommunications industry).

It is responsible for administering the Prices Surveillance Act 1983, and also has responsibilities under several other pieces of legislation.[3] The ACCC is the only national agency dealing with broad competition matters and the only agency responsible for enforcing the competition provisions of the TPA.

The mission of the ACCC is 'to enhance the welfare of Australians by promoting effective competition and informed markets; encouraging fair trading and protecting consumers; and regulating infrastructure services and other markets where competition is restricted'.[4]

The ACCC's corporate direction is focused by three specific objectives:

- to encourage competitive market structures, behaviour and performance;
- to seek compliance with the consumer protection laws and to achieve appropriate remedies when the law is not followed for the long-term benefit of consumers; and

- to inform the community at large about the Trade Practices Act and Prices Surveillance Act and their implications for business and consumers.

The ACCC is committed to fostering a competitive culture where individuals and their businesses (large and small, at all levels of production) have the opportunity to trade in an efficient and fair way. Effective competition means that purchasers (both business and non-business) can have the means and freedom to make informed choices, and to enjoy the benefits of competitive prices and quality goods and services.

The ACCC's primary responsibility is securing compliance with the competition and consumer protection laws. In doing so, it uses a wide range of responses such as litigation, education and consultation. This necessitates a vigilant and responsive approach to complaints and non-compliant behaviour.

As noted earlier, the ACCC is both the enforcement agency and adjudicates and arbitrates on certain competition law and regulatory matters.

The competitive culture that the ACCC seeks is an important element in its economic regulation and pricing activities. The ACCC makes decisions that balance the interests of providers, users and final consumers striving to achieve outcomes comparable to those which occur under competitive conditions.

10.1.10 Some Features of Australian Competition Law History

In 1906, Australian introduced law that mirrored the US Sherman Act and the then 1889 Canadian Combines Act. The Australian law was declared largely unlawful by the Australian High Court in 1912.

In 1965, Australia introduced its post-war restrictive trade practices legislation. That legislation and the activities of the Office of the Commissioner for Trade Practices lead to the creation of the still current 1974 Trade Practices Act. Although the 1974 Act has been reviewed and changed many times since 1974, the fundamentals of the 1974 Act still constitute the current law.

The 1974 Act saw a move away from British style restrictive trade practices legislation with examination by an enforcement agency to an outright prohibition regime but with the opportunity for authorisation. The Act also saw the introduction of consumer protection law, merger law and mandatory implied conditions and warranties.

The 1974 Trade Practices Act was introduced with a big bang. It was highly publicised in the media and a major advertising campaign. Industry was apprehensive and claimed that it would be 'the end of the world' as they knew it. To a large degree they were right. The 1974 Act posed an even greater threat to the myriad of interlocking anti-competitive agreements that had existed in the Australian economy since the Depression and had been consolidated by the war and post-war eras than the 1965 Act.

The initial response by business to the 1974 Act was to lodge some 20 000 applications for authorisation. Many were agreements that had previously been registered, and hence exempted, under the old law. These were relodged in the hope that they would be exempted under the public benefit test.

To some extent the new TPC encouraged business to lodge applications for authorisation by indicating that anyone who lodged by February 1975 would be given automatic interim authorisation. As a result, around 20 000 interim authorisations were granted.

Consequently, the early days of the Commission were dominated by the authorisation process. There were many public hearings and landmark decisions. In many cases, authorisations were appealed to the then Trade Practices Tribunal (now the Australian Competition Tribunal).

The Commission also conducted a number of court cases. While court successes in the competition area were limited, the Commission was more successful in consumer protection cases.

It is sometimes said that in Australia little has been done in relation to the competition cases. This view overlooks the authorisation role and the role of the Trade Practices Tribunal. In the early days, the matters that went to authorisation in Australia were often the subjects of court cases in other jurisdictions, especially in North America.

The Commission's authorisation work continued for many years. It is a slow process by its very nature and there were some dramatic discussions in relation to issues such as newsagents, stock exchanges, motion picture distributors and IATA.

Ironically in its early days the ACCC's role was somewhat more regulatory as most of its work was not responding to market place conduct but to applications for approval of specific conduct.

The second half of the 1970s were a rocky time for Trade Practices law. It was the era of the business dominated Swanson Committee,[5] which recommended cutbacks, and the generally unsupportive Government which issued formal directions on what the ACCC could do. The political environment at the time was generally hostile towards Trade Practices law, particularly within the Commonwealth and State Bureaucracies. Business was also opposed to the law.

Nevertheless, the Act stayed alive and there were continuing major authorisation issues such as Stock Exchanges[6] and IATA[7] in the early 1980s. The Act's consumer protection provisions had been so successful that States and Territories adopted them in a mirror fashion in the early 1980s.

The heady days of 1974 were long gone and there was a clear fight to survive.

The 1980s were a period of consolidation and reconsideration of some of the previous ideas and influence. The 1980s saw another review of but no change to the merger test.[8] The 1980s also saw consolidation in the consumer protection area through mirror state legislation and consolidation in relation to the ACCC's enforcement and adjudication role generally.

A new merger wave emerged in the 1980s and the ACCC was heavily involved in a number of significant cases but blocked few mergers. In 1977 the merger test had been changed from substantial lessening of competition to dominance or increased dominance. In the 1980s, the ACCC assessed and did not oppose a number of well-known cases using this new test.

Not only was the merger test changed but also the ACCC lacked the power to seek enforceable undertakings or other methods of controlling merger outcomes.

Yet the 1980s set the foundation for the future developments. It was late in the 1980s that discussions started which eventually resulted in the formation of the Committee which reported on National Competition Policy.

The 1980s did not have the drama of the previous decade. From the mid 1980s there started to be more sympathetic political support for the Commission's role. A number of reviews enhanced some of the Act's and the Commission's powers. The 1980s prepared the Act and the Commission for the enormous leap forward in the 1990s.

10.1.11 The 1990s

The 1990s saw a considerable deepening and broadening of the Trade Practices Act. Indeed, the scope of competition policy was broadened significantly to include issues which went well beyond the application of the Trade Practices Act.

During the 1990s, the Commission (both as the TPC and the ACCC) took a number of successful landmark actions. In particular, two cartel cases stand out as being significant.

The first concerned the TNT/Mayne Nickless/Ansett Freight Express market sharing agreement. The ACCC alleged that the arrangement had existed for many years and had been sanctioned by high-level staff in each organisation. TNT and Mayne Nickless did not oppose the ACCC's action. Moreover, the TPC and the parties presented agreed penalties of around $6 million for TNT and around $7 million for Mayne Nickless to the Federal Court which accepted them as reasonable.[9] The Court also clearly indicated that it was prepared to countenance agreed penalty proposals and to accept them if they were within a range that the Court judged to be reasonable. The magnitude of the fines (levied when the maximum penalty per offence for companies was A$250 000) had a significant deterrent effect on anticompetitive behaviour by many firms in Australia and indeed alerted corporate Australia to the far-reaching implications of the vigorous application of the Act.

The second cartel case involved the concrete industry. In 1995, the newly formed Australian Competition and Consumer Commission secured a total of

$21 million in penalties against Boral, CSR and Pioneer for market sharing and price fixing arrangements,[10] reinforcing the significance of the provisions of section 45 for the whole of corporate Australia and, incidentally, putting the newly formed ACCC on the maps of both corporate and consumer Australia.

Authorisations became much fewer, and were granted much more infrequently than in the past, often in relation to conduct that technically breached the law rather than serious anti-competitive effects.

There were also landmark cases under Part V (consumer protection) of the Act. Prior to the 1990s, there had not been a great deal of litigation under Part V of the Act. The ACCC's first substantial consumer protection action was against life insurance companies which had sold life insurance policies in an unconscionable and deceptive and misleading fashion to approximately 3000 aboriginal consumers in far north Queensland and the Northern Territory.[11]

This high profile case was followed by the AMP case in 1994, in which the ACCC secured refunds of around $100 million for over 275 000 consumers who had purchased life insurance policies on the basis of misleading and deceptive promotional material.[12] The promotional material claimed that 80 per cent of their investment would be guaranteed against any adverse movement in the stock market when in fact none of the investment was so protected.

The 1990s also saw some high profile cases concerning the telecommunications industry. Telstra was required to publish major corrective advertising for misleading price comparisons[13] and in another case, the ACCC obtained refunds for consumers from Telstra of A$45 million for a misleadingly marketed wire repair plan which imposed charges (to the magnitude of A$45 million) on many hundreds of thousands of consumers and small businesses without their consent.[14]

These and other actions sharply lifted the profile of both the ACCC and the Trade Practices Act. This in turn had significant deterrent effects on businesses which otherwise would have ignored the Act.

Public support for the Act and the ACCC was strengthened. The actions also had some political side effects in that they helped generate greater public support for competition policy.

The ACCC made no secret of its interest in having a high profile. It believed that this would contribute to effective enforcement of the law and better compliance because few firms like negative publicity. The ACCC's high profile was clearly justified by the benefits of educating the business community, as well as the general community, about the Act and its requirements.

In 1993 Parliament steeply increased the penalties under the Act from a maximum of A$250 000 per offence for companies to a maximum of A$10 million per offence. Since 1993 there have been a number of cases conducted under the new penalty provisions and penalties in the millions are now commonplace.

Another important change in the first half of the 1990s was the change in the merger law from a test of dominance to a test of substantial lessening of competition. The criteria to be considered to establish a substantial lessening of competition were incorporated into section 50.

Other important recent changes include the power in the ACCC to take action on behalf of consumers and business for damages resulting from conduct in breach of the TPA.

Another very important set of changes arose following the decision of the Heads of Government (the Prime Minister, State Premiers and Chief Ministers of Territories) to establish the Review of National Competition Policy.

The Committee's report also strongly emphasised the fact that the Act until then had only applied to private sector anti-competitive behaviour and not to many government operated business, particularly those embodied in legislation.

10.1.12 Lessons from Australia

- Competition law and its administration to be effective must develop gradually, as there is a need to socialise business and government.
- Gradual development facilitates building up the necessary skills in government and business.
- Enforcement of the law is vital to assist in the socialisation process and hence compliance with the law.
- The administration must be transparent to both business and the wider community. This is particularly important for foreign businesses operating or planning to operate in Vietnam.
- An exemption process is important but must be public and stringent. Competition law is serious law and has high penalties and hence exemption from the law should not come easily.
- Learn from others but do not accept others' dogma as correct.
- Learn from others but each matter investigated is on a case-by-case basis and local issues become critical.
- The main opponents of competition law are often other government agencies and the fact that the 'specialised laws in Vietnam override the general' will strengthen the hands of the opponents.
- Establish overseas links to share information, small economies are major beneficiaries of that process.
- Work closely with any neighbours that have similar law and share resources and undertake joint investigations.
- Develop regular consultative mechanisms with business and others to facilitate compliance and market place feed back.
- Develop a proconsumer, procompetition culture.
- Develop a culture focusing on outcome and not process.
- Develop a culture of speedy outcomes as you will be dealing with

- dynamic market issues and if not handled rapidly that failure in itself may have anti-competitive outcomes.
- Any agency established to administer the law must be properly resourced, however that does not need be at high cost. Skill base, technology and networks are most important.
- Finally, assume that most issues you face will not be new. Call up other more established international bodies and see what you can get from them. Do not necessarily follow what they have done but their earlier work may save you a lot of time and effort.

10.2   PARTICULAR NEEDS OF DEVELOPING ECONOMIES

The following is a checklist of measures that are likely to be necessary in a developing economy contemplating programmes such as privatisation or other economic reform measures.

10.2.1   Legislative Level

- National competition and consumer laws with complementary law and codes providing a framework for efficient incentive regulation of essential service providers enjoying natural monopoly or significant incumbent advantages.
- Government and legislated commitment to the independence of any regulatory agency.
- Introduction of appeal bodies for the protection of integrity in decision-making.
- Government and legislated commitment to full public participation in regulatory review processes.
- Public consultation in the development of community service obligations.

10.2.2   Regulatory Level

- Establishment, preferably on a national level, and resourcing of a regulatory body capable of taking an integrated approach to the solution of competition, consumer protection and essential services regulatory issues.
- Capacity building in that body to prepare for the reform of infrastructure utility industries and other reforms.
- Compliance education of the business sector and community education generally.

- Coordination with other government agencies, advocacy bodies, parliamentarians and relevant business to ensure that communication problems arising from literacy and remoteness are overcome.

10.2.3   Institutional issues

The establishment and maintenance of an effective institution is vital and the following outlines some necessary factors.

Significant debate exists around the globe as to the most appropriate framework for administering economic, technical and competition regulation.

Among the issues considered have been the merits of general versus industry specific competition regulation and of integrated versus separate administration of economic, technical and competition regulation.

10.2.4   General Versus Industry Specific Competition Regulation

This general approach promotes consistency, certainty and fairness in the universal application of the competition law. It also enhances the regulator's ability to take an economy-wide perspective; reduces the risk of regulatory 'capture' by industry, and minimises duplication. There are also potentially material administrative savings.

10.2.5   Integrated Versus Separate Administration of Economic, Technical and Competition Regulation

Technical regulation and some significant aspects of economic regulation are administered in some economies by industry-specific bodies or more general government regulators. This recognises that the national competition authority should focus on anti-competitive conduct and not become embroiled in overly detailed or complex technical regulatory matters unless they have a clear connection with competition issues in, for example, network industries.

Separation of regulatory duties between competition, technical and economic regulators does entail the risk that competition regulators will not always have the same level of technical knowledge that can be achieved by an integrated industry regulator.

Where such separation occurs, cooperation and coordination is obviously vital to avoid inconsistent and investment-discouraging application of the two sets of policies. Cooperative links therefore need to be forged between competition offices and sector-specific technical regulators.

The risks are less in industries where the regulator has both an economic regulatory role as well as its normal competition role. It also has various mechanisms in place to improve coordination between the various regulators. Examples include:

- frequent information exchange through regular liaison meetings and the exchange of publications or other information; and
- overlapping membership of regulatory bodies.

10.2.6 Transparency and Accountability

This concept is essential to ensure that businesses and consumers know under what legal conditions they operate and to facilitate inter-governmental cooperation. It applies both 'ex ante' (that is, formulating clear rules for potential economic operators) and 'ex post' (that is, making those concerned aware of enforcement decisions).

- Law(s) and regulations should be made publicly available.
- Any current gaps in coverage should be specified. Consideration should also be given to a 'standstill' or 'roll back' of such gaps. If any special rules exist for certain sectors, they should also be specified. All exceptions to laws and regulations should be publicly stated. Where the law(s) provide(s) for exemptions, exemption criteria, whether predetermined or through rule of reason analysis, should be set out in the published legislation or guidelines, or judicial opinions.
- Provisions should also be made that modifications to laws and regulations are regularly published (and if appropriate, a contact point be made available for foreign authorities or private agents in bilateral contacts).
- Transparency of enforcement policy could include publication of priorities, guidelines, case selection criteria and exemption criteria.
- Where competition authorities make a negative decision on a case, publication/explanation of such decisions by the competition authorities should be pursued where doing so would be administratively feasible and would not be unduly burdensome.
- Competition authorities should be required to protect commercial secrets and other confidential information.

10.2.7 Competition Enforcement Agency

The mission of any competition enforcement agency will generally be to enhance the total welfare of the economy's people by achieving comprehensive compliance with the competition legislation and its objectives. Compliance will be attained by timely and efficient enforcement action, competition policy advocacy, information dissemination and increasing market transparency.

For the competition agency to provide timely and efficient administration and enforcement of the competition legislation, it is important that management adopt a predictable and transparent approach – both internal and external to the organisation.

Internal openness can be created by regularly communicating management goals and objectives, minimising reporting layers, developing efficient IT systems and providing the necessary support and empowerment to employees to establish an interested and motivated workforce.

External openness would include the development of easily readable brochures concerning the legislation and the creation of a web-site on the Internet which could explain the purposes and structure of the organisation, facilitate complaint handling, provide information on the various provisions of the competition legislation and public notices of decisions.

A specially designated public communication/press officer to act on behalf of the competition agency should also be a consideration.

10.2.8   Competition Appeal/Adjudicative Body

In order to promote transparency and accountability for decisions, it is considered important that an appeal body exists to consider matters that are dealt with by the competition enforcement agency. An appeal body is necessary to protect the integrity of the decision making process. It is also important that this level of accountability is both real and perceived in the wider community.

10.2.9   Independence

This point ties in with several others that have already been discussed, namely institutional structures and transparency. It is important that the competition agency is functionally and operationally independent from government, even though it is likely to be publicly funded.

If this independence is not achieved, both in actual fact and in the perception of the community, then the competition agency will be, or be seen to be, influenced by the politics of the government of the day, and therefore subject to other political agendas, which obviously need not necessarily be in the best interests of competition and achieving competitive market outcomes.

10.2.10   Enforcement

However, having comprehensive legislation and a well-structured institutional framework for competition, consumer protection and economic regulation are only part of the equation.

Even if there are the right 'systems' in place, these systems will be worthless unless the implementation, administration and enforcement of these systems is also effective.

It is vital to keep in mind that enforcement is not an end in itself, but rather a tool to achieve the primary objective of achieving compliance with the law in order to foster competitive, efficient, fair and informed markets.

Enforcement action should be taken, not simply to win in court, but to achieve results in the market place. These results include:

- stopping the conduct quickly;
- compensating any person who has suffered loss or damage as a result of the contravention of the law;
- undoing the effects of the contravention;
- preventing a future contravention of the law, both immediately and in the longer term;
- providing a deterrence in the community at large and in particular in the industry concerned by means of publicity; and
- punishing the offender.

It is important in any enforcement action that investigations and any resulting litigation are well planned, working towards the identified objectives of the enforcement action while working within an organization's stated priorities. Effective investigation planning allows the achievement of timely and fair outcomes in an efficient manner.

The appropriate approach to investigation planning involves ensuring that investigation outcomes are identified at an early stage, and then tailoring the investigative approach to achieve those results.

The need is to focus on outcomes, not merely on processes.

10.2.11 Access to Remedies – Due Process

As an important element of effective and non-discriminatory domestic enforcement, it is important that firms be given, on a non-discriminatory basis, effective access to domestic judicial or administrative remedies. Consideration should be given to the following types of provisions.

- Rights of complainants to petition competition authorities and seek explanations for inaction on matters.
- Rights of complainants to bring complaints before the competition authorities.
- Rights of private parties to access the judicial system to seek remedies for injury suffered by anti-competitive practices.
- Due process for all parties in administrative or judicial procedures including protection of confidential information.
- Where competition authorities make case decisions, publication/ explanation of such decisions by the competition authorities.
- Appropriate access to avenues of appeal.

10.2.12 Institutional Challenges

A competition institution and its legislation have particular management challenges. The particular issues are:

- maintaining independence;
- developing the necessary legal, economic and administrative skill base;
- give appropriate weight to all roles;
- build and maintain a constituency;
- foster and maintain transparency and accountability;
- learning to exist in an adversary enforcement environment;
- developing proper compliance strategies in the market place;
- developing and maintaining a culture based on compliance and based on outcomes in the market place;
- relations with special service providers such as private sector lawyers;
- relations with other government agencies both in the policy sphere and other administrators;
- maintaining a secure environment so that business has the confidence of the agency and confidential information;
- handling the media;
- keeping up with technology developments in order to remain effective and relevant;
- withstand attacks from both friends and enemies;
- avoid capture;
- handle complaints speedily and professionally;
- ensure staff professionalism; and
- maintain staff morale and always support staff but move decisively if improper conduct.

10.3   OBSERVATIONS ON INSTITUTIONAL ISSUES OF RELEVANCE

The following observations have been made on institutional issues relevant to competition policy and law.

10.3.1   High Ethical Standards in Administration and Business

In any competition law regime it is essential that the administration maintain the highest level of ethical standards even if that is not the case in the external environment.

Competition law administration is highly sensitive to pressures involving ethical questions and any suspicion by the community that the regulator is not totally ethical will badly compromise its work and make the obtaining of information from the market place almost impossible.

As part of this ethical standard business must by totally confident that information that it provides the regulator in confidence stays confidential.

10.3.2   Educating Government and Business

One lesson that all regulators learn quickly is the need to educate the community and in particular business and in the case of developing economies government officials.

Experience from other jurisdictions is that this role is not taken seriously and even viewed with trepidation, as they do not see it as their role to educate.

However such education is critical to both ensure compliance with the law and to build up a constituency.

The form of such education will depend on local practice but publications and ready access to rulings are an essential part of such processes. It is also adds to the transparency of the organisation.

10.3.3   International Cooperation and Information Sharing

It is now very common for competition law regulators to enter into cooperation agreements and to exchange information to the extent the law allows them.

Interagency cooperation is getting more and more important as issues become global, highlighted by the recent surge in global cartels, such as the vitamins cartel.

Having domestic competition law is almost a pre-requisite of such cooperation and is one of the benefits of domestic law. In most cases without international cooperation it will be most difficult to get evidence to pursue these cartels in one's own jurisdiction as much of that evidence is overseas but has in many cases been obtained by regulators in another jurisdiction.

The other benefit of international cooperation is the help more mature agencies can give in developing a skill base and providing information on cases and strategies in relation to competition law and its administration. Whilst each administration is different there are significant similarities.

10.3.4   Interaction with Government Generally

Competition agencies have to interact with many other parts of Government and many levels of Government. Further they are often drawn into becoming an advocate for competition issues and concept.

10.3.5   Culture of Transparency and Accountability

Much has been said about transparency and accountability. This cannot be understated and underpins the whole integrity of the agency and the law it administers. This is not only important in the domestic market but also internationally.

Business and consumers expect and need the agency to have a strong culture of accountability and transparency. This is a challenge and one that has to be actively sponsored from the top.

10.3.6   Competition Law Needs Ongoing Support

Unlike some other areas of law, competition law needs constant work and support. Commitment must be long term.

NOTES

1   *Competition Principles Agreement.* Agreed between the Commonwealth, State and Territory Governments of Australia on 25 February 1994, s. 5 (1).
2   Nevertheless the ACCC merger guidelines recognise that efficiencies may promote competition and hence in some cases may be considered as part of the competition analysis in mergers.
3   These include, the Broadcasting Services Act 1992, Telecommunications Act 1997, Telecommunications (Consumer Protection and Service Standards) Act 1999, Australian Postal Corporation Act 1989, Trade Marks Act 1995, Airports Act 1996, ASIC Act 1989, Gas Pipelines Access (Commonwealth) Act 1998, and the Moomba-Sydney Pipeline System Sale Act 1994.
4   ACCC Corporate Plan and Priorities: 2001–02.
5   Parliament of Australia. Committee to Review the Trade Practices Act 1974 (1976), *Report to the Minister for Business and Consumer Affairs*, Canberra: Australian Government Publishing Service.
6   Trade Practices Commission Annual Report 1981–82, pp. 48–50.
7   Trade Practices Commission Annual Report 1980–81, pp. 52–3.
8   Parliament of Australia. House of Representatives. Standing Committee on Legal and Constitutional Affairs (1989), *Mergers, Takeovers and Monopolies: Profiting from Competition?*, Canberra: Australian Government Publishing Service; Parliament of Australia. Senate. Standing Committee on Legal and Constitutional Affairs (1991), *Mergers, Monopolies and Acquisitions: Adequacy of Existing Legislative Control*, Canberra: Australian Government Publishing Service.

9 Trade Practices Commission Annual Report 1993–94, pp. 12–13 and Trade Practices Commission Annual Report 1994–95. pp. 13–15.
10 ACCC Annual Report 1995–96, pp. 11–13.
11 Trade Practices Commission Annual Report 1992–93, pp. 27–9.
12 Trade Practices Commission Annual Report 1994–95, pp. 26–8.
13 Trade Practices Commission Annual Report 1993–94, p. 27.
14 ACCC Annual Report 1996–97, pp. 59–60.

11. Competition Policy, Global Competitiveness and Trade and Business Development in Asian Economies: The Future and Prospects

Tran Van Hoa

11.1 ISSUES IN FOCUS

In the preceding chapters, we have discussed and critically analysed major aspects and issues of competition policy and anti-trust laws (CPA for short) and global competitiveness (GCO) from a number of perspectives. First, we have surveyed the philosophy and the microfoundation underlying the concepts of CPAGC and as adopted in the international literature and institutions that are specialised in this field of enquiry. This philosophy and foundation have often been neglected in previous studies on the subject matter. Second, we have discussed the development and implementation of CPAGC in a number of major APEC countries in the Asian region, both developed and developing, and critically analysed aspects and issues as well as achievements, obstacles and challenges in the practices of CPA of these countries for possible adoption or adaptation by other economies that have not yet had their CPA.

11.2 GLOBALISATION AND COMPETITION AND COM-PETITIVENESS

With the advent and acceptance, reluctantly in some cases, of globalisation and the inevitable penetration of its companion concept, international competitiveness, we believe that the material we have presented and discussed in the preceding sections, while focused on selected countries in Asia and comprehensive in analysis but concise in its presentation, would be a wealth of timely and useful information relevant to serious studies on the subject matter by academics, students, economic and trade policymakers, business analysts, government economists and corporate executives. More importantly, the material would be used effectively to contribute, in a practical policy sense, ultimately to the facilitation of cross-border flows of goods and services in the case of the WTO, the improvement in domestic competition trade in the case of the APEC, and the enhancement of regional trade in the case of the ASEAN.

We have noted that, in many countries under study in our book, CPA and GCO are seen essentially as the outcomes of the philosophy and concepts of a laissez-faire economy or market, strongly advocated by the West, mainly the US and the EU, with the support of big transnational companies. As a laissez-faire economy is known to have optimal benefits in resource allocation and income distribution and maximum welfare generation, it has also been known to have its Achilles heel, namely market failures. This may explain why in major market economies with a socialist orientation in Asia, such as China and Vietnam, CPA and GCO have not been whole-heartedly welcome by government officials and the public alike. And this perception, rightly or wrongly, has hindered the development and implementation of CPA and GCO. It is interesting to note, from the report of the preceding chapters, that this perception and attitude has, with increasing globalisation and the growing influence of the WTO memberships, slowly changed very recently.

To minimise the occurrence and impact of market failures in order to gain optimal benefits of a truly laissez-faire economy model or something close to it, governments in both developed and developing countries have set up their own trade or competition commissions with ministerial power and function to supervise corporate structuring and operation. It seems that, according to the information we have recently surveyed on the Internet, no single country from all major trading blocs in the world has not embraced, for its local and international trade and industry policies, the ideas and concepts of CPA and GCO and developed or are developing CPA and aspects of GCO.

For these countries, the embracing is a necessity as trade and investment liberalisation can only improve their growth and economic development, enhance their business environment, increase the welfare of their populations, alleviate their poverty, and facilitate their integration into the global economy. It is also a necessity as the international pressure on adopting and implementing CPA and GCO has been intense from the international organisations such as the WTO, the World Bank and the International Monetary Fund, or even from such regional organisations as the APEC, the ASEAN or even the ASEAN+3 (that is, ASEAN+China, Korea and Japan) and ASEAN+5 (ASEAN+3 and Australia and New Zealand).

11.3   THE FUTURE AND PROSPECTS

In view of these reasons, the future of more collaboration between our major APEC countries in Asia and developed economies in North America and the EU and even the Oceania to liberalise trade and investment and to achieve high growth and development outcomes looks promising. By the same token, the prospects for these countries in appropriately and successfully developing and implementing their own versions of CPA and GCO and with the collaboration of countries that have had experience with CPA and GCO can be seen as good to excellent.

Index